TIM FLANNERY

EXPLORING THE INCREDIBLE WORLD OF ANIMALS

WEIRD, WILD, AMAZING!

ART BY
SAM
CALDWELL

Norton Young Readers

An Imprint of W. W. Norton & Company
Independent Publishers Since 1923

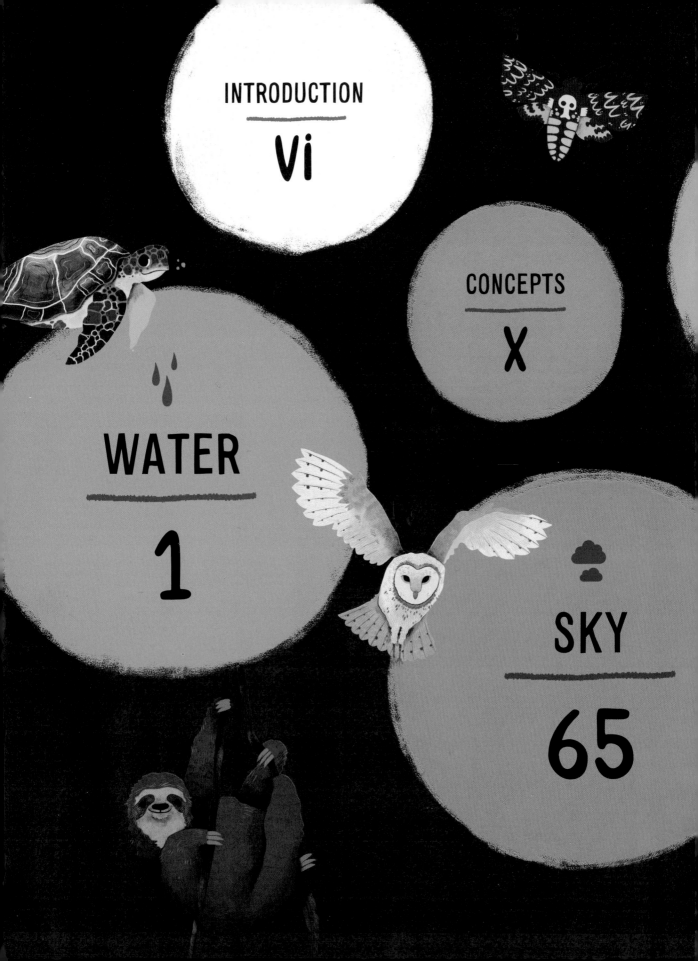

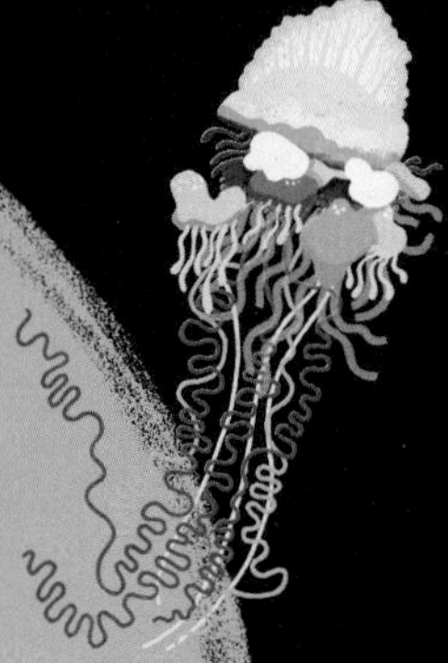

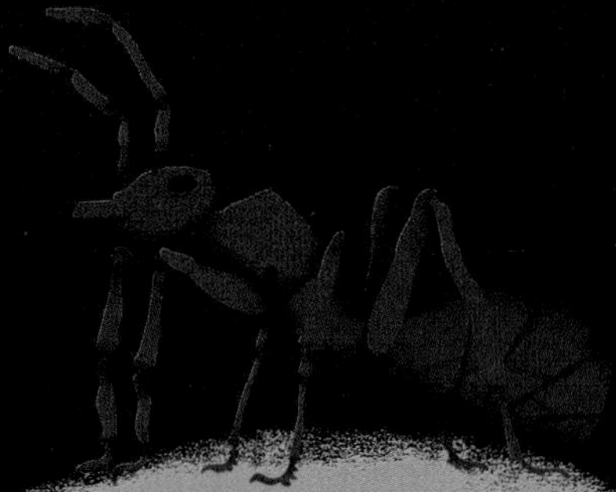

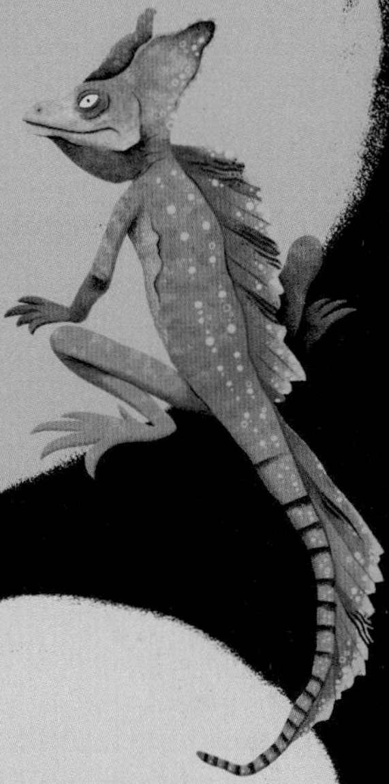

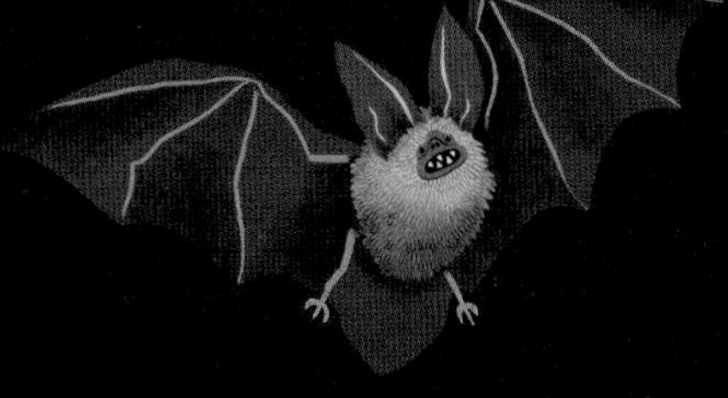

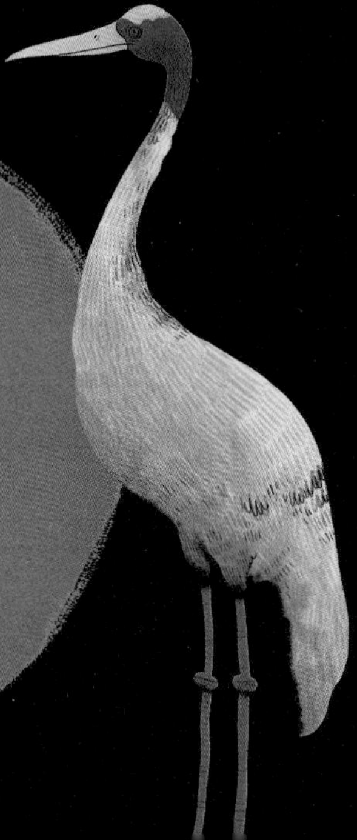

INTRODUCTION

I've been interested in animals and fossils for as long as I can remember. One of my earliest memories is from when I was four years old. I was playing in a vacant block beside our house, created when a neighbor's house burned down, and found a lump of molten glass. I felt sure that it was a fossilized dinosaur brain! When I was a kid, one of my favorite things to do was explore the tide pools at the beach and stick my finger into the sea anemones, just to feel the way they pulled my finger inward before releasing it when they realized that they couldn't eat me.

I grew up in the suburbs of Melbourne, Victoria, Australia, and there weren't a lot of opportunities near my home to see cool creatures. But when I was eight years old, I was walking on a sandbank at low tide and saw a strange rock. It had markings on it, and I suspected it was something special. I took it to the local library, where the librarian told me to take it to the museum.

The entrance to the museum was awesome, with doors tall enough to fit a Tyrannosaurus! Inside was a vast hall, full of stuffed creatures.

WEIRD!

There was a small door on the side, saying "visitors." I knocked on it, and a museum guard appeared, asking what I wanted. I showed him the strange rock, and he went away. Sometime later, a man in a white coat appeared and asked me to follow him. We went up a huge stairway, through another set of giant doors, and into a dark corridor. I could make out an Egyptian mummy in a sarcophagus on the floor, and some enormous bones. We turned a corner, and I found myself in a long hall, filled with gray steel cabinets.

The man in the coat opened one, pulled out a drawer, and lifted out a rock identical to mine. "It's *Lovenia forbesi*," he told me, "the fossilized remains of an extinct sea urchin. They are quite common in the rocks near my home." It was, he thought, about 10 million years old. I was awestruck. Then he asked, "Are you interested in dinosaurs?"

I WAS MORE THAN INTERESTED. I WAS OBSESSED.

The man put the fossilized sea urchin back, closed the drawer, and opened another. "Hold out your hand," he said, as he placed an odd pointed rock on it. "This is the Cape Paterson Claw. It's a claw from the foot of a dinosaur, and it is the only dinosaur bone ever found in Victoria."

I held the Cape Paterson Claw! I was so excited that I could hardly speak. Learning about fossils led to a big breakthrough for me: I discovered that I could visit the lands of amazing creatures in my imagination.

In the months and years that followed I learned to snorkel and scuba-dive in the bay near where I found that first fossilized sea urchin. A reef of fossil-bearing rocks was exposed there underwater, where I found extraordinary remains. I remember one winter afternoon, when the water was freezing but clear, I spied a length of fossil whale jaw, nearly as long as me, lying on the bottom. Another day, I chanced upon the tooth of a megalodon shark lying in the shallows. In my imagination I swam in that ancient Port Phillip Bay, full of giant sharks and whales.

I never found out who the man in the white coat at the museum was. And he probably had no idea of the passion he had sparked in me! When I was a little older I started to volunteer at the museum, cleaning and cataloging fossils.

It was incredible to actually hold the bones of extinct creatures, and to chip away the rock encasing them. As I cleaned the bones, I was aware that I was the first human ever to see them revealed. I wanted to see where they'd come from, so my cousin and I visited Cape Paterson, about 90 miles from Melbourne, where the claw had been found.

WE DISCOVERED A DINOSAUR GRAVEYARD!

The bones were hard to see because they are soft and weathered away so only a cross-section is visible. At the time the creatures lived, Victoria was near the South Pole. The famous Australian palaeontologist Dr. Tom Rich has spent a lifetime searching the rocks for more bones, and his studies have revealed a strange world inhabited by big-eyed and feathered dinosaurs that thrived in the freezing conditions.

I started my scientific career as a paleontologist—someone who studies fossils. As I searched for fossils I also explored the creatures of the living ocean around Melbourne. Each year elephant sharks would leave the depths of the Southern Ocean to breed in the shallows. Just 2 feet long, silvery and with strange protruding noses, they haven't changed much since the age of dinosaurs. Sometimes great schools of whitebait would arrive, and I'd swim among the fish, watching as barracuda and small sharks tried to hunt them.

As I grew up, I went further and further afield, into the Australian desert and Great Barrier Reef, where I encountered water-holding frogs, red kangaroos and magnificent coral. When I was 26 I was studying the evolution of kangaroos, and joined an expedition to Papua New Guinea. Over 9,000 feet up in the high mountains of eastern Papua I discovered a rat that was almost 3 feet long, and a wallaby not much bigger, that were both new to science.

I eventually became a mammologist—someone who studies living mammals. For 20 years I was the curator of mammals at the Australian Museum in Sydney. I visited most of the islands between eastern Indonesia and Fiji, discovering new species of marsupials, rats, and bats. By the time I left the job I'd been on 26 expeditions into the islands north of Australia and discovered more than 30 new living mammal species, including four kinds of tree kangaroos that are some of the largest mammals native to New Guinea. Along the way I've also named six of New Guinea's seven megafaunal marsupials: these were giant wallabies and panda-sized wombat-like creatures that

inhabited the island until humans arrived around 45,000 years ago.

To study the animals I had discovered, I went to the United States and Europe, where I worked in museum collections. People understood how expensive and difficult it was for me to travel all the way from Australia, so they gave me 24-hour access to the American Museum of Natural History. It was very cool being in the museum at night, and a little bit spooky!

Then I became interested in climate change and became Australia's climate commissioner. I call myself an evolutionary ecologist because I'm really interested in how ecology changes as evolution proceeds. For example, thousands of years ago Australia was home to giant marsupials. They affected the vegetation that grew by eating it, which in turn changed how much fire there was—they ate a lot of the plant matter that fire would otherwise burn.

When you think like an evolutionary ecologist, you notice amazing things. In Australia I've seen trees that still produce thorns to protect their leaves from being eaten by giant marsupials that have been extinct for millennia. I know that the ancestors of the humble striped frog originated in Africa 100 million years ago before hopping across the now vanished supercontinent Gondwana. When you think like an evolutionary ecologist, the world becomes a rich and amazing place.

If you're interested in animals and nature, you don't need to wait until you're older before you start your studies. There are lots of ways of starting right now. You can volunteer at a museum or on a dig, participate in a citizen science program like the Great Backyard Bird Count, or just start your own studies in a local tide pool or pond. If you decide to do a study by yourself, you need to take careful notes and send them to an expert in a museum or university to check them.

You might think that the world is fully explored now. But that's not true. There are still lots of mammals, and other creatures, to be found around the world. And we have barely scratched the surface of diversity in the deep sea.

THERE'S LOTS OF NATURE ON YOUR DOORSTEP, PROVIDED YOU KNOW WHAT TO LOOK FOR.

Beachcombing is great fun. You never know what the tide has washed up. And tide pools, creeks, and ponds are full of life. But be sure to stay safe as you investigate! If you don't live near a beach, you can study nature in a local park or backyard. The soil and plants will be filled with living things, including birds and insects. Museums and aquariums are the best places to learn about nature, while zoos, nature reserves, and even local parks are good places to be among the animals.

If you're interested in fossils, keep your eyes on the rocks. Even the stones used for buildings often have fossils embedded in them. Look out for curious shapes. They might be ancient fossil seashells that quarry saws have sliced into. And if you do find something, photograph it, or if it is small and portable (say a beach pebble), take it to your local museum. Most have services to help identify it.

When I was very young I often wished that I had a fun book that would tell me about the weirdest creatures on Earth. That's what I've tried to create here, for you. I hope that you find reading it to be a great adventure in itself, and that it leaves you wanting to see more of the wonderful and mysterious world around us.

Tim Flannery

CONCEPTS

EVOLUTION

Evolution is a word that describes how animals and plants change over generations. Each generation of living things is made up of individuals that differ a little from each other: some might be bigger, or more brightly colored, for example. And in nature, more animals are born (or germinate, if they're plants) than the environment can support. This means that the individuals that do best in their environment are most likely to survive. For example, if bigger, brighter animals or plants survive better, with each new generation the population will be made up of bigger, brighter individuals. Over many generations, the changes brought about by this "natural selection" can be so great that new species are created.

CLIMATE CHANGE

Earth's climate is changing because of pollution that humans are putting into the atmosphere. Greenhouse gases like carbon dioxide from burning coal, gas, and oil are causing the ground, oceans, and atmosphere to warm up. This might sound good if you live in a cold place, but many consequences of the warming are bad for living things. For example, warmer conditions mean that less water is available in some places, and creatures living in the warming oceans often have less food and oxygen. As seas rise and rainfall changes, and the atmosphere warms, entire habitats are disappearing, causing species to become threatened or even extinct.

SO SAD.

HABITATS

Habitats include places on land, in water, and even in the air. They are the places where animals live, and they vary greatly all across the world. Deserts are very dry habitats, tundras are very cold ones, while rainforests are very stable ones (with little temperature change, for example, between winter and summer). As animals and plants evolve, they become better adapted to their particular habitat. In this book, habitats are grouped into four very broad categories: water, sky, forest, and desert/grasslands. Within each there are many different habitats—far too many to list.

FOSSILS

Fossils are the remains of plants and animals that lived in the past. The chances of you, or any living thing, becoming a fossil is very small. Maybe one in a billion! The first step toward a fossil being created happens when the remains of a plant or animal are buried in sediment like sand or mud. If the conditions are right, over thousands of years the sediment turns to rock, and the remains become "petrified" (which means turned to rock) or preserved in some other form, like an impression (such as a footprint).

COMMON NAMES ⓥ. SCIENTIFIC NAMES

EXTINCTION

Animals and plants have two kinds of names: a common name and a scientific name. The common name of a species is the name that you generally know them by, and these names can vary in different areas. For example, "wolf" is a common name in English, but wolves are called "lobo" in Spanish, and have many different names in other languages. But the scientific name never varies. This means that by using the scientific name, an English-speaking scientist and a Spanish-speaking scientist can understand each other, even if they can't speak a word of each other's language.

Scientific names have two parts. For wolves, the scientific name is *Canis lupus*. The first part (*Canis*, in this case) is known as the genus name, and it is shared with close relatives. For example, the golden jackal's scientific name—*Canis aureus*—also begins with *Canis*. But the combination of genus and species name is unique. For wolves, the species name (*lupus*) means "wolf" in Latin.

Scientists use terms like "vulnerable," "threatened," and "endangered" to describe how likely an organism is to become extinct. Extinction occurs when the last individual of a species dies. If an animal is endangered, it means that very few individuals exist, and that they might soon become extinct. If an animal is threatened, it means that they are likely to become endangered in the future, while an animal being classed as vulnerable means that they are likely to become threatened.

ANIMAL TYPES

Animals and plants are classified according to their evolution. Animals, for example, can be divided into those with backbones (vertebrates) and those without (invertebrates). You can't always tell which group a plant or animal belongs to by just looking at them. Sometimes looks can be misleading! Falcons are related not to eagles or kites, which they resemble, but parrots. Parrots and falcons are classified in a group called "Austroaves," meaning "southern birds," because they originated in the southern hemisphere.

CONSERVATION

Conservation means taking care of nature and all of its plants and animals. Conservation is something that everyone can be part of. Governments help by creating national parks, and fining litterbugs and polluters. Scientists play an important role in conservation by studying how we can help various species. You can be a conservationist in your own backyard: just plant a native tree that will become a home to the birds.

CONSERVE TO PRESERVE!

JELLYFISH

You might have come across a jellyfish washed up on the beach, or if you're really lucky you might've seen one floating gracefully along in the water. They're a fascinating mix of extreme beauty and super-slimy weirdness, and that's just how they look—they have some seriously bizarre habits, too. If you're curious about how something gets the name "snotty jelly," or whether zombie jellyfish could possibly be real, buckle up—you're about to find out.

I DON'T THINK YOU'RE READY FOR THIS JELLY!

WHERE CAN I SEE A JELLYFISH?

It doesn't matter where you live in the world—if there's an ocean near you, chances are there are jellies in it.

THE PERFECT NAME

Although jellyfish have the word "fish" in their name, they're actually not fish at all. They're related to things like sea anemones and coral. You can call them "jellyfish" or just plain "jellies."

Jellies belong to a group of animals with the scientific name Cnidaria, meaning "nettle," because many jellies and their relatives have a **OUCH!** sting just like a nettle plant.

Jellies all have official scientific names, but most of them have common names too. These common names are like nicknames that really suit the particular kind of jelly.

► **Cauliflower jellyfish** have big, lumpy arms that look like fluffy cauliflower florets.

► When it's in the water, the **snotty jellyfish** is a regular jellyfish shape. But when it's washed up on the sand, all of its different body parts melt together into something that looks really disgusting—like a huge pool of slimy snot.

► **Fried egg jellyfish** have a golden yolky bump in their centers and a pale ring around their outsides that's like an egg white. Their texture is pretty similar to an egg, too—gelatinous and just a little bit rubbery.

► **Flower hat jellyfish** have a hat-shaped dome covered with brightly colored shapes and patterns.

FANCY!

SIZE MATTERS

FROM PEANUTS TO PIANOS

► **Irukandjis**, the world's smallest jellies, can be almost half an inch long—about the size of a peanut with the shell cracked off.

actual size

► **Lion's mane jellies**, the largest jellyfish in the world, can weigh up to nearly 2,200 pounds—the same as two grand pianos. They have thick masses of tentacles that look like a lion's shaggy mane.

ANCIENT JELLIES

Jellyfish fossils are some of the oldest animal fossils ever found. Many different kinds of marine animals appeared about 550 million years ago, and, before that, jellyfish may have had the open oceans pretty much to themselves. Sharing the oceans with hordes of other creatures doesn't seem to be cramping the jellies' style, though—they keep on multiplying and spreading at alarming rates.

RISE OF THE MEGA JELLY

Portuguese man-of-war and **long stingy stringy thingies** (yes, they're both real animals!) might look like regular jellies, but they are both actually made up of heaps of different creatures—kind of like a bunch of children stacked up in a trench coat to disguise themselves as an adult. These creatures, which are called "zooids," work together like a single jelly. Each individual does a different job, including catching food, digesting it and defending the team against predators. These mega jellies can be enormous—more than 140 feet long, or about half as long as a football field.

UP CLOSE AND PERSONAL WITH . . . A SEA WALNUT

Sea walnut seems like an unusual name for a jelly, right? But it suits this one perfectly. These jellies have small bodies covered in lumps and bumps, so they look an awful lot like walnuts. Also, they live in the sea. They've practically named themselves!

Sea walnuts begin laying eggs when they are just 13 days old, and pretty soon they're laying 10,000 eggs *every single day*. Obviously this keeps them pretty busy, but somehow they still find time to eat regular meals. Sea walnuts have seriously impressive appetites—they can eat more than ten times their own weight in food each day! They can double in size in a single day—all that food has to go somewhere.

Here's the really cool thing about these jellies—if you cut a sea walnut into pieces, you won't slow it down all that much. Each piece of gelatinous goop will grow into its own separate jellyfish, and they'll all be off living their own lives in just two or three days.

NO JOKE!

DON'T PEE ON ME!

Some jellies have powerful venom in their tentacles. **Irukandjis** are tiny, but they have a sting that is 1,000 times stronger than a tarantula bite! Even touching a little bit of **box jellyfish** tentacle can make you really sick, and if 15 feet of it touches your skin you might have only four minutes to live—or even two.

You might have heard that if a jelly stings you, someone should pee on the affected area to relieve the pain. You'll be happy to know there's no reason to ever get soaked in urine—this is definitely a myth. If you get stung you should seek immediate help from a doctor, but pouring vinegar over the area might help with the pain in the short term, depending on the type of jelly that stung you.

DO JELLYFISH LIVE FOREVER?

THEY KIND OF DO, ACTUALLY.

R.I.P.

If jellyfish fall on hard times they have a secret power—they can "degrow." They shrink down to a tiny size so that they can eat a lot less food and still scrape by. When food is plentiful again, they grow back to their normal size. But that's not all jellies do to avoid death:

▶ **Moon jellies** can grow whole new body parts. They can also age backward, turning themselves back into baby jellies anytime they want. Imagine if humans could do those things!

▶ One kind of jellyfish literally lives forever. When it "dies" it begins to rot, which is pretty much what you expect from a dead body. But then something strange happens. Tiny parts of the rotting jelly find each other and come back together to form a baby jelly. All of this happens within five days of the "death," which is a pretty short timeframe in which to raise the dead. Their name won't surprise you— what else could you call them but **zombie jellies!**

▶ No one could call a jellyfish a quitter—lots of jellies keep on stinging even after death! They don't mean to sting things at this point, but their tentacles are still full of venom that will be released when touched.

CLIMATE CHANGE AND JELLIES

Climate change is bad news for just about everyone on the planet—but it may actually benefit jellyfish. This is because climate change will lead to oceans warming up. Warm water contains less oxygen—so some species will struggle to survive. But jellies don't need as much oxygen as other animals to breathe, so they'll be fine— tropical jellies (like those pesky and very poisonous **Irukandji**) will likely spread further around the world.

Jellyfish might even have the ability to speed up climate change. Jellyfish make loads of carbon-rich feces and mucus (poo and goo) that bacteria use to breathe, which is just about the grossest thing ever. Not all bacteria are bad— some are really useful! But this particular kind produce a whole lot of carbon dioxide.

Jellyfish also eat vast numbers of things like plankton, which take a lot of carbon dioxide out of the atmosphere and oceans. Losing too much plankton will mean there's a lot more carbon dioxide in our oceans, which will speed up climate change.

WANT TO LEARN MORE ABOUT CLIMATE CHANGE? FLIP TO PAGE X!

5

SOLAR-POWERED JELLYFISH

On a small island in the Pacific Ocean, part of the island nation of Palau, swarms of **golden jellyfish** live in the aptly named Jellyfish Lake. These jellies follow the path of the sun as it moves through the sky each day, floating from one side of the lake to the other to make sure they stay in the sun's rays. But why do they do it? Not to get a tan, that's for sure! These particular jellies have a type of algae living in them that get their energy from the sun. The algae need the jellies to carry them around, so they supply the jellies with food and energy as a kind of trade for carrying them wherever the sun goes.

A GROUP OF JELLYFISH IS CALLED A SMACK. THEY CAN ALSO BE CALLED A BLOOM OR A SWARM.

SOUND THE ALARM!

Alarm jellyfish live deep in the ocean, where it's REALLY dark. Really dark, and also full of all kinds of weird creatures. A lot of these creatures have glowing lights to make living in the dark easier, and the alarm jelly is no different. But, unlike other glow-in-the-dark animals, this jelly doesn't use its lights to hunt. It uses them to avoid being eaten! When it's attacked, the alarm jellyfish launches into a dramatic performance with lots of flashing and spinning lights. This incredible show attracts a whole lot of other predators to the scene, which might seem like a bad idea. Surely hordes of dangerous predators are worse than just one, right? But there is logic behind the jelly's plan! It knows that all the new predators will probably go after the original attacker, giving the jelly a chance to escape.

SNEAKY!

ARE JELLIES EVERYWHERE?

Jellies can thrive where few other species dare to go. Humans use scuba gear to breathe underwater, and some jellies use their body parts to do a similar thing! They absorb oxygen through their bells and hold on to it, kind of like taking a big gulp of air, which lets them swim into oxygen-less water without running out of breath.

Jellies can live pretty much anywhere in the ocean, but they don't just live in the salty water of the sea! A few tiny, stingless types of jelly can live in fresh water, too. So, yes, the world is pretty much bursting at the seams with jellies.

JELLYFISH v. EVERYONE

Jellies are cute, and the small ones look about as harmless as a shower cap. But don't be fooled! Jellies can cause a whole lot of trouble.

▶ Who would win—jellyfish or fishing boat? One average-sized jelly might not do much damage, but when a swarm of giant jellies is scooped up in a fishing net it can be heavy enough to tip an entire boat over. We're not talking about a tiny little dinghy, either—this once happened to a fishing trawler weighing 10 tons!

▶ Jellies are often sucked up with sea water into the cooling systems of nuclear power plants. Up to 150 tons of jellies are removed each day from some power plants just to keep them operating—that's millions of individual jellies sliming their way into machines and gunking them up until they stop working. Gross, but kind of impressive!

▶ In the Philippines, people were plunged into darkness one night when a huge swarm of jellies shut off the electricity! A large power plant had sucked up 50 truckloads of jellyfish through its cooling system, which shut off all the power and sent the plant into an actual blind panic— no one could see anything in the dark!

WHO'S HUNGRY?

Some jellies don't need to eat at all—they absorb tiny pieces of nutrient in the water through their skin. Most jellyfish don't try very hard to hunt for food—they just drift through the water, trailing their tentacles like nets to catch prey. But not all jellies are willing to wait for their food to come to them! When it comes to hunting, different species have their own special tricks.

▶ **Box jellyfish** are the only jellyfish with eyes and brains! They're wildly clever hunters that are able to get up some serious speed as they go after fish and crabs.

▶ **Australian spotted jellyfish** have a sneaky way of catching plankton. They shoot a special foam into the water to thicken it and make it harder for plankton to move around. Once the plankton are swimming in slow motion, the jellies glide in and gobble them up!

HOW DO THEY MOVE?

By pulsating their bells, some jellies can actively propel themselves through the water in a hypnotic movement. They actually pull themselves through the water, by creating a negative pressure in the water ahead of them, as they pulsate.

PIRANHAS

Piranha means "tooth fish" in Tupi, an indigenous language of Brazil. It's no surprise they were named after that particular feature—they have seriously fearsome grins. They live in freshwater lakes and rivers, including the Amazon River, and they can also commonly be found in the nightmares of people petrified of being eaten alive while swimming. True, piranhas are incredible hunters that are attracted to the smell of blood, but you'd be surprised at the things they'd choose to eat before sampling your toes!

SCAREDY FISH

Piranhas have huge teeth, but there are still plenty of larger, fiercer predators that can eat them, including caimans—relatives of alligators. Traveling in crowds makes them feel less open to attack—there's safety in numbers!

A FISH OR A DOG?

Red-bellied piranhas bark to frighten off predators.

WHERE CAN I SEE A PIRANHA?

Piranhas live in South America.

A GROUP OF PIRANHAS IS CALLED A SHOAL.

WHAT DOES A PIRANHA EAT?

Piranhas are known for having a taste for flesh, but plants are actually a common part of many piranhas' meals. Some of them are even vegetarian!

- ▸ Seeds, nuts, and riverweeds make tasty snacks for piranhas.

- ▸ Meaty prey commonly includes things like worms, crustaceans, snails, fish, and any dead animals or birds that they find in the water.

- ▸ If there isn't much food around, they can turn to cannibalism and start eating each other!

CAN A PIRANHA EAT ME?

A piranha certainly wouldn't turn its nose up at nibbling on human flesh, but the human would have to be dead or very close to it before piranhas made a proper meal of them. They generally only go after large prey such as humans or capybara if they're dead or severely injured. If there isn't a lot of other food around and you splash noisily into a piranha-infested river with a bleeding foot, you might be risking a piranha bite. That said, people regularly swim in rivers with piranhas without it turning into a bloodbath.

CRUNCH!

Wimple piranhas swim quickly at their prey, barreling up and taking a firm bite before their hapless prey knows what's hit them. They aren't actually going after flesh, though—their favorite food is fish scales. They ram into fish to dislodge their scales, which they crunch down on as their frightened prey swims off (a few scales lighter!).

YUM!

FISH SCALES

TEAMWORK MAKES THE DREAM WORK

Red-bellied piranhas are great at sharing! They look for food together, often lurking in underwater plants and waiting to spring out to surprise unsuspecting prey. When one fish comes across something meal-worthy they let the rest of the shoal know, and everyone gathers around to take turns tearing a mouthful out of their shared dinner. Piranha dinnertime isn't always so polite, though. These fish can go into a feeding frenzy when they're hungry and come across prey in the water, with masses of fish thrashing and flipping around to fight for a bite before their friends gobble it all down.

FROGS AND TOADS

Frogs and toads are more similar than you'd think. They're both amphibians and even share a scientific name, Anura, which means "without tail" in Latin. Anurans with smooth skin are usually called frogs, while ones with warty skin are usually called toads. But both smooth and warty-skinned types can occur within the one Anuran family. Frogs and toads are a lot more brutal than they look. Did you know there's a frog that can inject poison into its attackers using the horns on its head? Or one that breaks its own bones to use as weapons? And they're only the modern ones—ancient species were tough enough to tangle with baby dinosaurs!

WHERE CAN I SEE A FROG OR TOAD?

Frogs live on every continent except Antarctica.

A GROUP OF FROGS IS CALLED AN ARMY, A GROUP OF TOADS IS CALLED A KNOT.

BIG
AND SMALL

The smallest frog is the *Paedophryne amauensis*, which only grows up to one third of an inch long. The entire frog is the same size as a pea!

The largest frog is the **goliath frog**, which is about 1 foot long and can weigh more than 7 pounds—the same as a brand new human baby, but a whole lot slimier.

FLANNERY FILE

Some time ago I was working in a very remote village in New Guinea. One day, a woman brought in a gigantic frog and sat it down on the table in front of me. This frog was the size of a dinner plate! I thought maybe it was dead, because it was completely still. Then, with no warning, it leapt off the table and onto my chest! It got me right around the throat with its arms, kind of like a big frog-hug. Everyone in the village screamed—they thought I'd been attacked by this giant frog. But I couldn't stop laughing—the frog was just like a big baby. I picked it up and popped it back on the table, and it quickly bounded away.

THE PERFECT NAME

- **Rocket frogs** have a pointy nose that looks like the tip of a rocket ship—and they can launch like a rocket, too. The Australian rocket frog can jump 13 feet high!

- **Ornate Pac-Man frogs** have super-wide jaws, just like the famous yellow computer game character they are named after. They snap up their prey just as enthusiastically, too!

- **Venezuelan pebble toads** have bumpy, pebble-colored skin. When these tiny mountain-dwelling toads feel threatened they roll up and bounce away downhill just like a loose pebble.

- **Little devil frogs** are bright red, the same color as a cartoon of the devil, and they're packed full of poison, too.

- **Mossy frogs** have lumpy skin that is covered in mottled green patches. They look just like tiny, moss-covered rocks!

- **Glass frogs** have completely see-through skin, so when you're looking at them you can see all of the organs working away inside.

- **Wolverine frogs** are also known as hairy frogs or horror frogs. They have masses of hair-like growths sticking out near their back legs, a bit like Wolverine's shaggy sideburns. But that's not all! Just like the comic book character, these frogs have the ability to snap their own bones and force the bone spikes out through the skin of their feet to protect themselves. Once they've neutralized the threat they pull the broken bones back inside their bodies and start to heal. INCREDIBLE!

FROG FOOD

Tadpoles can eat plants, but mature frogs and toads are carnivorous. They'll eat just about any insect or animal that will fit inside their mouths, including larger prey such as mice, fish, other frogs, and even small snakes. That's pretty brave!

Why do frogs blink so much as they eat? Well, frogs can push their eyes so far back into their heads as they blink that their eyeballs help push the food down their throats.

WILD!

EGG ADVENTURES

Frogs and toads often lay their eggs straight into the water, but sometimes they lay them on part of a plant that's hanging over a body of water instead. When these tadpoles hatch they slither off the plant and into the water below.

NIFTY!

- In Japan, the female **forest green tree frog** produces a fluid similar to egg whites, which she whips into a thick foam using her back legs. She makes a large, baseball-sized sphere of foam that will hold all her eggs securely up in a tree until they're ready to hatch.

- Frog eggs look like a tasty snack to many animals, but **red-eyed tree frog** eggs aren't quite as helpless as they look. If they sense a predator, the tiny tadpoles start to wriggle furiously inside their eggs. They release a special chemical that helps them break through the egg wall, letting them hatch early and dive into the water below.

CLIMATE CHANGE

Changes to the temperature of their homes or to water levels can make it much harder for frogs and toads to survive. The **golden toad** of Costa Rica may have already been driven extinct by the changing climate.

IS BEING A TADPOLE COMPULSORY?

Surinam toads skip the tadpole stage altogether—they pop out of their eggs fully formed. Mothers lay up to 100 eggs at a time, which settle onto their flat, broad backs and become embedded in the skin. When they're ready to hatch, the baby toads tear holes in the skin and burst through! Luckily the holes heal over afterwards.

CAN A FROG KILL YOU?

Frogs are pretty cute, so you might think there's no way they could be dangerous. But you'd be wrong! Not only are some frogs poisonous, but some are toxic enough to kill you.

▶ The **golden poison dart frog** has enough poison to kill ten adult humans. **DEADLY!**

▶ Some frogs don't make their own poison—instead, they eat a range of toxic insects and reuse their poison for their own protection.

▶ Many poisonous frogs are brightly colored and have elaborate patterns. These colors work as a warning to predators, who know that brightly colored frogs are likely to give them a nasty surprise (i.e., pain and death) if they try to eat them.

▶ **Greening's frogs** have spiky growths on their skulls that they use to inject their poison instead of waiting for it to absorb through the skin.

FLANNERY FILE

I was once camped in the desert in Central Australia during a thunderstorm. There was lots of thunder before any rain fell, and I heard frogs calling from the bone-dry sand dune I was camped on. You might think deserts are too dry for frogs to live in, but some species bury themselves in the sand and rest for long periods until it rains. The frogs I heard must have been roused from their slumber by the sound of the thunder. By morning enough rain had fallen to create a lake at the foot of the dune, and it was completely full of frogs!

ANCIENT DINOSAUR-EATERS

Frogs and toads have been around in some form or another for more than 200 million years. The fossilized bones of one ancient species were found in Madagascar. The species has been given the name **devil frog** or "devil frog from hell." This frog lived about 70 million years ago and was a large, aggressive predator that may have even eaten baby dinosaurs!

13

WHALES

Whales can grow to sizes that are, quite frankly, very intimidating. Don't let that scare you, though—even though they're the biggest animals in the ocean, most whales enjoy chomping down on teeny-tiny prey such as krill. They have excellent singing voices, strangely useful poop, and a whole heap of weird body parts—including giant heads, forehead teeth, and, if you go back far enough in history, legs.

SEASONED TRAVELERS

Gray whales have the longest migration of any mammal. They travel an astounding 10,000 miles each year between their summer feeding grounds near Alaska and their breeding grounds near the coast of Mexico.

WHERE CAN I SEE A WHALE?

Whales travel a lot to find the right climate for feeding and mating, so they can be seen anywhere from the freezing cold waters around the Arctic and Antarctic to tropical coastal areas.

A GROUP OF WHALES iS CALLED A POD (OR A GAM, PLUMP, OR HERD).

DIVING CHAMPS

Sperm whales can dive more than 3,000 feet deep in the ocean to look for giant squid, holding their breath for up to an hour and a half at a time. Their remarkable diving abilities might have something to do with a mysterious substance called "spermaceti." Their heads are packed full of the stuff, which is thought to help these whales adjust their ability to either float or sink in the water.

IS THAT A UNICORN?

Male **narwhals** have a giant spike sticking out the front of their heads. They're the big, blubbery unicorns of the sea! Despite looking like a horn, narwhals' spikes are actually ridiculously long teeth. This special forehead tooth can grow to more than 8 feet long, but scientists aren't sure why they grow that way. Maybe it's to attract a mate, or to use as a weapon—either way, they look pretty magical.

SINGING STARS

Whales can be incredibly loud! **Toothed whales** and **baleen whales** make different kinds of sounds, and they make them for different reasons, too:

▶ Toothed whales make a range of clicks, whistles, clangs, and groans. These noises help them communicate with each other and find their way around in the ocean. Their clicking sounds travel long distances through the water, bouncing off anything in their paths, including things like fish and rocks, and ricocheting back to the whale. When the altered sounds come back the whale can work out what they've bounced off—it's like they're mapping the ocean around them using sound.

▶ Many baleen whales, including male **blue whales** and **bowhead whales**, are known for singing complex and incredibly beautiful songs. Male **humpback whales** have some of the most famous whale songs. They're also the loudest animals in the world! Other whales can hear their songs from thousands of miles away. The reason whales sing is shrouded in mystery, but it is likely to be related to mating.

HUGE HEADS v. BIG BRAINS

Right whales have particularly huge heads— they take up one third of their entire bodies! They don't have the biggest brains, though—that award goes to **sperm whales**, which have bigger brains than any other animal in the world.

SLEEPING STANDING UP

Sperm whales don't need a whole lot of sleep—only about seven minutes at a time. They usually nap near the surface of the ocean, floating completely vertically!

SPA DAY

Bowhead and **beluga whales** use rocks to exfoliate! They rub up against rough rocks to get rid of the layers of dead skin that build up on their bodies. They'll even go out of their way to reach certain rocky outcrops that are effective exfoliants, traveling long distances just to have a good scrub.

SNOT STUDIES

AAA CHOO!

You can tell a lot about whales from their snot, including if they're pregnant, how good they are at turning food into energy, and even how stressed they are! For that reason, scientists often collect whale snot to study. Whales blow snot up out of their blowholes, so it's extraordinarily tricky to catch it before it goes shooting off into the water. Blowhole spray can reach up to 30 feet in the air! Scientists have discovered a clever way of getting their snot samples, though—they use drones to pick up the snot and deliver it to them!

A DENTIST'S DREAM

Some whales have teeth, others have baleen. What's the difference?

▶ Whale baleen looks like big furry combs inside their jaws. Baleen is made of the same thing as your hair and fingernails, only on a much larger scale—whales have hundreds of plates of baleen in their mouths, and each piece can be nearly 8 feet long. That means each plate is almost definitely taller than either of your parents! They eat by gulping huge mouthfuls of water, then letting the water drain out. As the water drains, the baleen catches the krill, plankton and tiny fish for the whale to gobble down. DELICIOUS!

Scientists recently discovered that these kinds of whales have a weird organ buried in their chins. It looks like a jelly blob with fingers, and it helps them judge when they have taken in enough water to sieve through their baleen.

▶ Whales without baleen generally have sharp, pointed teeth, which means they can eat bigger prey like fish, squid, and crabs. But they don't do a whole lot of chewing—they mostly use their teeth to hook onto their prey, which they then swallow whole.

FLANNERY FILE

My first job as director of the South Australian Museum was to arrange an expedition to collect a rare, gigantic **southern right whale** skeleton. The museum curator led a team to the beach where the dead whale had washed up. As soon as she arrived, she put on her rubber boots and waterproof pants and waded right into the whale's rotting body so she could cut the remaining flesh off the bones. But just as she got inside the whale's skeleton, a huge wave came up and pulled the carcass out into the water. It was quickly surrounded by a pack of six great white sharks that started feeding on the whale meat. Everyone thought, *Oh no! She'll be eaten alive!* But, luckily, the next wave washed her and the carcass back onto the shore. Even after she'd been washed back up, she didn't abandon the job. It was stinky and gross and scary, but she didn't care! She was so passionate about getting this skeleton back to the museum.

Once all of the bones had been collected, the team loaded them into the museum truck and drove back to the city. That afternoon, I got a very angry phone call from someone saying, "I'm going to sue the museum for damage to my car!" I thought, *What on EARTH? How can this day get any weirder?!* He said, "I was driving behind your museum truck and something was leaking out. It's stripped all the paint off my car!" The heat had melted the oil in the whale bones, and it had dripped out of the truck and splattered onto this poor guy's car. The oil was so powerful, it stripped the paint clean off! We had to pay to fix his car, of course.

WHALE MILK

Baby whales grow up fast. Newborn **blue whales** can gain 200 pounds a day for the first part of their lives! Part of the reason they grow so astronomically quickly is that whale milk is super fatty—human milk is about 4 percent fat, while whale milk is more like 40 percent fat! Their milk is also extraordinarily thick—almost like toothpaste.

A WHALE WITH LEGS?

Whales didn't always live in the ocean—their ancient relatives originally lived on land! One of the earliest types of whale was called **Pakicetus**, and these ancient mammals had four legs and sharp teeth. They were much smaller than modern whales—more like the size of a wolf. They moved into the sea and lost their legs about 50 million years ago.

THE BIGGEST ANIMAL EVER

The largest whale is the **blue whale**. These ocean giants can grow to more than 100 feet long, which is about one third the length of a football field. They can weigh as much as 220 tons—as much as a house! They are the biggest animals to EVER live on Earth (including the dinosaurs).

The smallest whale is the **dwarf sperm whale**. The biggest ones weigh about 660 pounds, which isn't even half the weight of a cow, and the longest are up to 9 feet.

CLIMATE CHANGE

A warming planet means melting ice in the polar regions, which actually makes it easier for some whales, like **humpbacks** and **bowheads**, to find food. As the water warms they can stay for longer in their colder feeding grounds. But carbon dioxide is affecting the acidity levels in the ocean, which will continue to affect the availability of whale food—krill won't do so well in more acidic waters.

FLANNERY FILE

I once went out in a canoe into the tropical sea north of Bali to look for whales. It was a still, quiet morning, the sea as still as glass. We saw a serrated shape ahead and paddled carefully towards it, and it turned out that there were two **sperm whales** resting at the ocean's surface, as well as half a dozen dolphins cavorting around them. We drifted until we were really close. Then one of the whales slowly arched its back, raising its tail high above our heads as it slid gracefully into the sea. The second whale followed, and our canoe was left alone on the vastness of the ocean.

POOP AND PEE

- Among other things, **blue whales** eat krill. Krill eat tiny life forms called "phytoplankton," which need iron to grow. Blue whales have a lot of iron in their poop, so every time they poop more phytoplankton bloom in the water. That leads to more krill, which means more tasty snacks for the whales. So they're attracting food just by pooping, and then as they eat they poop even more. It's a beautiful (though stinky) cycle!

- It is hard to measure how much whales pee—they live in the water, so any pee spreads out around them pretty quickly— but one study suggested that **fin whales** release 257 gallons of pee *each day*. That could fill up four bathtubs! Every now and then whales can be seen lying on their backs and letting a plume of pee burst upward like a fountain.

A HEALTHY APPETITE

Whales don't get to be as big as they are by picking at their food—in fact, they eat almost constantly. **Sperm whales** munch down about 1,000 pounds of fish and squid each day, and **blue whales** can eat more than 7,500 pounds of krill over the same period of time.

IMPRESSIVE!

I'LL *RACE* YOU!

Male **humpback whales** get wildly competitive when it comes to mating, racing against each other in something called a "heat run." During a heat run, up to 40 males will compete for one female. She sets off at a fast pace with a horde of males thrashing along behind her. The males noisily flap their tails and fins against the water to intimidate each other, jostling to get closest to the female. When they really get going the males begin to collide with each other, and leap out of the water onto one another. As you can imagine, a fully grown humpback whale crashing down on you can really slow you down!

OTTERS

Otters are aquatic members of the weasel family, and they can live either in the ocean or in fresh water. Otter dads don't usually stick around for long, so moms and their babies live together—and they make ridiculously cute families. Go ahead and look at pictures of otters holding hands—you'll agree. Otters love going down waterslides as much as the average kid, and they're really into brushing their fur. Really, REALLY into it. Read on to find out why otters carry rocks around and what the deal is with their poo.

WHERE CAN I SEE AN OTTER?

Otters live in waterways on every continent except for Antarctica and Australia. Sea otters live along the coast of the Pacific Ocean in North America and Asia.

SEA OTTERS PLAY WITH ROCKS, THROWING AND CATCHING A NUMBER OF THEM IN THE AIR, KIND OF LIKE JUGGLING.

A GROUP OF OTTERS ON LAND IS CALLED A ROMP, BUT IN THE WATER A GROUP IS CALLED A RAFT.

DiNNERTiME!

All otters are carnivores. **Sea otters** eat things like squid, fish, crabs, and sea urchins. **River otters** eat things like frogs, crabs, fish, and crayfish. Most otters can eat up to 15 percent of their body weight each day, but **California sea otters** eat on a whole other level—they can eat up to 25 to 35 percent.

▶ River otters have long, sensitive whiskers that pick up on tiny movements in the water, helping the otters to sense nearby food.

▶ Sea otters have favorite foods, just like you. Well, not just like you—unless you enjoy eating black snails or sea urchins. Parents teach their children to go after the same types of food that they enjoy, so favorite foods are passed down through generations.

▶ River otter mothers help their pups learn how to hunt by catching fish and then letting them go so that their pup can practice chasing them down.

▶ Sea otters really enjoy eating shellfish and clams. Their teeth are much stronger than yours, but they're still not tough enough to crack open a clam. So they use rocks! Sea otters each carry around their own special rock, tucking it into a pocket of skin under their armpit when they're not using it. When they want to chow down on some seafood they balance the rock on their chest, clasp the unlucky shellfish in their paws and smash it over and over again into the rock until it cracks open. **GENiUS!**

There are 13 different types of otter. Numbers are shrinking for nearly all of them—the **North American river otter** is one type that is doing really well. Five species of otter have been classified as endangered. One of the reasons otters are struggling is their history of being hunted by humans for their fur.

13 OTTERS TO LOVE

1. **Sea otter** ENDANGERED

2. **European otter** (Eurasian otter)

3. **Hairy-nosed otter** (this one was thought to be extinct for a while) ENDANGERED

4. **Spotted-necked otter** (speckle-throated otter)

5. **Smooth-coated otter**

6. **North American river otter**

7. **Southern American river otter** (large river otter) ENDANGERED

8. **Amazonian river otter** (long-tailed otter)

9. **Giant otter** ENDANGERED

10. **Asian small-clawed otter**

11. **African clawless otter** (African small-clawed otter)

12. **Congo clawless otter**

13. **Marine otter** ENDANGERED

TOUGH GUYS

Groups of otters can gang up and make loud calls to scare off predators. They might not look scary, but **river otters** have been recorded frightening off jaguars!

BUILT TO SWIM

Sea otters occasionally come onto land to rest and **river otters** sleep in burrows called "holts" and sometimes hang out on land, but all otters spend a lot of time in the water. They have a whole host of features that make swimming a breeze.

▶ Otter feet have webbing, kind of like built-in flippers to help them swim.

▶ Otter ears and noses can close off in the water so that they don't get clogged up with water when they're diving.

▶ The broad, powerful tail of an otter is called a "rudder," which helps otters push through the water like an extra limb.

▶ Otters have powerful lungs that allow them to hold their breath underwater for up to eight minutes. **IMPRESSIVE!**

▶ Otters have two layers of incredibly thick fur—a layer of short fur underneath and a second layer of long fur on top. Their fur traps air close to their skin, keeping it warm and dry even as they're swimming in icy water.

SWIMMING LESSONS

All otter babies can naturally float as soon as they're born—they bob around in the water like a cork—but they can't swim right away. Luckily baby otters don't take long to learn how to swim—after a couple of lessons from their mothers they're zipping around like pros.

HOW BIG IS AN OTTER?

The **giant otter**, as its name suggests, is the largest otter. It grows up to almost 5 feet, 11 inches, which is taller than many adult humans! It's not the heaviest otter, though—that award goes to the **sea otter**, which can weigh up to 90 pounds.

The smallest otter is the **Asian small-clawed otter**. These little critters only weigh 11 pounds at the most—about half the weight of a wiener dog. They're short, too, only growing to about 3 feet long.

STICKING TOGETHER

While their babies are still learning how to swim, otter mothers have to make sure their little ones don't float off down the river or across the waves. They have a few ingenious (and adorable) ways of keeping tabs on them:

- Otter mothers float on their backs, clasping their baby in their arms on top of their bellies.

- Mother and baby pairs can both float on their backs together, holding paws to make sure they don't get separated by the current.

- **Sea otters** sometimes bundle their babies up in floating masses of seaweed so they can go and hunt without their baby drifting off!

MESSAGES IN THE POOP

Otter poo has a special name—it's called "spraint," and otters are very particular about it. Like humans, they don't poo just anywhere—they have a designated spot for it. Otters can tell a lot about each other by sniffing piles of poop, including how old another otter is and what sex they are. Taking a big whiff of poo sounds like a pretty gross way to get to know someone, but some people think otter poop actually smells quite nice—like jasmine tea or freshly mown hay! Not everyone agrees on that point, though—others think it stinks like rotting fish. If you ever come across some otter poo, give it a sniff and see what you think!

EW!

DOLPHINS

Picture a dolphin. You're probably thinking of a sleek gray creature frolicking off the coast of a tropical island. Maybe one with a cute smile and a sweet, chirruping call. Well, you're right—many dolphins are just like that! But did you know that dolphins also live in freshwater rivers? Or that **melon-headed whales** and **orcas**, also known as **killer whales**, are actually both types of dolphin? Dolphins are full of surprises—and they have some deeply weird habits.

River dolphins live in freshwater rivers in South America and Asia. **Ocean dolphins** live all around the world. Many dolphins prefer warmer coastal waters, but even the colder and deeper parts of the ocean have dolphin residents, including the mighty **orca**.

A GROUP OF DOLPHINS IS CALLED A POD.

SURF BROS

Dolphins like to surf! They use their bodies to catch waves, including the waves caused by boats as they cut through the water.

RAD!

WHAT'S SO GOOD ABOUT
SEA SPONGES?

Sea sponges are big lumps of sponge that grow in the ocean. They might not sound exciting to you, but dolphins love them!

▶ Male **humpback dolphins** have been seen giving sea sponges as gifts to females they like. It's the dolphin version of giving your crush a bunch of roses.

▶ The **bottlenose dolphins** from Shark Bay in Australia have some weird habits. They tear off pieces of sea sponge and stick them over their snouts. As far as fashion goes, this might look a little questionable, but the dolphins aren't doing it to be cute. They use their snouts to seek out food on the rough surface of the ocean floor, and the sponges stop their noses from getting scratched and damaged. **CLEVER!**

RIVER DWELLERS

Some ocean-dwelling dolphins can occasionally venture into fresh water, but there are only a handful of species of dolphin that live exclusively in fresh water. They have more flexible necks than ocean dolphins, allowing them to turn sharply to avoid obstacles. They can also swim upside down! The life of a **river dolphin** isn't all fun and games, though—pollution, hunting, and construction are making it harder and harder for these creatures to survive.

! SHARK ATTACK

Sharks attack and eat dolphins, but these powerful predators are regularly thwarted by clever pods of dolphins that don't want to become dinner.

▶ Dolphins are much more agile in the water than sharks. They have the ability to swim steeply up and down, while sharks swim best going forward. That makes it much easier for dolphins to evade capture.

▶ Pods of dolphins gang up to scare away sharks. They're fearless in a fight, ducking in and beating the shark with their tails to frighten it away.

▶ Sometimes dolphins will swim up underneath a shark to attack its soft underbelly, hitting it with their snouts. It doesn't seem like a nose jab would do that much damage, but a dolphin snout is strong enough to stun a shark, or even kill it.

BABY MUSTACHE

Imagine if you were born with a beard. Well, that's almost the reality for baby dolphins. They're born almost completely hairless except for a row of hairs across their snout, like a baby mustache, which falls out after about a week.

HITCHING A RIDE

Baby dolphins can't swim very well at first, but they have a nifty trick to help them keep up with their super-speedy mothers. By swimming right up close to their mom, they get sucked into her slipstream. They barely have to work to keep up; they can just relax and get pulled along.

LAZY?

OR INSPIRED?

GOING FOR A SPIN

Dolphins are famous for their graceful leaps out of the water. **Spinning dolphins** and **spotted dolphins** are particularly high jumpers—they can reach over 15 feet in the air! Spinning dolphins do something a little special as they leap—as their name suggests, they spin like ballet dancers! They start spinning under the water to build up power, and then burst up into the air, where they keep spinning. They can make seven full turns in just one second before crashing back down into the water.

SPITTING

Snubfin dolphins don't spit their food out, they spit *at* their food! They hunt in groups, spitting powerful jets of water to herd fish together so they can catch them more easily.

FLANNERY FILE

Once I was filming a documentary in Australia's Shark Bay, and we saw a pod of wild dolphins quite a long way from the shore. I swam out toward them, and they didn't move away. In fact, one of them came right up over my shoulder! I had a GoPro camera with me, so I took a selfie with the dolphin resting its head on my shoulder.

TERRIBLE TABLE MANNERS

Dolphins don't really chew their food—despite having sharp teeth, they have quite weak jaw muscles. That doesn't stop them from eating, though! They use their teeth to grab onto their prey, which they usually swallow whole.

Sometimes dolphins shake their food or rub it against a rough surface to break it into pieces. Imagine if you tried eating like that at the dinner table! **Bottlenose dolphins** sometimes beat cuttlefish to get rid of their ink, or scrape them along the ocean floor to remove their bony parts. They've also been observed removing the heads of catfish before eating them to avoid being poked by their sharp spines.

THE NEWEST DOLPHINS

Only three new species of dolphin have been discovered since the 2000s. The **Burrunan dolphin**, living around the coast near Melbourne, in Australia, was recognized as a new species in 2011. Other new additions to the dolphin gang are the **snubfin dolphin**, discovered in 2005 in New Guinea, and the **Australian humpback dolphin**, in 2014. A case was put forward in 2014 for a new type of river dolphin living in Brazil, called the **Araguaian boto**. But scientists can't agree if this dolphin is a close relative of the **Amazon river dolphin** or part of the same species.

SOUND MAPS

Many dolphins use echolocation to find food and map out their surroundings. They make up to 1,000 clicking sounds per second, and these sounds travel through the ocean and collide with objects or other animals, sending back echoes to the dolphin to let them know what is nearby. The messages these echoes pass on to the dolphin are amazingly detailed—they can find out how far away things are, how big they are, and what shape they are.

MODERN FAMILIES

Male **orcas** don't raise their own babies. After mating, they leave their partner and move back to live with their mothers! That might sound a little irresponsible, but male orcas are actually very helpful in other ways. They're really good at babysitting their younger relatives, often helping to look after their nieces, nephews, and younger siblings. Many other dolphins, including **bottlenose dolphins**, live in larger pods where everyone helps take care of any babies in the group.

DOLPHIN TO THE RESCUE!

Dolphins are known for being remarkably compassionate. If one of their group is injured they will help it up to the water's surface so it can breathe, and they even come to the rescue of other animals. Moko, a **bottlenose dolphin**, famously helped rescue two pygmy sperm whales that were stranded on a New Zealand beach. Humans had been trying to rescue them for some time, but the whales kept washing back onto the sand. Moko swam up and helped guide them away from the beach and out into open water.

WHAT A HERO!

DID YOU SAY MY NAME?

Each **bottlenose dolphin** has its own signature whistle that helps the pod communicate and keep track of each other. The whistles are like names—dolphins use their whistle to identify themselves, and if they hear another dolphin call it out, they'll respond.

ORCAS ON THE HUNT

Orcas are apex predators, so they spend most of their time thinking of ingenious ways to catch food instead of worrying about being eaten. They often live in cooler parts of the ocean, with plenty of ice around, and different clans specialize in catching different types of food. Some eat only salmon, and others only seals—a bit like the way some people like toast for breakfast and others prefer cereal.

▶ Orcas often work in groups to take down prey, such as seals. They don't settle for gobbling up the ones swimming in the water—they go after the ones on the ice, too. They splash water over chunks of ice floating on the ocean surface to wash the hapless seals off, or dive underneath the floes and knock them from below to make them tilt or even split apart.

▶ Even whales aren't safe from orcas. One of the ways they overpower such enormous prey is flopping on top of them—weighing them down in the water to tire them out. It's a bit like an older sibling sitting on you so you can't run off; only in that case, you don't end up being eaten!

BEST FRIENDS

Male **bottlenose dolphins** form lifelong friendships, and often bond closely with one or two others, working together to impress females. These bonded dolphins are often seen swimming side by side, jumping through the air in unison, rubbing against each other, and overlapping the fins on the sides of their bodies—a bit like holding hands.

SWEET!

PUFFERFISH

Pufferfish have huge eyes and big, full fish lips, but don't let their cuteness fool you! These sweet-looking fish have a surprisingly large number of ways to cause discomfort and even death for anything that tries to eat them. You can find them in oceans and fresh water, nibbling on some shocking things and getting all puffed out of shape when someone bothers them.

HOW BIG IS A PUFFERFISH?

The **dwarf pufferfish** is about 1 inch long, or the width of a one-dollar coin. You could hold a whole handful of them at once, but you probably shouldn't!

WHERE CAN I SEE A PUFFERFISH?

Pufferfish prefer warmer waters, especially tropical parts of the ocean. They sometimes live in subtropical waters, and even venture into fresh water, but never cold water.

PUFFERFISH CAN SWIM BACKWARD AS WELL AS FORWARD —A VERY RARE SKILL FOR A FISH.

TOE BITERS

One type of pufferfish, **ferocious pufferfish**, has been known to bite. Its teeth are so powerful that they can tear off large chunks of human flesh, usually out of people's feet.

YUCK!

BACK OFF

Pufferfish aren't great at swimming, which is unfortunate for an animal that lives in water. Luckily, they have a lot of other cool skills to make up for it!

- When they sense danger, pufferfish swell up to enormous sizes. They don't hold their breath to do it—they suck in large amounts of water, and can still breathe even when they look like balloons. If a pufferfish inflates after it's been seized by a predator, it can block up the attacker's throat and make it impossible to breathe—it's not giving up without a fight!

- Pufferfish don't have scales—they're covered in tough skin instead, which can change color to help them blend into their environment.

- Lots of species of pufferfish are covered in spines, but they mostly lie flat against their bodies. The spines can be hard to spot until the fish puff up—then they're impossible to miss!

- Many pufferfish are chock-full of a poison called "tetrodotoxin." One pufferfish can be poisonous enough to kill five ice hockey teams—that's 30 people! The poison starts by making your lips and tongue go numb, then your entire body gradually becomes paralyzed before you eventually die. This poison is super toxic to most other animals, too—only a few sharks are able to snack on a pufferfish and live to tell the tale.

UNDERWATER ARTISTS

White-spotted pufferfish males go to a lot of effort to find a mate. They spend about a week working 24 hours a day to build an elaborate nest on the sandy ocean floor. The nests look like a work of art—they're shaped like a sunburst, with peaks and valleys of sand radiating out from a circular center. The male fish builds these shapes by wriggling through the sand, and even decorates his masterpiece with carefully collected pieces of shell and coral! After finding a mate, the male stays in his nest until the eggs hatch, then he abandons it! The male only uses each nest once before moving on to build a fresh nest for a whole new set of eggs.

THAT'S DEDICATION!

BOYS AND GIRLS

Dwarf pufferfish are not born male or female—they take on a sex later in life. If they become male they are able to release a special hormone into the water that makes sure other pufferfish living nearby become female—that way, they can become the alpha male with no competition.

31

CRABS

Crabs are crustaceans, relatives of lobsters and prawns. You're probably familiar with them—you might have seen one of these eight-legged creatures scurrying along a beach, or a cartoon version singing about living under the sea in *The Little Mermaid*. There are more than 4,500 different species of crab, though, and not all of them are ocean-dwellers. Many crabs live on land, and some even live in trees!

WOULD YOU CUDDLE A CRAB?

Some crabs, including **teddy bear crabs** and **orangutan crabs**, have luscious locks across their bodies. They might look soft and fuzzy from the outside, but don't be fooled—there's still a hard shell and two snapping claws underneath all that fluff!

A GROUP
OF CRABS IS
CALLED A CAST

(NOT THE KIND YOU
PUT ON A BROKEN ARM,
OBVIOUSLY).

ON THE HUNT

Some crabs eat meat, others eat plants. They have a number of ingenious methods for finding their dinner:

- **Soldier crabs** hunt together in large troops, clearing out every speck of food hidden on a beach, one section at a time. The smooth beach becomes covered in tiny bumps of displaced sand as they dig for food.

- **Pea crabs** are tiny, pea-sized crabs that live inside the shells of creatures like oysters, mussels, and clams. They don't need to hunt—when food filters into the shell of their host, the sneaky little crab steals it!

- **Sand bubbler crabs** eat by shoving sand into their mouths with their claws. They eat tiny bits of food from between the grains, spitting out the leftover sand and rolling it into a ball that they throw behind them as they move. And they move fast! At low tide they quickly comb through the sand and then bury themselves beneath it so that the waves don't sweep them away.

EXTRA ARMOR

Carrier crabs, also called "urchin crabs," have hard shells like most other crabs. But they aren't content with their built-in armor—they want extra protection! They pick up things like sea urchins, rocks, and shells from the ocean floor and carry them around on their backs like a shield, often choosing poisonous urchins with vicious spikes. The urchins don't seem to mind—they get carried to new places where they can find food—but it does mean the crabs only have four legs left to walk with. The other four are busy clinging on to their shield!

THE SPIDER AND THE PEA

Not all crabs are the cute little critters you see scurrying around on the beach—the **Japanese spider crab** has a leg span of more than 13 feet! To put that in perspective, the tallest human to ever live was 8 feet, 11 inches. That's SERIOUSLY big. Japanese spider crabs live for up to 100 years, so they have plenty of time for growing. The tiniest crab species is the **pea crab**. As the name suggests, these crabs can be as small as a quarter of an inch, or about the size of a pea.

TWO TUMMIES

wow!

Crabs have two stomachs, and one of them has teeth inside it! Because they don't have any teeth inside their mouths, crabs need a toothy stomach to help them break down the chunks of food they swallow before passing it on to the second stomach to complete the act of digestion.

GIMME A C!

The **pom-pom crab** has tiny little claws, but you barely notice the size of them—you're too busy staring at the miniature pom-poms it's clasping like a crabby cheerleader. The pom-poms are actually sea anemones, which the crabs use to ward off predators. If they lose one of their pom-poms these crabs do something pretty brutal—they tear the remaining one in two! Luckily the sea anemones are very hardy, and regenerate into two whole anemones quite quickly. The crabs sweeten the deal by sharing some of their leftover food with their claw decorations, so it's not all bad.

UP CLOSE AND PERSONAL WITH . . . A CHRISTMAS ISLAND RED CRAB

As their name suggests, these crabs live on Christmas Island—and their shells are an eye-catching red.

▶ These flashy crabs eat mostly plants, rifling through leaf litter on the forest floor to find snacks.

▶ They live on land, but they still need to keep their gills moist so they can breathe. That means no basking in the sun! They avoid the heat by hanging out in the shade and digging burrows to sleep in. During the hottest part of the year they spend up to three months in their burrows, even blocking up the doorways so they don't dry out inside.

▶ Adult crabs live on land, but their babies spend their first month or so in the ocean. That means that when the crabs are ready to start their families, they need to head to the beach. They choose when to go based on when the tide is highest, which means millions of crabs flood out of the forest and toward the ocean at once. As you can imagine, seeing hordes of bright red crabs on the move is pretty incredible, and these crabs aren't shy about making a spectacle. Over a couple of weeks they tramp across roads in waves, scaling cliffs, and even venturing into houses on their way to the ocean. It's pandemonium!

DESERT DWELLERS

Inland freshwater crabs make their home in very dry parts of Australia. During heatwaves or long periods of drought, they dig deep burrows in the earth where they can keep cool and live off their stores of fat until the rains arrive. They can keep this up for an impressive six years!

TREE CLIMBERS

SOME CRABS LIVE ON LAND AND SOME LIVE IN WATER, BUT THERE ARE A FEW ADVENTUROUS TYPES THAT WANT TO BE UP IN THE TREES!

▶ The *Kani maranjandu* lives in the hollows of trees in India, using its slender, sharp-tipped legs to scamper around on the bark. Like many other land-dwelling crabs, it needs to keep its gills wet so it can breathe—it does it by dipping them into pools of rainwater that collect in tree hollows.

▶ **Coconut crabs** live on land, but regularly climb trees to cut down coconuts, which they are able to crack with their extraordinarily powerful claws. These monster crabs can weigh more than 8 pounds and stretch to 3 feet wide. As well as feasting on coconuts, they've been known to hunt birds! They clamber up into trees, latch on to their unlucky prey, and tear them apart, using their powerful claws to crunch through their bones with ease.

WARRIOR CRABS

Some crabs have dips and creases across the surface of their shells that look uncannily like human faces. The **heikegani crab** from Japan is sometimes called the "samurai crab," because many people think their shells look like the faces of fierce samurai warriors.

WHERE CAN I SEE A CRAB?

Crabs can be found in oceans all around the world. Some crabs also live on land or in fresh water, and these crabs generally prefer warmer, tropical countries.

FLANNERY FILE

Christmas Island, off the northwest coast of Australia, is a kingdom of crabs! There are hardly any other large kinds of land animals living on the island, but you can see **red crabs**, **blue crabs**, and **coconut crabs** everywhere! There are tens of millions of them. I went to a local school where the janitor had begun to feed leftover lunch scraps to the coconut crabs living behind it. I went to take a look and found myself standing among the rocks with hundreds of gigantic coconut crabs milling around and waiting for food. These crabs can be enormous, and they look a bit like giant spiders.

SPOOKY!

SEAHORSES

Seahorses' faces look distinctly horsey, hence the name. Despite their odd likeness to large hoofed creatures, seahorses are in fact a type of fish. Seahorse babies, which are truly tiny, are called "fry," giving everyone the perfect opportunity to use the expression "small fry" in a completely correct scientific context. Seahorses are laughably bad swimmers, especially considering they're fish, but they make up for it by being really good at playing hide-and-seek.

WHERE CAN I SEE A SEAHORSE?

Seahorses are usually found in warm and shallow coastal waters around the world, although a few types live in slightly cooler waters off the coast of places like Ireland, England, and Japan.

A GROUP OF SEAHORSES iS CALLED A HERD.

DROPPING ANCHOR

Seahorses rely on their remarkably flexible tails to stay anchored. They curl them around seagrass, coral, or anything else they can get a solid grip on so that their delicate bodies don't get buffeted around in the water. Even when they want to move from place to place, they often hold on to a loose piece of plant life or debris to help weigh them down and give them more control as they ride the currents.

LIFE IN THE SLOW LANE

Seahorses have many skills, but they're firm failures in the swimming department. In fact, **dwarf seahorses** are the slowest fish in the entire world!

▶ A seahorse's odd, elongated body shape isn't built for speed, and the fact that they swim completely upright doesn't help.

▶ Seahorses don't have a lot in the way of fins. They have two small ones on the sides of their heads to help them steer and one slightly larger one on their back to propel them through the water . . . slowly!

▶ A seahorse can move its back fin from side to side an impressive 35 times every second, but even then it still only travels 5 feet per hour. That means if an average 12-year-old human were lying down, it would take a seahorse an entire hour to swim from their toes to the top of their head.

▶ Seahorses do have some things going for them—they have a body part called a "swim bladder" that can be pumped with varying amounts of air, helping them float at the right depth in the water.

WHAT DO SEAHORSES EAT?

Seahorses might be small, awkward swimmers, but that doesn't stop them from being voracious hunters!

▶ Seahorses don't have to chase down their prey; they wait for it to come to them. They latch on to a plant or piece of coral with their tails and wait, and then eat anything that drifts by.

▶ Seahorses suck up their prey through their snouts, which are great for reaching into small spaces. Depending on how much food they're trying to scoff down at once, their snouts can get bigger to fit it all in.

▶ They eat huge amounts of plankton and small crustaceans. Some species can eat a mammoth 3,000 brine shrimp in just one day!

▶ Seahorses don't have teeth or stomachs, so their food moves through them pretty quickly. It's hard to feel full when you don't have a stomach, which is why they're always eating!

HiDE-🔴AND🔴-SEEK

Seahorses are small, they don't have the ability to bite or sting, and they definitely can't outswim predators—so how do they stop themselves from becoming dinner for one of the many dangerous beasties dwelling in the ocean? It's a simple strategy—they hide!

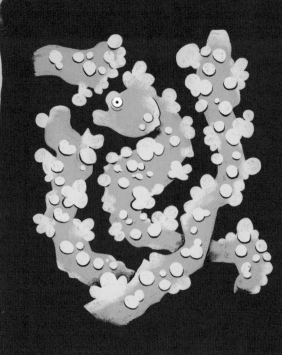

- Seahorses have special cells full of pigment near the surface of their skin, which help them quickly change color to match their surroundings when they're under threat.

- Not all color changes are caused by danger—they can also show how the seahorse is feeling. When it's dancing with its mate, the shifts in color are often elaborate.

- Some seahorses develop a permanent color to match their home. Some types of **pygmy seahorses** will turn purple or orange, depending on the color of the coral they live on. Two orange parents can end up with purple offspring if the fry drift off and land on purple coral.

- Seahorses can change the texture of their skin to blend in even more seamlessly with their environment. They can develop lumps, bumps, and rough patches to look more like coral, as well as algae and other plant life.

HOW BIG IS A HORSE?

Big-belly seahorses are the largest species. They grow up to 14 inches long, which is about half the length of a skateboard. As their name suggests, they have a particularly rotund tummy! The smallest seahorses are called "pygmies." One of the tiniest, the **Japan pig**, is about the same size as a grain of rice. They live near the coast of Japan and *apparently* look like baby pigs—that comparison might be a bit of a stretch, but you'd probably agree that they're as cute as piglets.

DEDICATED DADS

Unlike just about every other animal, seahorse dads are the ones that get pregnant—at least in a sense. During mating, the female puts her eggs into the father's special brood pouch. He fertilizes them and then carries them around until they're ready to be born. After about 30 days the seahorse eggs turn into squiggly little seahorse fry, which shoot out of their father's pouch like streamers from a party popper. He can give birth to an astounding 2,000 fry in one go, and get pregnant again with the next lot the very same day.

CLIMATE CHANGE

Because they often live in such delicately balanced environments, the slightest changes to the climate can wreak havoc for seahorses. As climate change affects things like coral reefs and seagrass beds, seahorses are struggling, leading to 11 different types being classified as vulnerable or endangered.

FLANNERY FILE

You rarely see seahorses in the water, because they're so well disguised. When I went snorkeling as a kid, I sometimes saw them. But, more often, I would find them washed ashore after a winter storm. They seem to appear in the most surprising places—I often find them at my local beach. You have to look *so carefully* in the seaweed to spot them. When I do find one, it always feels exciting—no matter how many I've seen before. There are plenty of other things to find on the beach after a storm, too—paper nautiluses, pufferfish, and lots of good shells.

STRICTLY BALLROOM

Male and female seahorse pairs mate for life, and they can often be seen twining their tails together so they don't get separated. As if that's not cute enough, they also dance together every morning to build their attachment to each other. With their tails curled together they spin around, changing color as they sway gracefully through the waves.

BRAINY FISH

Seahorses have an odd connection with your brain. No, they're not telepathic—just brain-shaped. The part of your brain that deals with your memories is called the "hippocampus," which is also the scientific name for seahorses. This vital chunk of brain looks like an elongated, curved ridge with bumps along it—just like a seahorse.

EASY, TIGER

Seahorses make a growling sound when they're feeling upset.

CROCODILES

Crocodiles are often seen lazing about in the water or lumbering along slowly on land, but don't underestimate them! They're excellent at sneaking, hiding, and general lurking, but can also be incredibly fast and surprisingly athletic when they need to be. Most animals (and you should probably count yourself among them) can't think of anything worse than getting a close-up of a crocodile's mouth, but, for a special few, the inside of a crocodile's mouth isn't a bad place to be. Crocodiles might be fearsome hunters, but they also have a softer side!

WHERE CAN I SEE A CROCODILE?

They live in Australia, Asia, South and North America, and Africa.

WHEN THEY'RE ON LAND, A GROUP OF CROCODILES IS CALLED A BASK. IN THE WATER, THEY'RE CALLED A FLOAT.

WHO WOULD BABYSIT A CROCODILE?

BUS

SONG AND DANCE

▶ Crocodile mothers have to guard their eggs so that predators don't eat them. It's a big job, sometimes lasting more than three months, so some mothers hire help. **Nile crocodiles** have worked out a deal with nesting curlews—the birds help keep an eye on the eggs, and in return the mother crocodiles protect the bird babysitters from predators.

▶ When crocodile babies are ready to hatch they start to make sounds inside their eggs, telling siblings in neighboring eggs that it's time to break free. Their mother can also hear these tiny sounds, so she'll be ready to scoop up her babies and carry them to the water as soon as they hatch. How does a crocodile carry babies? Not in its tiny arms, that's for sure. They open up their mouths, let the babies clamber in and carry them there among all those sharp teeth!

Crocodiles wriggle around, slap the water, blow bubbles, and make bellowing sounds to attract a mate. Males can also release a stinky musk, a bit like how humans put on perfume or cologne, which you can see like an oily slick on the surface of the water.

GROSS!

HOW BIG IS A CROCODILE?

Saltwater crocodiles are the biggest reptiles living on Earth today. The largest one ever found weighed over 2,370 pounds, about the same as two grand pianos, and was an astounding 20 feet, 3 inches long. That's over *three times* the height of LeBron James.

The smallest are the **dwarf crocodiles**, which can weigh as little as 40 pounds and are generally about 5 feet long. They're considered small for a crocodile, but if they stood on their tail they'd most likely still be taller than you!

The largest crocodile to ever live was probably the ***Sarcosuchus imperator***, which was alive 110 million years ago, weighed 10 tons and was 36 feet long.

HOW DO YOU TELL THE DIFFERENCE BETWEEN A CROCODILE AND AN ALLIGATOR?

One easy way to tell the difference is by taking a look at their teeth—from a safe distance, of course! When an alligator's mouth is closed you can't see any of its teeth. Not crocodiles, though! They have two large teeth on their bottom jaw, one on either side, and they stick out even when their jaws are shut.

SUPER SENSES

Crocodiles have lots of small bumps all over their bodies, with extra on their heads and near their teeth. These bumps are more sensitive than the tip of your finger—if they're swimming underwater, their bumps help them feel something as small as a raindrop hitting the water's surface.

CROCODILE TOOTHBRUSHES

A crocodile with gaping jaws and small birds hopping around between its teeth is a very odd sight, but quite a common one. The birds are called plovers, and they don't have a death wish—they just know that the crocodile won't eat them because they do an excellent job of cleaning parasites from its gums!

KEEPING COOL

When crocodiles get too hot they open their jaws up really wide, a bit like how a dog pants to cool down. No matter how hot they get, crocodiles never sweat.

DISPOSABLE TEETH

Crocodiles lose and regrow teeth all the time—they go through about 8,000 teeth in a lifetime.

WHAT BIG TEETH YOU HAVE!

Crocodiles have very strong jaws—they can bite through bone with ease—but they're only strong when they're biting down on something. Crocodiles have barely any power to open their jaws, so all it takes to keep a crocodile from snapping is a piece of string tied around its jaws.

ON THE HUNT

Crocodiles are carnivorous, and they're also apex predators. So they're doubly dangerous! Some species go after smaller prey, including fish and birds, but the larger species need bigger meals—they eat things like monkeys, buffalo, hippos, and even sharks!

▶ Because their eyes and nostrils sit on top of their heads, crocodiles can stay almost completely submerged in water while still breathing and looking around. Crocs lurk like this near the edge of the water, lunging out to attack animals as they bend down to drink.

▶ **American** and **marsh crocodiles** sometimes lie under the water with sticks balanced on top of their heads. They only seem to do this during nesting season, when birds are particularly keen to gather sticks to build their nests. When the birds get close enough, lured by the sticks, the crocodiles surge out of the water and snap them up.

▶ Despite having heavy bodies and short legs, crocodiles can propel themselves out of the water with great speed—they use their long, powerful tails to launch.

▶ Crocodiles often do something called a "death roll" where they hold on to part of their prey's body and roll over multiple times to tear it off. They can do this both on land and in the water and will keep on rolling until their prey stops struggling—usually when it dies.

WILL A CROCODILE EAT YOU?

Yes, many types of crocodiles will attack and even eat humans. The saltwater species can be particularly dangerous, so if you're heading into their home territory make sure to take care where you swim.

FLANNERY FILE

When I was in my twenties I went on an expedition to Papua New Guinea. We walked for a couple of days to reach a remote village. I thought I'd take a shortcut back and inflated my airbed and floated down the river. It was a great day, circling gently in whirlpools and watching wildlife, including birds of prey such as kites circling overhead. But when I returned to our starting point a village man looked angrily at me. He took me to his house, which had the skull of an enormous crocodile on the wall, then pointed to the river I'd rafted down on my airbed. I'd been very silly indeed.

SHARKS

Sharks have a reputation for being fearsome hunters, which is very much deserved for certain species. Many sharks don't pose any threat to you, though—from the tiny sharks that don't have mouths big enough to bite your ankle to the gentle giants that only eat plankton. You'd also be surprised at some of the things that can hurt a shark. Spoiler alert: one of these things is the water they live in! Sharks do things that are endlessly fascinating, like eat their pesky siblings and live in volcanoes. Yes, that's really true.

WHERE CAN I SEE A SHARK?

Sharks live in every ocean on the planet, from freezing arctic waters to warm tropical beaches.

ANCIENT GIANTS

Megalodons are extinct sharks that lived between 2 million and 25 million years ago. They were 50 feet long and had jaws strong enough to crush a car—or a whale, which is what they hunted (cars didn't exist then).

WHALE SHARK PATTERNS

The patterns on whale sharks are highly varied, like human fingerprints—no two whale sharks have the same pattern.

HUNTING AND EATING

Most sharks are carnivores. Common shark snacks include fish, sea lions, seals, dolphins, turtles, rays, and plankton, but hungry sharks have been known to eat all sorts of things. The skull of a polar bear was once found in the stomach of a **Greenland shark**!

▶ **Whale sharks** take in a huge amount of water as they gulp down mouthfuls of plankton and tiny fish. They can't drink it all, so they filter in the food and spit the unwanted water back out. They can expel up to 400,000 gallons of water per hour, which gives you an idea of how much these giant sharks eat.

▶ For some sharks, the smell of blood in the water is enough to send them into a feeding frenzy. A **great white shark** can sense just one drop of blood in 26 gallons of sea water.

▶ **Thresher sharks** are so flexible they can bend their bodies in half. Their tails can be as long as their entire body, and they use them to hunt by flipping them forward so violently that the fish they hit are smashed into pieces!

▶ **Cookie-cutter sharks** are only about 1 foot long, but they have huge, triangular teeth in their lower jaws. They feed by swimming up to whales and other large marine mammals and biting, then twisting, to cut out a circle of flesh. Whales are sometimes covered with the circular scars left by these sharks.

DON'T POKE MY EYE!

Sharks are pretty tough, but they still have weak spots: their eyes. Some sharks have an extra eyelid, which is a thin but strong membrane that sits underneath their external eyelids and gives an extra layer of protection to their eyeballs. Not all sharks have this, so they have to find another way to keep their eyes safe from their flailing prey. The **great white shark** uses a pretty basic solution—it just rolls its eyes back so you can only see the whites of the eyes. One handy side effect is that it makes them look even more intimidating!

A GROUP OF SHARKS IS CALLED A SHIVER.

LONG LIVES

Greenland sharks can often live for 272 years, and possibly even up to 400 years. That's longer than any other vertebrate on Earth! These sharks keep growing as adults, but only grow a third of an inch each year.

Knowing how old a shark is can be tricky, and there is plenty of room for error. The most common method is by counting the rings of cartilage that build up over time on their spines. This is similar to the way trees can be aged by counting the rings within their trunks. You can tell how old Greenland sharks are by counting the layers on their eyeballs, which grow new layers over time.

PESKY PARASITES

Ninety percent of **Greenland sharks** have a parasite that lives and feeds on their eyeballs. These parasites cause so much damage that the sharks become blind. Luckily they spend most of their time deep in cold, dark waters, so they're not dependent on eyesight.

CAN SHARKS DROWN?

Some sharks need to swim constantly so that they can breathe. Sharks don't actually breathe through their nostrils; they only use those for smelling. They use their gills to breathe—pulling fresh water in through their mouths as they swim, absorbing the oxygen, then passing the water out through their gills. If they stop swimming, their access to fresh supplies of oxygen-filled water also stops. Some types of shark do have a nifty way around this—instead of waiting for water to flow through their mouths and gills, they actively suck water in and force it out through their gills, which means they can stop swimming and still access oxygen-rich water.

SHARKCANO

It sounds too wild to be true, but a group of scientists have discovered sharks living inside an underwater volcano! It's not a dormant volcano, either. The volcano's name is Kavachi and it sits underneath the surface of the Pacific Ocean. The water around it is hot, acidic, and cloudy, which makes it hard for lots of marine creatures to live there, so scientists are still looking into how the sharks are able to survive. Researching this incredible discovery is tricky, because sending a human into such a volatile area isn't wise. But the scientists have found an incredibly cool way to gather the information they need—they're sending in robots!

AMAZING!

One of my favorite sharks is the **wobbegong**. It can grow up to 10 feet long, and has strange, seaweed-like protrusions around its mouth. It spends most of its time on the sea bottom, or in sea caves. When I used to scuba-dive off the coast of Victoria I often found them lurking, sometimes covered in small crayfish, in submarine caves. They were very docile. But you must never touch their tails, because they can turn around with lightning speed and bite you if you do! I've swum with sharks a number of times, and, to me, sharks are really very similar to dogs. They're friendly and inquisitive creatures; you've just got to be a bit cautious, like you would be with a big dog. Having to share a space with sharks teaches you a new respect for nature. In the Pacific Islands, people swim with sharks and crocodiles all the time, because they know their movements and habits. Likewise, the crocodiles and sharks know people's movements and habits. Some of the sharks and the crocodiles are probably as old as the people who are swimming!

BEACH BATHING

We often think of sharks hanging around beaches, but although some sharks do like to be near coastlines, plenty of sharks prefer the open ocean or even the deep sea where there is no sunlight. **Basking sharks** spend most of their time deep underwater, where humans can't see them, and only about 10 percent of their time near the ocean's surface. Some sharks, such as the **bull shark**, can live in fresh water as well as salt water, swimming inland through rivers.

HOW BIG ARE SHARKS?

The **whale shark** is the largest fish in the world. They can grow to 40 feet long and weigh up to 28 tons, more than four African elephants. At the opposite end of the spectrum, the **dwarf lantern shark** can be as small as 6 inches long.

KEEPING THE TOOTH FAIRY BUSY

Sharks have an astounding number of teeth that grow in multiple rows in their mouths. **Great whites** have up to 300 teeth and some sharks have even more! Sharks regularly lose their teeth (one of the hazards of being so keen on biting things), so they need to have plenty of teeth ready to replace the ones that fall out. When they lose a tooth, one from the row behind moves forward to fill the space, kind of like a conveyor belt filled with teeth.

FAST MOVERS

Shortfin makos can swim up to 60 miles per hour and are the fastest sharks in the world, followed by **salmon sharks** and **great whites**.

A SHARK CAN GO THROUGH 50,000 TEETH OVER ITS LIFETIME.

WHAT DOES ELECTRICITY HAVE TO DO WITH SHARKS?

Sharks have something called "electroreception," which is pretty much a superpower. They have a whole lot of pores on their snouts that are filled with a special kind of jelly that is very sensitive to electric energy. This jelly allows sharks to sense tiny electric currents caused by fish and other marine animals moving in the water. The jelly can even pick up on a movement as tiny as the heartbeat of a fish, allowing sharks to home in on their prey with ease. **NEAT!**

CLIMATE CHANGE

As oceans warm with climate change, some sharks are spreading out to follow their food sources. Other sharks that used to migrate with the seasons to reach warmer waters are staying put, because their home is now warm enough year-round.

As an apex predator, sharks are vital for keeping delicate marine ecosystems in balance.

OLDER THAN DINOSAURS

There are more than 450 different species of shark swimming in oceans all around the world, and many of them are relatives of ancient creatures.

▶ The **sixgill shark** has ancestors that lived 20 million years before dinosaurs.

▶ The **frilled shark** has been around for about 80 million years and hasn't changed much in that time. The modern frilled shark has a long, snake-like body and a hinged jaw packed with 300 thin, super-sharp teeth.

SINGLE PARENTS AND SIBLING RIVALRY

Some female sharks, like **bonnethead** and **leopard sharks**, can give birth without ever meeting a male! This usually only happens when there are no males around, and babies born in this way are always female.

Sand tiger sharks have two wombs. Why? Because these brutal babies eat their weaker siblings in the womb! If these sharks didn't have two wombs to keep their murderous offspring separate, they'd only ever have one baby at a time. It's survival of the hungriest!

PLATYPUSES

When platypuses were first discovered, some scientists thought someone had stitched together the body parts of different animals—like a swimming version of Frankenstein's monster—just to trick them! That's because platypuses look like a strange mix of a duck, a beaver, and an otter. Their scientific name, **Ornithorhynchus anatinus**, even means "bird-snout duck-like." Platypuses don't just *look* weird, they also act weird—the way their babies are born (and fed!) is particularly odd—and they're not quite as cuddly as they seem, either.

WHERE CAN I SEE A PLATYPUS?

Platypuses live in the eastern and southeastern parts of Australia.

CLIMATE CHANGE

Climate change could affect platypuses by reducing rainfall and increasing evaporation. This could dry up the streams and rivers that they depend upon.

PLATYPUSES ARE RARELY FOUND IN GROUPS, BUT A GROUP OF THEM WOULD BE CALLED A PADDLE.

UNDERWATER BUFFET

Platypuses live in riverbank burrows, and although they can walk on land they spend most of their time swimming and hunting in the water. They generally go for small prey like insect larvae, tadpoles, shrimp, and the kinds of beetles and bugs that swim. If an unsuspecting flying insect lands on the surface of the water it could also become a tasty snack!

▶ Platypuses hunt for an astounding 10 to 12 hours every day.

▶ They can eat their body weight in food over the space of 24 hours.

▶ Platypuses can't see, hear or smell underwater, but their remarkable bills are able to pick up on tiny electric currents caused by their prey moving through the water. You could say their bills are their secret weapons!

▶ Platypuses can stay underwater for 30 to 140 seconds. When they're looking for food, they make lots of quick dives, scooping insects, gravel, and leaf litter from the riverbed and filtering through it for things to eat. They store whatever food they find in special cheek pouches until they come back up to the surface, where they float as they eat.

TURTLE CRUNCHERS

Scientists have found a fossilized tooth from an ancient type of platypus called **Obdurodon tharalkooschild** (what a mouthful!), which lived between 5 million and 15 million years ago. These creatures are thought to have grown to about 3 feet long and weigh four times as much as the platypuses living today. They also had heaps of powerful teeth that might have been strong enough to crunch up baby turtles!

BUILT TO SWIM

Platypuses have bodies that are decidedly ungraceful on land, but in the water it's a whole different story.

▶ Their thick fur is waterproof, keeping them cozy as they swim.

▶ Their feet have webbing between the toes, making them perfect for paddling and steering through the water. It's kind of unhelpful to have webbing when you're trying to dig a burrow, though, so they have the ability to retract the webbing to give their claws all the room they need to dig!

▶ When platypuses dive, they close their eyes and ears with special flaps of skin. They even have a built-in nose seal that stops water from filling their nostrils when they dive. Handy!

▶ Platypuses are SPEEDY under the water. The bodies that waddle on land are suddenly capable of zipping along at 3 feet per second.

MILK FED

When platypus babies hatch, they're only slightly larger than a jelly bean. Their mothers feed them milk, but not in the usual way. The milk oozes out of pores in the mother's belly instead—kind of like how sweat appears on your skin after a bike ride. A platypus baby has to lick the milk right off its mother's stomach!

WOW!

FLANNERY FILE

I got to help name the fossilized remains of the oldest ancestor of a platypus ever discovered. The fossil was one of the weirdest I've ever seen—it was a jaw with teeth that had all turned into opal! It was very beautiful, with colorful flashes and parts so clear that you could see right through them! We named it *Steropodon*, which means "lightning tooth," because it had been found at a place called Lightning Ridge in New South Wales.

HOW BIG ARE THEY?

Platypuses are usually between 15 and 23 inches long, about the size of a small dog.

POISONOUS COWBOYS

Platypuses are one of the only venomous mammals in the world! Males have special venom glands that are connected to sharp, half-inch-long spurs near their back feet, kind of like the spurs on cowboy boots. The venom that comes out of the spurs is powerful enough to kill a dog, but luckily isn't lethal to humans. It is very painful, though!

CONGRATULATIONS ON THE BIRTH OF YOUR . . . EGG

Most mammals, including humans, give birth to fully formed babies. But not the platypus! They're one of only two mammals in the entire world that lay eggs (the other is the echidna). Platypus mothers don't sit on their eggs to keep them warm in the burrow—they cradle the eggs against their stomachs and fold up their wide tails to hold them in place.

MISSING BODY PARTS

▶ Carnivores need teeth, right? Wrong! Platypuses don't have any, just flat plates to grind their food against. They use the bits of rock scooped up along with their food as temporary teeth to help mash the food inside their bills. Weirdly, platypus babies actually have small teeth when they're first born, but they fall out pretty quickly.

▶ Platypuses don't have a stomach. Their gullets connect straight to their intestines, meaning their mouths and butts are one step closer than they are in your body. A stomach is generally pretty vital for breaking down food, but platypuses eat things that can be digested without the help of one.

• FLANNERY FILE •

Platypuses are super-secretive animals. They spend most of the day snoozing in their riverbank burrows, and when they leave their hidey-holes they usually dive straight into the water, so they can be hard to spot. When I was a teenager I was walking along a creek in western Victoria. It was early in the morning, and I had no idea that there were platypuses living in the creek, which flowed through farmland. I reached a small bluff and there, just below me, was a platypus, resting on top of the water. Luckily it didn't see me, so I stood still for around 15 minutes and watched as it dived, swam, and fed in the clear water. It was one of the most magical experiences of my life.

TURTLES AND TORTOISES

Turtles and tortoises are both types of Testudines (say that tongue twister three times fast!). "Testudines" means "shell," and you can't miss that feature on these creatures—their shells cover most of their bodies. So how do you tell the difference between turtles and tortoises? It all comes down to where they live—turtles can spend time on land, but they generally prefer the water. Some live in the ocean, others prefer fresh water. Tortoises always live on land. Turtles and tortoises have been around since the dinosaurs, so they've had plenty of time to develop some weird habits, including breathing through their butts, imitating worms, and growing green mohawks.

WHERE CAN I SEE A TURTLE OR TORTOISE?

There are turtles or tortoises on every continent except Antarctica.

HOW DO TURTLES BREATHE?

Some turtles come to the water's surface regularly to breathe, but certain freshwater turtles hibernate all winter underwater, and others barely come up for air year-round. So, how do they do it?

▶ The **mata mata turtle** uses its bizarrely long snout like you would use a snorkel.

▶ The **common musk turtle** has a special tongue that is covered in little buds that draw oxygen out of the water, so it breathes through its tongue as it swims.

▶ The Australian **Fitzroy River turtle** absorbs oxygen through its cloaca, or, in simple terms, it breathes through its butt. Yes, seriously. **CLEVER!**

STINK ATTACK

Musk turtles, also called stinkpot turtles, are small enough to sit in your hand. When they feel threatened, they release an overpoweringly bad smell from musk glands underneath their shells. It smells so bad that most predators will back off.

WHAT'S FOR DINNER?

Tortoises eat plants, and some turtles are partial to plant-based snacks as well, but for the most part turtles are carnivorous—and they've come up with some pretty ingenious ways to catch their meals.

▶ The **alligator snapping turtle** lives in rivers and lakes in the United States. It has a sneaky way of hunting that involves poking out its long, pink tongue and wiggling it around so it looks like a worm. Passing creatures that are lured in to try to eat the "worm" get snapped up in the turtle's powerful, beak-like jaws.

▶ **Leatherback turtles** have a whole lot of spiny barbs inside their throats that help them eat jellyfish. The barbs point toward their stomach so it's easy for jellies to slide down, but if they try to slither back out they get spiked! These turtles can eat more than 220 pounds of jellyfish each day, so they play an important part in controlling jellyfish populations.

▶ **Cantor's giant softshell turtles** bury themselves in the mud in the water, leaving just their eyes and mouths poking out. They only go to the surface to breathe twice a day! They stay completely still, and then when a fish or crab wanders past they snap it up with lightning speed. Their dinner never sees them coming.

▶ **Wood turtles** love eating worms, and they've developed a clever way to catch them. The turtles stomp their feet to imitate the sound of raindrops hitting the ground, luring earthworms out into the open where they can be gobbled up by the waiting turtle.

Mary River turtles are often called by a much more unusual name—the green-haired punk turtle! They get their name from their super-weird hairstyles—they sport tufts of bright green hair that often look like mohawks. Here's the twist, though—the "hair" is actually a type of algae. These turtles also have two fleshy spikes sticking out from under their jaws, which look like a strange beard or even two pointy teeth. I once saw a Mary River turtle in the wild, with its long, green "hair." What really amazed me was how big it was! Its tail alone was as thick as my arm. Mary River turtles are butt-breathing turtles—they breathe through their cloacae—hence their massive tails. These amazing animals have probably lived in the Mary River in Australia for millions of years. They used to be in many other river systems as well, but they have only survived in one. I felt like I was in the presence of reptilian nobility!

A GROUP OF TURTLES IS CALLED A BALE (OR A NEST), WHILE A GROUP OF TORTOISES IS SOMETIMES REFERRED TO AS A CREEP.

A PORTABLE HOME

Unlike hermit crabs, turtles and tortoises don't outgrow their shells. They never have to go looking for a new, bigger shell, because their shell is part of their skeleton—it's just outside of their body instead of inside, like ours. Some turtles and tortoises can pull their heads and feet inside their shells for protection, but not all of them are that lucky—some are stuck with permanently exposed limbs.

CLIMATE CHANGE

The sex of baby sea turtles is decided in the egg by the temperature of the sand they are laid in. Typically, males hatch from eggs that are kept at less than 80 degrees Fahrenheit, and females hatch from eggs that sit in temperatures higher than 86. With climate change warming our planet, scientists are finding that the number of female sea turtles is jumping way beyond the number of males, which will make it trickier for them to mate in the future.

⌇ TEENY TiNY ⌇
OR UNBELIEVABLY BIG

South Africa's **speckled Cape tortoise** is the smallest type of Testudines. They can weigh as little as 3.5 ounces and their shells are only 2 to 4 inches long! That means the smallest of these miniature tortoises can be held in the palm of your hand.

The biggest type of Testudines is the **leatherback turtle**, which lives in salt water and can weigh a whopping 2,000 pounds. That's the same weight as 150 bowling balls, and if you've ever been bowling, you'll know how heavy just one of those is.

BORN ON THE BEACH

All female turtles need to come onto land to lay their eggs, and sea turtles like to return to the exact same beach they were born on to lay their eggs. They usually haven't seen that particular beach since they were a coin-sized hatchling (which might have been decades ago) so nobody knows how they manage to find their way back! Sometimes they travel thousands of miles to lay their eggs. When they get there, female sea turtles dig a deep pit in the sand with their flippers and lay up to 200 eggs before filling it up with sand and swimming back into the ocean. After two months the eggs hatch, and the tiny baby turtles need to dig their way out of the sand and race down the beach into the water. If they're not quick, animals such as crabs, lizards, and birds scoop them up and eat them!

A TURTLE IN A TREE?

Even though turtles can walk around on land you probably wouldn't expect to see one in a tree. But **big-headed turtles** aren't your average turtle—they've been seen using their big beaky jaws and long tails to clamber up into bushes and trees! As you can guess by the name, these turtles have a comically large head that is about half the size of their entire shell, complete with huge jaws.

OCTOPUSES

You can tell just by looking at them that octopuses are weird. They're smart, secretive and really good at avoiding trouble—sometimes by pretending to be a lump of coral, other times by shooting ink everywhere like an exploding pen. Their bulbous, brainy bodies can squeeze into tiny spaces, because they're almost completely boneless, and sometimes they even break off one of their arms—you'll never guess why!

WHERE CAN I SEE AN OCTOPUS?

Octopuses live in oceans all around the world. Many prefer shallow waters in slightly warmer areas, but some live in deep, dark, and very cold parts of the sea.

A GROUP OF OCTOPUSES iS SOMETiMES CALLED A CONSORTiUM, BUT THEY VERY RARELY HANG OUT iN GROUPS—THEY PREFER TO BE ALONE.

ON THE HUNT

Octopuses are carnivores, usually targeting smaller marine animals such as crabs, shrimp, lobster, and fish.

- Many octopuses, including the **pale octopus**, use their powerful arms to pull apart shellfish and eat the flesh inside. They can even pull open oysters! Their beaks are powerful too. They're shaped like a parrot's beak and can crack into shells.

- If it comes across a shell that is too tough to pull open or crack, the **common octopus** has a toothed tongue that it uses to drill into shells. It has toxic saliva that it can inject into the holes to disarm the animal inside and make it easier to pry open the shell.

- Sharks can sometimes fall prey to hungry octopuses. They use their many arms to hold the sharks tight and their surprisingly sharp, beaky mouths to tear into their flesh.

- Octopuses often drop down onto their prey from above, using the suckers on their arms to latch on to their prey and force them into their mouths.

- If *you* want to taste something you need to put it in your mouth, but octopuses can taste with every part of their skin. Imagine being able to squish some ice-cream onto your elbow and immediately be able to tell if it was strawberry or chocolate flavored! The suckers on octopuses' arms are extra sensitive, with about 200 tastebuds packed onto each arm.

EATING JELLY

Some types of octopus are immune to jellyfish venom, so they can safely make a meal out of them. It's one thing to gobble down a jelly, but multiple types of octopus have also been seen toting around venomous Portuguese man-of-war and fried egg jellies after catching and killing them. The reason is really clever—they're using the trailing stingers of the jellies to catch food, as well as to protect themselves.

LADIES AND GENTLEMEN

Male and female octopuses are often startlingly different sizes. Female **blanket octopuses** are about 6 feet wide, but males are a mere 1 inch! The females of this species are also 40,000 times heavier than the males and have huge sheets of red, patterned skin between their arms. As they swim, they can unfurl these sheets of skin and trail them like a billowing cloak.

WATER • OCTOPUSES

59

MIRACULOUS BODIES

▶ Octopuses don't just have one heart—they have three! One pumps blood around the body and the other two pump blood to the gills. The heart that supplies blood to the body stops beating when they're swimming, which is one of the reasons octopuses prefer to walk when they can.

▶ Human blood is iron-based, which makes it red. Octopus blood is copper-based, which makes it blue. The copper in their blood helps carry oxygen around their bodies at very low temperatures, so the octopuses that live in the freezing water around Antarctica have extra copper in their blood. That means their blood is extra blue!

▶ Octopuses can release a black, inky substance into the water when they're scared. The ink, which is partly made of mucus, makes it harder for predators to smell, taste, and see. The ink is so powerful that it can hurt the octopus, too, so the octopus needs to make a speedy getaway while its enemy is busy being blinded with black snot.

▶ If an octopus loses an arm—maybe in a fight, or escaping a predator—it can regrow the missing limb. **HANDY!**

THROWING A *TANTRUM* ARGH!

Some octopuses living on the Australian coastline have been seen picking up shells and throwing them at each other. That's taking antisocial behavior to a whole new level!

HAPPY FAMILIES

The decision to start a family is a risky business for octopuses.

▶ Male octopuses have eight arms, just like females, but one of their arms is pretty unusual—it's full of sperm. Female octopuses often kill and eat males after mating, so some males have come up with a clever way to avoid becoming dinner. They snap off their special baby-making arm, give it to their mate and make a quick escape. Drastic!

▶ Female octopuses lay tens of thousands of eggs—sometimes more than 100,000 in one go. The mother protects them from predators, keeps them clean, and makes sure they're getting enough oxygen until they hatch, which sometimes takes months. The mother regularly goes without food over this time and will actually eat her own arms before she'll leave her eggs to find food!

▶ A female *Graneledone boreopacifica* octopus—a species that lives in the deep sea—has been recorded taking care of her eggs for a mammoth 53 months. That's nearly 4½ years!

ON THE ROAD AGAIN...
WITH A MOBILE HOME

Coconut octopuses carry a portable house around with them, like humans use camper vans. These clever critters find two halves of a shell and tuck them underneath their bodies, using a few arms to hold them in place as they waddle along. It's not graceful, but it does mean that if they come across anything frightening they can climb inside one shell half and use their suckers to slam the other half shut on top of themselves.

MASTERS OF DISGUISE

With their bizarrely shaped bodies you'd think octopuses would stand out, but they can be amazingly hard to spot.

▸ Octopuses have thousands of cells on the surface of their skin that are filled with different colors. By expanding or tightening their skin they can choose which colors are visible, letting them change to match whatever they're near. They can even create stripes or spots of color.

▸ As long as their bony beak can fit, octopuses can twist and contort the rest of their boneless bodies to squeeze into tiny gaps and cracks.

▸ By contracting special muscles across their bodies octopuses can change the texture of their skin from smooth to rough, spiky, or wispy, depending on what kind of rock, sand, seaweed or coral they need to blend into.

▸ Some octopuses bury themselves in the sand to hide—the **hammer octopus** stays buried all day and only emerges at night to hunt.

▸ One type of octopus is so good at disguises that it has been given the name **mimicking miracle octopus.** These tricksters can mold their bodies to look like a whole host of different animals, including sea snakes, eels, and lionfish. If there is a predator approaching the octopus can either imitate an animal that looks dull and inedible so it doesn't get eaten, or mimic an animal that the predator is afraid of so that it hightails it out of there.

GENIUS!

ON THE RUN

Octopuses have been known to climb out of the water for short periods of time when it suits them, but why would an octopus ever want to be out of the water? In the wild, they might make a quick foray out onto a rock to catch a crab or some other snack. In captivity, the stakes are much higher! In New Zealand, an enterprising octopus named Inky staged a miraculous escape by climbing out of his tank, walking through the aquarium, squeezing into a narrow pipe, and slithering down into the sea.

The ancient Romans recorded octopuses climbing out of the sea at night to raid the factories where the famous fish sauce garum was made.

CLIMATE CHANGE

The blue blood that octopuses have is sensitive to acid levels in the water. Too much acid makes it hard for their blood to keep moving oxygen around the body. As oceans become more acidic with climate change, they'll find it harder to get enough oxygen.

GET OUT OF MY ROOM!

Octopuses are secretive creatures that spend a lot of time skulking in caves and rock crevices. Their hidey-hole is called a "den," and if they can't find one that suits them they'll build their own. They pick up rocks and stack them to make walls, and even make rock doors that they can pull shut. Octopuses also decorate the area around their dens with the shells of snails and clams they've eaten—making an octopus's garden.

TAKING YOUR
BREATH AWAY

Blue-ringed octopuses are small, incredibly dangerous octopuses that live in coastal waters around Australia. They're quite common on rocky beaches, even near big cities, but they're shy and hard to spot. When they're scared, their brown skin flashes with electric blue rings, warning predators to back off. Their powerful venom can easily kill a human, but they're really shy and won't attack unless threatened. The stinging part of their body is so small that you don't always feel it when you're stung, but it's hard to miss the symptoms caused by their poisonous saliva—you'll have difficulty breathing, your lips and tongue will go numb, and your breathing muscles will eventually be completely paralyzed.

SCARY!

ANCIENT OCTOPUSES

The oldest octopus fossil that has been found belonged to a creature called *Pohlsepia*, which lived 296 million years ago, millions of years before the dinosaurs.

BRAINS IN THEIR ARMS?

Neurons are nerve cells that let us know what's going on in different parts of our bodies. For example, when you touch something hot, your neurons are what make you pull your hand away. For humans, a lot of our neurons are in our brains. Octopuses have neurons, too—like all animals—but instead of being mostly in their brains, 65 percent of them are in their arms! That means their arms are really good at doing lots of different things at once. You might find it hard doing two different things at once with your hands, like patting your head and rubbing your tummy, but an octopus can use each of its eight arms to do eight different things at once. They're multitasking champions!

BUSES AND BEANS

The biggest octopus in the world is the **giant Pacific octopus**. The largest one ever found was more than 30 feet wide, which is a little longer than one of the original red double-decker buses from London, and weighed more than 600 pounds. The smallest is *Octopus wolfi*, which is often shorter than 1 inch. These tiny creatures weigh less than a single jelly bean!

SQUEE!

ALBATROSSES

The albatross is a type of seabird that spends most of its time flying over the ocean, a really long way from land. From a distance, you might think albatrosses don't look all that different from seagulls. You'd be wrong, though! For starters, albatrosses are huge. As in, bigger-than-you huge. They can also dive deep underwater to catch their prey, fly ridiculously long distances and make some seriously weird sounds. And wait until you find out where they sleep!

WHERE CAN I SEE AN ALBATROSS?

Most of them inhabit the great Southern Ocean, but a few types also live around the North Pacific Ocean.

A GROUP OF ALBATROSSES IS CALLED A FLOCK, A ROOKERY, A WEIGHT, OR A GAM.

GLOBE-TROTTING BIRDS

Albatrosses travel for most of their long lives. Some birds are still gliding around when they're 60! The average albatross will travel more than 4.3 million miles in a lifetime —enough to circle the world about 180 times, or make more than six round trips to the moon.

SALTY SEA WATER

Because they spend most of their time over the ocean, it's tricky for albatrosses to find fresh water—so they have to drink sea water. Drinking sea water is TERRIBLE for humans—we get even thirstier and start to hallucinate when we do it—but albatrosses have a nifty system to deal with all that salt. They have a special passage above their beak that leaks out the salt that builds up in their blood.

CLIMATE CHANGE

Declining fish populations mean that there is less food available for albatrosses, and rising sea levels make it harder for them to build nests in some of their usual places.

MOO!

?

A DATE WITH AN ALBATROSS

Albatrosses date for a really long time before settling down to have a family—sometimes more than two years! During this time they dance for each other, groom each other, and make all kinds of bizarre sounds to impress each other, including one that makes them sound like a cow.

HUNTERS

Albatrosses gobble down a surprising variety of foods—almost anything they can fit down their gullets. They love squid, and they have more than one way of catching them.

▶ Albatrosses can spend hours paddling around in circles in the middle of the ocean. This looks innocent, but is actually a sneaky albatross trap! It's thought that this odd behavior stirs up bioluminescent creatures, which in turn attract squid to the surface of the water, where the albatross can catch them.

▶ Albatrosses don't have to wait for squid to come to the surface—they can dive 41 feet underwater to chase their prey! Squid don't make it easy for albatrosses to catch them, but it's tricky to avoid a bird that can dive with the speed and precision of an albatross.

▶ It's easiest to scavenge for dead squid because they float toward the surface of the water, where the albatross scoops them up using its large beak. And, of course, dead squid don't try to escape!

HOW BIG IS AN ALBATROSS?

All albatrosses are large, but the biggest of all is the **wandering albatross**. It's a true giant, weighing up to 26.5 pounds—twice as big as a bald eagle. It also has a 11.2-foot wingspan, the largest of any bird. Your bed probably isn't even 7 feet from top to bottom, which gives you an idea of how huge these birds really are!

FLANNERY FILE

Once I was on a Russian research vessel sailing through Drake Passage, which is a stretch of water between Antarctica and South America. It's one of the stormiest places in the world! Our boat was caught in a storm, and I was struggling to stand upright. It was a big boat—an icebreaker—and it was made for the conditions, but it was still being tossed about. So there I was, stumbling around and feeling very sick, when I looked out to sea and spotted an albatross flying by. It was soaring within a fraction of an inch of the rolling waves, and it was under perfect control. It was just cruising! Albatrosses are masters of that turbulent environment. It was breathtaking. I thought, *How can this fragile bird deal with these hammering winds and these massive waves so perfectly?* This albatross made it look like it was nothing.

SHARKS ALIVE

A young albatross's first flight is brief, typically involving a splashdown in the sea near its nest. Huge tiger sharks often lie in wait in these areas, but the albatross babies are so excited about being out of the nest that they're oblivious to the danger. They bob about in the shallows, casually staring down the advancing sharks or even giving them a cheeky peck on the snout as they plough past. But it doesn't take too long for the young birds to catch on to the danger lurking below. After all, the birds that don't learn fast are likely to become a shark's snack!

SUPER PARENTS

When they have a baby, albatross parents don't have time for anything but taking care of their chick. They take it in turns to leave their cliff-top nest to find food, and often travel more than 600 miles for a single chick-sized meal! They don't carry food all that way back in their beaks, either—they swallow it and then vomit it up for their chick to eat. Gross! With all that travelling, albatross parents hardly ever see each other. They usually only have a few seconds to catch up in between one bird arriving home and the other one setting off. It makes sense that albatross pairs only have one baby at a time. Raising an albatross chick is hard work!

ALBATROSSES DON'T SLEEPWALK, THEY SLEEP*FLY*

Albatrosses spend more of their lives aloft than almost any other kind of bird. They don't have big enough chest muscles to fly by flapping their wings. Instead, they stretch out their huge, heavy wings and cleverly use the wind to glide through the air, a bit like how a human uses a hang-glider. They can't fly if there isn't any wind. Flapping to take off is hard, but once they're up in the sky they can relax and let the wind carry them. Some albatrosses stay in the air close to 24/7 for the first six years of their lives, only stopping occasionally to rest on the ocean surface. That doesn't mean they stay awake for six years straight, though—they just sleep as they fly! We know this because a dozing bird occasionally flies into a boat—talk about a wake-up call!

BIRDS IN PERIL

Many species of albatross are critically endangered. The main threats to their health are fishing hooks and plastic waste. When they try to eat bait from fishing lines hanging off the sides of boats, they can get stuck on the hook and dragged underwater. The birds can confuse plastic waste with food, and when they eat it the plastic fills their stomach so they can't fit any real food in. So make sure you never litter—your waste could end up in the ocean, where an albatross could eat it.

BATS

There are about 1,300 different types of bat, and they're the second most abundant mammal in the world after rodents. Rodents might come out on top when it comes to sheer quantity, but bats are the clear winner in other categories—they're the only mammal that can fly! The stories about bats sucking blood like vampires are true, but not all bats are scary—some bats are adorable little bundles of fluff, and others use their moose-like noses to make hilarious honking sounds. They're very versatile!

WHERE CAN I SEE A BAT?

Bats live in most parts of the world, but they prefer places that are warmer. You won't find them in Antarctica or the Arctic—too cold!

A NEED FOR SPEED

Brazilian free-tailed bats can fly up to 100 miles per hour.

A GROUP OF BATS iS CALLED A COLONY OR A CLOUD.

UP CLOSE AND PERSONAL WITH . . .

VAMPIRE BATS

Yes, **vampire bats** are real—but don't worry, you're unlikely to get bitten by one because they prefer the blood of animals like horses and cows. The good news is that the prey of a vampire bat usually survives the attack, just with less blood!

▶ Because blood is mostly made of water, vampire bats need to eat every night to get enough nutrition. They can skip one meal if they absolutely have to, but if they skip more than that they won't survive.

▶ Vampire bats don't catch their prey by swooping in from the air—they approach on the ground, sometimes running along on all fours to chase their dinner.

▶ Vampire bats have sharp fangs that they use to slice into the veins of their prey. Blood is designed to thicken when you're injured so that your wounds can heal over, but vampire bats have a special kind of saliva that stops the blood from thickening while **INGENIOUS!** they're eating.

▶ Vampire bats have built-in infrared vision, so they can see their prey moving in the dark by sensing the heat of their bodies.

▶ Vampire bats are really generous. They share their meals with other vampire bats, but the way they do it is pretty gross. They vomit up the blood that they just ate so that their friend can eat it!

BLIND AS A BAT

You might have heard the expression "blind as a bat," but a bat's eyesight can be three times better than the average human's. And their hearing abilities are even more incredible! Bats make sounds that echo back in different ways depending on what is nearby. These complex call and echo patterns allow bats to create a highly detailed map of their surroundings. The sounds they make can be incredibly loud, but you can't hear them because they're at a pitch that human ears can't pick up.

BURROWING BATS

Bats don't just fly and walk on the ground—some of them dig under the ground, too! These burrowing bats live in New Zealand and are able to fold up their wings so that they can dig through rotting trees and under the earth.

FLANNERY FILE

In 1991 I discovered a kind of bat that was thought to have been extinct since the Ice Age. **Bulmer's fruit bat** is the world's largest cave-dwelling bat, with a wingspan of about 3 feet. The bats once lived all over Papua New Guinea, but by the time I found them they only lived in a single cave. The cave was a vertical shaft about half a mile deep, and a few survivors of human hunting had found a refuge there. To confirm what I'd discovered, I had to climb up a tree hanging over the cave at night and set a net. It was very scary!

I once discovered a new species of flying fox on New Ireland in Papua New Guinea. When I was searching for bats I had to climb a mountain of bat poo and wade through a lake of bat pee inside a huge cave. The bat that I discovered is called **Ennis' flying fox**. Its wings look like dead banana leaves, and by day it hangs in banana plants and other trees.

THE BAT CAVE

The biggest bat colony is in a cave in Texas—about 20 million **free-tailed bats** live there. They sleep inside the cave during the day and flood out at night to feed on insects, filling the sky with a swirling black mass of wings.

BABY BATS

Dyak fruit bats are one of the very few animal species whose dads produce milk to help feed their young.

FOXES AND BUMBLEBEES

Flying foxes are the biggest bats in the world. Despite their name, they're not related to foxes—they just have a foxy-looking face. They're a type of fruit bat and can have a wingspan of close to 6 feet. Even though these bats are very large, they don't weigh much—the largest ones only weigh about 3 pounds, which is the same as half a brick. That's one of the reasons they can hang upside down without feeling ill—they're too light to have the same "blood rush to the head" feeling that we do after hanging upside down for too long.

The smallest bat in the world is the **bumblebee bat**. It isn't only the smallest type of bat, though—it's also the smallest mammal in the world! It weighs less than a tenth of an ounce, which means two of these bats put together still weigh less than an average piece of letter paper. They're usually about 1 inch long, which is a little shorter than a paperclip.

THE PERFECT NAME

- The **Yoda bat** has big green-and-yellow-tinged ears that stick out to the side and a wide mouth stretched into a gentle smile. Many people think this type of bat looks particularly wise and kind, like a certain small Jedi.

- **Leaf-nosed bats** have large, oddly shaped noses. The shape of their noses varies, but it often looks like some kind of crinkled leaf has fallen from a tree and landed on the bat's face.

- **Spear-nosed bats** have a large, fleshy spike protruding above their pig-like noses.

- Most bats have pretty sizeable ears, so you know the **big-eared bat** must have REALLY big ones to earn its name. These bats have tiny faces that are dwarfed by the long rabbit-like ears that stick straight up from their heads.

- **Clear-winged woolly bats** have a particularly soft, fuzzy body and, unsurprisingly, see-through wings!

- The average **wrinkle-faced bat** probably has more wrinkles than your grandparents. These bats have masses of grooves in the bare, pink skin of their faces, as well as flaps and folds of loose skin.

CLIMATE CHANGE

Increasing temperatures are difficult for bats to deal with. In Australia, soaring summer temperatures can cause large numbers of bats to die from overheating and dehydration.

THE CUTEST BAT IN THE WORLD

The **Honduran white bat** is tiny, with fluffy white fur. Its ears, nose, feet and parts of its wings are bright yellow and orange, and its ears are shaped like little leaves.

These bats love to go camping, and make their own tents by slicing the large leaves of tropical plants so that flaps fold down on both sides to create a cozy green shelter. These tents help keep the bats hidden from predators and protect them from the weather.

CUTE!

CLEVER!

MOTHS

Is a moth just a less exciting version of a butterfly? Absolutely not! In fact, some moths are so ridiculously beautiful that spiders take one look at them and let them go instead of eating them (there's a bit more to that story, but we'll get to that later). They love pretending to be things they're not, like hornets or eyeballs or lumps of poop. Speaking of poop—the way they go to the toilet is like nothing you've ever heard of. They also love to eat nectar and honey and other sweet things (except for the ones that have more . . . Transylvanian tastes).

MOTHS AND BUTTERFLIES

Moths are closely related to butterflies, as they evolved from the same ancestor about 250 million years ago. Moths are far more common than butterflies—there are around ten moths to every single butterfly in the world.

A GROUP OF MOTHS IS SOMETIMES CALLED A WHISPER.

WHERE CAN I SEE A MOTH?

Moths live all over the world.

WHAT'S THE DEAL WITH MOTH MOUTHS?

Moths generally eat a lot more when they're caterpillars because they're building up energy to transform into moths. Moths and caterpillars eat different kinds of food, too.

100% BIRD TEARS

▶ Caterpillars particularly enjoy eating plants. Sometimes a moth's name gives you a clue about its favorite thing to nibble on when it's a caterpillar, such as the **cherry dagger moth** or **oak moth**, which feed on cherry trees and oak trees respectively.

▶ Once caterpillars turn into moths they generally lose their chewing mouths and develop a long, thin proboscis, which they use like a straw to suck up liquid foods like plant nectar. Some moths keep their mouths and continue eating firmer parts of plants such as pollen.

▶ Some moths don't have mouths or proboscises at all, so they can't eat anything once they've developed beyond their caterpillar stage. They have to eat a lot as caterpillars so that they get all the nutrients they need to last them through their short lives as moths.

▶ Moths with a long proboscis, such as the **hummingbird moth**, drink plant nectar from mid-air. They hover above a flower and let their proboscis uncurl down into the middle of the flower where the nectar is stored. **Darwin's hawkmoth** has a proboscis that can be longer than a ruler, which allows it to reach inside the particularly deep tropical flowers.

▶ A blood-sucking **vampire moth** that lives in Siberia pushes its proboscis, which is covered in tiny spikes and barbs, under the skin of animals to reach the blood flowing underneath.

▶ Some moths use their proboscis to spear through the eyelids of sleeping birds to reach the salt-rich stores of tears in their eyes. The proboscis is so thin that it doesn't hurt the birds—they can sleep right through it!

FLANNERY FILE

I was exploring high in the mountains of Papua New Guinea, and one drizzly night I visited a friend living in a nearby village. He lit a lamp when I arrived and as we sat and talked, moths became attracted to the light. Tens of thousands of them flew through the window and filled the hut! They were all different varieties—some were the size of a steering wheel, and others were as tiny as the nail on my pinkie finger. Eventually we could hardly see each other because there were so many moths fluttering through the air between us. It was a very hot night, so we were sweating quite a bit, and the moths were landing all over us to drink our sweat. It was an incredible sight!

UP CLOSE AND PERSONAL WITH . . .
AN ORNATE MOTH

HONEY RAIDER

Ornate moth caterpillars eat the rattlepod bush, a plant that produces a toxin that's meant to deter things from eating its leaves. Ornate moth caterpillars are one of the very few things that are immune to the toxins. These tough little bugs actually store the poison in their bodies to use themselves! After the caterpillar has transformed into a moth, it releases frothy, poison-laden blood from near the base of its wings. The poison is so lethal that predators have learned to recognize and fear the markings of this moth. For example, if an ornate moth is caught in a spiderweb, the spider will often carefully cut it free instead of trying to eat it. Interestingly, the poison isn't just used against predators. Males of the species rely on their toxins to attract a mate—if they're poison-free, female moths are not interested in them.

Death's-head hawkmoths, named after the distinctive skull-like markings on their backs, love eating honey—so they have developed several techniques to steal it from inside beehives. They make a loud screeching noise using an accordion-like action that confuses the bees. They are also able to produce a chemical that mimics the smell of bees, which helps them sneak into hives without being discovered. Finally, they have a partial immunity to bee venom, so if they only get a couple of stings as they're charging into the hive they might still make it out alive. Imagine risking your life every time you wanted a meal!

HOW BIG IS A MOTH?

Moths can be anywhere from as small as a period to as large as a dinner plate. **Atlas moths** are one of the largest in the world, with wingspans that can be as long as a ruler. The smallest moths, known as **pygmy moths**, have tiny bodies and wingspans of just one tenth of an inch. Those particular moths live all over the world, but they're so small that they're easy to miss.

CAMOUFLAGE OR COSTUME?

Many moths have intricate patterns and vivid colors on their wings that frighten predators, who know that these markers are indicators of toxicity. But it is not just poisonous moths that look this way—some harmless species imitate their intricate colors. These trickster moths evolved from more camouflaged species that gave up their protective coloring for a different kind of protection.

▶ The **buff-tip moth** curls its mottled brown wings into a tube shape when it sits on branches so that it looks just like a broken-off twig.

▶ The **hornet moth** has hornet-like coloring as well as a similar body shape and completely clear wings. These moths also copy a hornet's style of flight, making every effort to convince predators that they are not defenseless moths but hornets with a powerful sting.

▶ Some moths and caterpillars, including the caterpillars of some **hawkmoths**, have patterns on them that look like large eyes.

▶ The **pearly wood-nymph moth** looks just like a blob of bird poo! EW!

PINEAPPLE PERFUME

WHEN THEY'RE LOOKING FOR A MATE, MALE GOLD SWIFT MOTHS WILL RELEASE A SCENT THAT IS IRRESISTIBLE TO FEMALE MOTHS—THE SMELL OF RIPE PINEAPPLE!

HOW DO MOTHS GO TO THE TOILET?

Many moths, including *Gluphisia* moths, like to congregate around puddles and gulp down vast amounts of water. They're too small to need all that water to hydrate, so why do they drink so much? Well, there are small amounts of salt in the water, which is good for moths. They strip the salt out of the water as they drink, then get rid of the excess water—by shooting it out of their butts! They can squirt out around 20 of these powerful streams every minute as they drink—and each stream can be 1 foot long! This whole process has its own special name—it's called "puddling."

VULTURES

With their gloomy looks and strange, often bald heads, vultures seem pretty ominous—especially when they gather around injured animals, waiting for them to die so they can have a feed. But these meat-eating birds don't deserve their bad reputation—they rarely kill other animals, preferring to eat those that have recently died. They're basically tidying up gross messes as they eat, making them some of the most helpful birds on the planet.

A GROUP OF VULTURES IS CALLED A VENUE OR A COMMITTEE IF THEY'RE ON THE GROUND, BUT IF THEY'RE FLYING, THEY'RE CALLED A KETTLE. SOMETIMES A GROUP OF FEEDING VULTURES IS CALLED A WAKE.

WHERE CAN I SEE A VULTURE?

Old World vultures live in Asia, Africa, and Europe; the New World vultures live in the Americas. Between the different species, vultures live on every continent except Australia and Antarctica.

WHAT DOES A VULTURE SOUND LIKE?

Vultures aren't all that noisy. New World vultures don't even have vocal organs! Instead of singing or calling, these birds are more likely to grunt or even hiss as a way of communicating.

WOULD YOU EAT WHAT A VULTURE EATS?

Vultures generally eat animals that are already dead, including carrion, which is animals that have started to rot. But they prefer their meals to be fresh—animals that have recently died are ideal. Vultures will occasionally go after live prey, but in those cases the animal is already injured or weakened in some way. Animals such as zebras, wildebeest, elephants, hippos, and antelope are all common meals, but sometimes vultures eat things that are a little more surprising.

▶ Although meat is by far their most common food, vultures do eat some plant matter, including things like rotting fruits.

▶ **Palm-nut vultures** are almost entirely vegetarian! They eat some small animals, such as frogs and fish, but mostly large quantities of fruit from palm trees.

▶ **Egyptian vultures** have been known to use stones to break open the eggs of large birds, such as ostriches, then eat the gloopy insides.

▶ **Bearded vultures** mostly eat bones! They drop them from high up in the sky to smash on rocky areas below. Once the bones have shattered, which can take a few tries, the birds guzzle down the bone marrow, as well as shards of actual bone. They also use this trick to break open the shells of turtles so that they can get at the flesh inside.

FEEDING FRENZY!

Sometimes hundreds of vultures will feed on the same dead animal, especially one that is particularly large. With so many birds feeding at once, mealtimes can get pretty hectic. The birds flap around in a frenzy, pecking and stepping on each other to get at the food. Unsurprisingly, bigger vultures have the most success in a situation like this, with smaller and younger birds often forced to wait until the end to feed on the scraps.

A group of vultures can eat a carcass down to the bone in a matter of minutes. They tear off chunks of food and stuff them into a pouch in their neck called a "crop." Only after they've packed the crop full of food will they sit still and actually digest their meal. If they have chicks, they won't digest the food at all—they'll fly back to their nest and regurgitate the food for the chicks to eat.

STARTING A
FAMILY

Different vulture species nest in different ways—Old World vultures build large nests made from sticks, usually in trees or on cliffs, while New World vultures generally nest in bare holes dug in the ground, known as "scrapes." Some nests, particularly ones belonging to Old World vultures, are even bigger than queen-sized beds! Vulture eggs can be quite beautiful, and are often covered in brown or purple speckles. The chicks hatch with large feet and bare beaks poking out from the fluffy white down that covers their bodies. They look almost cuddly, but also very odd!

WEAPONIZED VOMIT

Some vultures, like **turkey vultures**, have highly acidic vomit, so if they throw up on the sensitive parts of a predator, it can actually hurt them. It also smells really, really bad! This isn't surprising, as its main ingredient is rotting, half-digested lumps of meat. There's another reason vultures throw up when they're threatened—puking up a large meal makes the birds considerably lighter, so they can make a quick escape by taking flight.

TOXIC WASTE

UNDER THREAT

As large animals such as elephants become less common, vultures will struggle to find food. Populations of these large birds are declining very quickly, partly due to a lack of food, but also because they are often hunted or poisoned by humans.

WHO'S WHO

There are three groups of vultures, all of which descended from different birds of prey. The first two groups, both known as Old World vultures, contain a total of 18 species. They find their food using their keen eyesight—they have a terrible sense of smell.

The third group is called the New World vultures. Some New World vultures, such as **turkey vultures**, have an excellent sense of smell. The part of their brain that processes scents is extra-large, helping them to find carcasses that are below the tree cover and not visible from the air.

WHAT'S THE DEAL WITH

VULTURES AND POO?

Vultures regularly poo and pee on their legs, and they do it on purpose. There are two very good reasons for doing something so disgusting. First, it helps them to cool down, a bit like tipping a glass of water over your feet—only a whole lot ickier. Their poo and pee also have a lot of something called uric acid in them, which helps kill any bacteria they might have picked up by traipsing around in dead bodies.

Egyptian vultures eat cow poo, and they especially love the yellow kind. The yellower the poo is, the more nutrients it has in it—plus it helps keep their faces a vivid yellow, which helps them find mates and intimidate other vultures.

HOW HIGH CAN THEY FLY?

A **Rüppell's griffon vulture** has been seen flying close to 7 miles above the ground, making it one of the highest-flying birds in the world—if not the highest.

PESTS OR HEROES?

Vultures have really strong stomach acids, which is how they're able to eat flesh that has sometimes already started rotting and could be carrying various infections or disease. They can even break down anthrax bacteria, which would kill you! By eating the bodies of dead and decaying animals, vultures are often helping to stop the spread of lethal bacteria. They might look creepy, and their diet might gross you out, but these birds are definitely your friends!

SERIOUSLY BIG BIRDS

The **Andean condors** are the biggest vultures. They can weigh up to 33 pounds, about the same as a large toddler. They also grow to 4 feet tall, which is more like the height of a seven-year-old child. Not bad for a bird! Their wingspan can extend to 11.5 feet, and they have the largest wing area of any bird in the world.

HOATZINS

Despite what they look or act like, hoatzins aren't an odd combination of bird and lizard, or bird and cow. They're the only survivor of a very ancient line of birds, which is part of the reason they look quite different from every other bird species. With their vivid blue faces, bright red eyes, and long, feathery crests, hoatzins are impossible to miss—especially when gathered in groups of 100, which can happen. And their appearance isn't even the weirdest thing about them . . .

HOW BIG IS A HOATZIN?

Adult hoatzins are about 2 feet tall, which means three of them stacked up would be as long as your bed. They're not heavy, though—even fully grown they weigh a little less than 2 pounds.

TAKE TO THE SKY! OR NOT . . .

Adult hoatzins can fly, but not very well. You're more likely to spot them perched in a tree doing their favorite thing (eating), or digesting.

WHERE CAN I SEE A HOATZIN?

Hoatzins live in South America, especially around the Amazon and Orinoco river basins.

SKY • HOATZINS

82

GRAZING ANIMALS

Hoatzins are herbivores. Their favorite foods are fresh leaves and buds—the younger and tenderer, the better. Many birds have a crop, which is a pouch in their throat used to store and digest food, but hoatzins' crops are unusual in a couple of ways. For a start, they're extremely large. They also have special ridges inside them that help grind and shred food after it is swallowed. Once the food has been broken up, hoatzins use a special mix of bacteria to ferment their food so that it can be fully digested. They are the only birds in the world that digest food in this way—other animals with similar systems are cows and sheep.

TERRIBLE AT SNEAKING

Whether they're flying or clambering through trees with their strong feet, hoatzins aren't exactly graceful. They're loud and clumsy as a general rule, so it's lucky they don't have to sneak up on their food. Aside from the noise they make crashing around through the trees or undergrowth, hoatzins also make a wide variety of hissing, grunting, wheezing, croaking, and rasping sounds. No cute little tweets here!

NOT YOUR AVERAGE BABY

Hoatzins like to build their nests on branches that hang out over water. That way, if a predator is approaching, their chicks—who are unable to fly—can escape by tumbling out into the water below. Plunging into a river might sound worse than taking a chance in the nest, but hoatzin chicks aren't your average baby birds! They can swim quite well and, as long as they don't get snapped up by a passing crocodile, they are able to paddle to shore and climb back up into the nest. Yes, you read that right—the chicks CLIMB back into the nest, using their claws. As if that's not weird enough, their claws aren't even on their feet—they're on their wings. Hoatzin chicks have two big, sharp claws on each wing, which means they can grasp onto branches and climb around until they're old enough to fly. When that time comes, usually a week or so after hatching, the claws simply fall off.

STINKING IT UP

Hoatzins are often called "stink birds" or "skunk birds" and, to be honest, they deserve the name. They smell terrible! Some people describe their stench as being similar to cow manure. The smell comes from the special way they digest their meals. As their food ferments it releases a smelly gas called methane. The birds then burp the gas out, sharing the pungent side effects of their digestion process with the world around them.

GROSS!

BURRRP!!

EAGLES

There are many different species of eagle, some more closely related than others, and they're also related to other large birds of prey, such as hawks and kites. Eagles are particularly huge, with hooked beaks, enormous wings, and powerful talons—they cut quite an impressive figure. Eagles are known as fierce hunters, elegant flyers, and intimidatingly regal birds. Which is all true! But they can also be awkward (just look at one trying to swim) and are surprisingly likely to steal their dinner rather than hunt for it themselves.

WHERE CAN I SEE AN EAGLE?

Eagles live in Africa, Eurasia, across the Americas, and in Australia.

A MISLEADING NAME

Bald eagles aren't bald, but because the feathers on their bodies are dark brown and the ones on their heads are white they do look a bit like they're featherless on top—especially from a distance.

A GROUP OF EAGLES iS CALLED A CONVOCATiON OR AN AERiE.

WHAT DOES AN EAGLE EAT?

Each species of eagle has its own favorite food, with common snacks including rodents, fish, reptiles, insects, and other birds. But they also eat things that are a lot more surprising! Turtles, small kangaroos, mountain goats, sloths, deer, flamingos, wallabies, and even small crocodiles are on the menu for some eagles.

Eagles eat every part of their prey—they're not picky. They have strong stomach acid that helps them break down their food, even the bones! The few bits and pieces that can't be easily digested, such as feathers, are coughed up as pellets that look a bit like chunks of poop. **YUCK!**

A BIRD'S-EYE VIEW

Eagles have excellent eyesight, about four or five times better than yours. They can see prey from over 2 miles away.

HOW **BIG** IS AN EAGLE?

The impressive size of an eagle is perhaps best seen in flight, when their unfurled wings are on show. Some of the biggest wingspans can stretch up to 8 feet across, such as on the **Steller's sea eagle** and the **white-tailed eagle**. The tallest basketball players in history don't measure up to that! Despite this immense size, even the heaviest of the eagles are not particularly weighty—the **Philippine eagle** and Steller's sea eagle are toward the top of the spectrum and still only reach a maximum of 18 to 20 pounds. That's about the same weight as a small beagle.

CALL OF THE WILD

Some eagles, such as **sea eagles**, have calls that are strong and loud. Others, like the **bald eagle**, have much less awe-inspiring calls. Sometimes, when you hear an eagle on TV, its call has actually been enhanced to sound more impressive. **SNEAKY!**

ON THE HUNT

EAGLES ARE CARNIVORES AND APEX PREDATORS, SOMETIMES KILLING ANIMALS MORE THAN FIVE TIMES BIGGER THAN THEM.

- Despite having a lethal-looking beak, eagles generally use their talons to catch their prey. The **harpy eagle** has claws at the back of its talons that can rival those of a bear in terms of size, and its legs can be nearly as thick as your ankle.

- Hunting often starts in treetop perches, where eagles sit silently and look out for prey moving below, swooping down to pounce on anything that catches their eye. Eagles also dive onto their meals from flight, and they occasionally even run after **YES, SERIOUSLY!** them on foot.

- Unlike you, eagles have the ability to see ultraviolet light, which helps them track their prey. All they have to do is follow the trails of pee left by animals marking their territory—the urine reflects ultraviolet light!

- Fish eaters, like the **bald eagle** and **African fish eagle**, snatch many of their meals straight out of the water. If their prey is heavy, they'll cling on to it with their talons and drag it toward land. Sometimes they'll even get into the water themselves, keeping a firm grasp on their dinner with their feet and using their wings like oars to paddle toward solid ground.

- Eagles often steal food from smaller birds and will even fight other eagles for food—especially in winter, when meals are scarce. A bald eagle was once caught on camera stealing a dead rabbit from a fox. The young fox wasn't giving up without a fight and was lifted into the air by the eagle as they tussled over the meal. Eventually the fox dropped back to the ground and trotted off as the victorious eagle flew off with its stolen dinner. **SHAMELESS!**

A BIG NEST FOR A BIG BIRD

Eagle nests are called "eyries," and they're huge! They're generally built in trees or on cliffs. Eagles use sticks for the base of their nests, and line the inside with grass, feathers, and moss to soften them. **Bald eagle** nests are particularly huge—they can be over 20 feet deep, so an average human adult standing inside wouldn't be able to see over the edge. They can also be over 10 feet wide and weigh over 4,400 pounds. That's heavier than a car!

ANCIENT GIANT

Haast's eagle is now extinct, but it was once the largest eagle in the world. It weighed close to 40 pounds and had a wingspan of 10 feet! This giant bird of prey lived in New Zealand, where it hunted giant flightless birds called moa.

FLANNERY FILE

Australian **sea eagles** mate for life. But first they test out the strength of a potential mate in an aerial battle, during which they lock talons and spiral downward through the air. I once saw a pair that were so evenly matched, they stayed locked until they hit the sea more than half a mile from shore. It was a windy day and they were exhausted, waterlogged, yet still fighting in the water! Overhead, a whistling kite circled, tight and low, waiting for one to die!

I set out in my dinghy armed with a yard broom. The kite flew off and the eagles separated. The smaller male had a gash on his breast—a spot of red on otherwise spotless white. I placed the broom under the larger female and she stood steadily on it, entirely unafraid, as I lifted her above head height. She took off, swooping so low over the water I feared she might go in again. Her yellow eyes, with their fearless, imperious gaze, were unforgettable—as was her fearsome beak! The wounded male was younger and more fearful. He kept swimming feebly away from me, but after a dozen attempts he gave up and I swept him into the boat, where he lay with wings hanging over the sides, his head drooping, utterly exhausted. I put him ashore on a rock, where he sat for hours before moving off. I often wonder if they stayed together.

SOARING AND DIVING

Instead of burning through energy by flapping their huge wings, eagles prefer to use warm currents of air to glide through the sky.

- Eagles can stay aloft for hours at a time and have been known to reach heights of 10,000 feet as they fly.

- Reaching speeds of nearly 30 miles per hour is not uncommon for flying eagles, and they can go even faster when they dive—some, like the **golden eagle**, can reach speeds of more than 120 miles per hour as they plummet toward the earth.

- If a **bald eagle** loses a feather from its wing, another feather will fall out from the same area on the other wing so that the eagle can stay balanced as it flies.

CRANES

Cranes are one of the world's oldest surviving bird groups. There are 15 different species of crane, and they're all very social. Large herds of them are often seen gathered near water, causing a ruckus as they call out to each other and take part in flamboyant dancing. Once you find out more about these incredible birds you might become a craniac—the name given to crane-obsessed humans!

LUMPS AND BUMPS

Cranes have incredibly long legs, but not everything is as it seems. Cranes' knobbly "knees" are really the heels of their feet. That means that their "feet" are actually their toes, so cranes don't actually walk—they tiptoe.

WHERE CAN I SEE A CRANE?

Cranes can be found in every part of the world except South America and Antarctica.

A GROUP OF CRANES IS CALLED A HERD, A SEDGE, OR SOMETIMES EVEN A DANCE.

CLIMATE CHANGE

Many cranes make their homes in wetlands—the perfect habitat for finding food and laying eggs. As the planet warms, the wetland homes of cranes are drying out and making it harder for cranes to thrive.

GETTING ROWDY

CRANES SEEM ALMOST IMPOSSIBLY GRACEFUL AS THEY SOAR THROUGH THE SKY OR STEP GENTLY ACROSS MARSHY GROUND. BUT THE NOISES THEY MAKE ARE ANYTHING BUT DELICATE!

HONK!

- **Gray crowned cranes** make a honking sound, and the bright red gular pouch under their beaks can inflate to help make their calls extra loud.

- **Sandhill cranes** have a raucous, rattling call that can travel over 1 mile.

- Pairs of mating cranes sing loud duets during breeding season.

- A crane's windpipe gets longer and longer as the bird matures. By the time it's an adult, the windpipe is far too long to just go straight up and down—it has to curl around like a complex brass instrument instead. The **whooping crane** has the longest windpipe—laid out flat, it would be 5 feet long.

STARTING A FAMILY

- Cranes usually mate for life, but if things aren't going well for a pair they sometimes "divorce" and find new mates.

- Their eggs are about 4 inches long, and when the chicks hatch they're about the size of a large apple. They don't stay that small for long, though! Crane chicks grow at an extraordinary rate, sometimes shooting up more than 5 feet in just a few months. Not many animals grow that fast— it would probably take quite a few years for you to grow a similar amount.

- Crane babies are advanced for their age—they can walk as soon as they hatch out of their eggs, and they're also born with their eyes open. There's a special name for baby animals that can see and walk right away—they're called "precocial."

TALL AND LEAN

Sarus cranes are the tallest flying bird in the world, stretching to 6 feet tall—taller than many adult humans. That's nothing compared with the length of their wingspan, though, which is well over 8 feet! These slender birds aren't the heaviest cranes—that title goes to the **red-crowned cranes**, which weigh up to 26 pounds.

SO YOU THINK YOU CAN DANCE?

Cranes often dance to impress a mate, pairing up and showing off their best moves. But they don't just dance for romance—they can dance year-round for almost any reason, sometimes in huge groups. Young cranes are taught to dance by their parents, and sometimes they practice their moves for years before whipping them out when they're ready to start a family of their own.

Crane dancing is weird. It can be very elegant, but it can also be downright hilarious. They bob their heads up and down rapidly, leap back and forth, flap their wings, bow toward the ground, and occasionally throw their heads back to make a loud call. They also show off by picking up food or sticks and throwing them high into the air.

CLOUDS OF CRANES

Many cranes spend winter in warmer areas and then fly back to cooler areas in spring to breed. The sight of a whole herd of cranes migrating across the sky is awe-inspiring, although once cranes are up in the air you can't always see them easily— some species can fly as high as 6 miles, which isn't too far off the height a plane flies at!

BIRDS IN DANGER

In 1941 there were only 16 **whooping cranes** left in the world, mostly due to habitat loss and hunting. People have worked hard to save these birds from extinction, and their numbers have grown, but there is still only one flock of these beautiful birds left in the wild.

STANDING OUT

- Aside from the red caps on their heads, **sandhill cranes** are mostly gray all over. That is, until they start to preen with their beaks—their beaks are often coated in mud from searching for food, and it gets rubbed into their feathers until they have a distinctive red or brown tinge to their coat.

- **Gray crowned cranes** don't need mud to stand out—they have a crown-like fan of pale, golden-hued feathers sticking up above their heads like feathered royalty.

I once visited the International Crane Foundation in Wisconsin. This group is working hard to create habitats where cranes can thrive, and it has every species of crane on Earth living there. You can see each type of crane in half an hour or so, instead of the months it would take to see them all in the wild.

CORN-FED CRANES

Cranes often hunt for water-dwelling prey such as fish and frogs, but they also gobble down insects, mice, and even snakes. Plants are on the menu, too—sometimes cranes forage in the wild, and at other times they make use of crops grown by human farmers. **Sandhill cranes** often make a pit stop during their migration, taking a break in Nebraska, to fuel up on corn left on the ground after the fields have been harvested. The cornfields are close to the Platte River, the perfect stopping place for cranes to gather, sleep, and feed, gorging themselves so they'll have energy later on.

OWLS

Because most owls are up and about at night, you might not have had the pleasure of seeing one in the flesh. So you could be surprised to learn just how big some owls can get, or that they have some seriously odd habits—including running along the ground on their huge, scaly feet or collecting their own poop.

There are two distinct kinds of owls: **true owls** and **barn owls** (and their relatives). True owls are a huge group—there are over 220 species, ranging from the huge **Eurasian eagle owl** to the tiny **elf owl**. Barn owls stand out because of their large heads with heart-shaped faces.

A GROUP OF OWLS IS CALLED A PARLIAMENT.

CLIMATE CHANGE

The habitats of some owls, like the alpine grasslands used by **sooty owls** in New Guinea, are being destroyed by climate change. Many owls also need large, old trees with hollows in them in order to nest, so deforestation is leading to habitat loss and making it harder for them to nest.

WHERE CAN I SEE AN OWL?

Owls live on every continent except Antarctica.

HUNTING HABITS

Owls use their powerful hearing to hunt. Some owls can even hear prey as it moves under the cover of dirt, leaves, or snow. When it comes to catching their prey, owls have lots of different techniques.

- Owls often perch on a branch, sometimes staying so still that they look as if they're sleeping. But they're just concentrating! When a suitable meal appears below them, the owl drops swiftly down from the tree to pounce on it.

- Hunting from flight is also a common technique. Huge wings allow owls to glide, and the soft, ragged edges of their wings help them move through the air silently. That means they can sneak up on their prey, swooping in before the poor creature has heard them coming.

- **Fish owls**, as their name suggests, love eating fish, plus other water-dwelling creatures, such as frogs. They often hunt for their prey by perching on a rock in or beside a river, then darting down to grab wriggling fish in their claws as they swim past.

- **Burrowing owls**, who spend a lot of time on the ground, are able to run after their prey! These odd owls also stockpile their poop, stacking it up around their burrows to tempt dung beetles. Once the beetles are lured close enough, the owls snatch them up and eat them.

OWLS EAT MICE, RIGHT?

Owls are carnivores, and they're not picky—some species eat more than 100 different types of prey. The smallest owls often eat insects, but others can hunt animals that are two or three times bigger than them! Common owl foods include mice, rabbits, and small birds, but they also eat a range of much more surprising things, such as koalas, raccoons, eagles, herons, monkeys, skunks, sloth, small deer, baby foxes, warthogs, and even hedgehogs. OUCH!

NIGHT OWLS

Although some owls hunt during the day, most owls sleep when the sun is up. The colors and patterns on their feathers help them blend into their surroundings, which means they don't need to bother finding a place to hide as they sleep in broad daylight—you could walk right past one having a snooze on a branch and not see it.

OWL  EYES

OWLS DON'T HAVE PERFECT EYESIGHT, BUT FOR EVERY FLAW THEY HAVE A COOL BONUS FEATURE THAT MAKES THEIR VISION TRULY REMARKABLE.

- Owls don't have round eyeballs like yours—theirs are like long tubes. This means their eyeballs can't move around in their sockets to see in different directions very well. To make up for it, they have double the number of vertebrae—the building blocks of bone in the spine—as other birds. That means they can easily turn their heads to look straight behind them.

- Owls don't have great color vision, but they can see extra well at night. They can see tiny contrasts between different shades of black and gray, so seeing even the smallest movements in their surroundings is possible on dark, shadowy nights.

- Owl eyesight is excellent for things that are far away, but it isn't very good for things that are right in front of them! To help them keep track of things close by, owls have a whole lot of whiskery feathers around their beaks called "filoplumes." These sensitive feathers help them sense things, including their prey, once they are too close to see.

- The **great horned owl** has the largest eyes of any owl. If these birds were as big as you, their eyeballs would be as big as oranges!

PUKING PELLETS

Owls often swallow their prey whole, only shredding it into strips if it is particularly large. Eating every part of an animal has an interesting side effect, which is that owls throw up every day, sometimes more than once. They're not doing it because they're sick, though! And their puke isn't gloopy like yours—it's quite a firm pellet, made out of all the little bits of animal that the owl couldn't digest, including fur, bone, and feathers. **ICK!**

TAKING A DIP

Owls can swim, although generally only if they really need to, such as if they accidentally fall into water. As you would imagine, swimming owls look quite awkward! Their heads stick out of the water, buoyed by their outstretched wings. They use their wings like oars to paddle toward land, their bodies bobbing up and down as their wings rotate to propel them forward. They can't take off from the water, so they need to swim to land and dry out their wings before they can get back into the air.

HOME SWEET HOME

- Some owls, such as **great horned owls**, take over the nests of birds like ravens and magpies.

- **Goggle-eyed Cuban screech owls** make their own nests, hollowing out a little nook in a tree—usually a palm tree!

- Some desert-dwelling owls, like **elf owls** and **ferruginous pygmy owls**, raise their owlets (baby owls) in cacti. They use nest holes that were originally hollowed out by woodpeckers.

- **Burrowing owls** don't nest in trees—they live in underground burrows. Sometimes they dig their own, but they will also take over burrows created by prairie dogs, armadillos, or ground squirrels.

- **Grass owls** only ever nest on the ground. They hollow out grassy tunnels, with a nest formed out of a tussock of grass tucked away in the center.

◄● FLANNERY FILE ●►

Powerful owls live in the botanic gardens in Sydney, Australia—it's one of the best places to see them. There are a couple of really big Moreton Bay fig trees in the gardens, and the owls are often perched in them. I once was walking through the botanic gardens and found a pile of possum guts on the ground. I knew what that meant! I looked up into the trees and, sure enough, there was a powerful owl with a ring-tailed possum gripped tightly in its claws. You need to look super carefully if you want to catch a glimpse of an owl. Start by looking on the ground for the leftover parts of their prey—like the wing of a flying fox, or the bones or guts of a possum or a mouse. As they eat, owls often drop little bits of their meal on the ground below. Look up, and don't be discouraged if you can't see anything right away. Eventually you'll probably see a great big feathery owl sitting where the leaves are thickest—you might even spot a whole family!

WHAT A MOUTHFUL!

The largest owl that ever lived, now extinct, was called the ***Ornimegalonyx***—try saying that ten times fast! It lived on the island of Cuba, in the Caribbean. It stood 3.6 feet tall, about the size of a six-year-old child, and weighed at least 19 pounds. It was a hunter, and easily able to kill the young of the giant sloths that are now extinct but once inhabited the island.

PELICANS

Nearly everything about a pelican is big—all eight species have large rotund bodies, giant scaly feet, and huge wings. But the most eye-catching body part is doubtlessly their enormous, record-breaking bill! Pelicans can do some seriously cool things with their bills, although fish would probably describe their bills as "terrifying" rather than "cool." It's all about perspective.

STARTING A FAMILY

Pelicans often come together in colonies to lay their eggs, with hundreds or even thousands of birds building nests close together. Both parents share egg-minding duties, often using their large feet to help keep them warm.

LUSCIOUS LOCKS

Dalmatian pelicans sport a crop of long feathers on top of their heads, which often look strangely like a human hairstyle, or even a feathery wig.

WHERE CAN I SEE A PELICAN?

Pelicans live on every continent except Antarctica.

A GROUP OF PELICANS IS CALLED A SCOOP.

DEEP DIVES

Brown pelicans have different eating habits from other pelicans. They fly above water, scouting for food with their keen eyesight. Once they spot a fish they dive toward the water at incredible speeds, slamming into their prey to stun them before gulping them down. All of that hurtling around and smacking into water would hurt a lot of other animals, but these birds have a stack of nifty tricks to stop themselves from getting injured.

▶ Tensing all of their muscles as they dive stops their necks from breaking when they hit the water.

▶ The body parts that help these pelicans to breathe and swallow (the trachea and esophagus) sit on the right side of their necks, so they turn toward the left as they dive to protect these delicate parts from hard collisions with the water.

▶ Inflating special air sacs under their skin helps soften the impact of their landing.

Australian pelicans are often wary of people, but at certain times of year they can get so hungry that they will come up and beg food from you, particularly around Sydney. One year, each time I went fishing on the Hawkesbury River, I had to reserve a fish for my pelican friend, which had taken to visiting me in my favorite fishing spot.

BILL OF CHAMPIONS

▶ Pelicans have the longest bills of any bird in the world, sometimes stretching to nearly 1.5 feet long. The pouch hanging below, referred to as the "gular pouch," is also impressively spacious—it can hold up to 3.5 gallons of water!

▶ **Australian pelican** pouches are usually a combination of soft pinks and yellows, but during breeding season these colors become much brighter and are also joined by splashes of vivid blue. Once the eggs have been laid, the colors tone back down.

▶ **White pelicans**, both male and female, grow a large lump on their beaks during mating season. It looks a bit like a horn and falls off once the eggs have been laid. It's thought that this special beak growth makes the pelicans more attractive to potential mates.

HOW DO YOU IMPRESS A PELICAN?

In breeding season, multiple **Australian pelican** males compete for the attention of a female. A parade of male pelicans follow a female as she walks around, trying to impress her by throwing fish, sticks, and other objects into the air and swinging their bills around. Eventually, the males start to drop off one by one—a bit like contestants being eliminated on a reality TV show—until just one is left.

FLANNERY FILE

I have heard some funny stories about pelicans occasionally eating other birds, and they've apparently even been reported to eat the odd chihuahua! I've seen pelicans going head to head with sea eagles quite a few times. When sea eagles are young, they're very silly—they don't know how to do anything, and they'll have a go at anything. They often learn to fly in the hungry part of the year, when there isn't a lot of food around, so they're always on the lookout for a meal. They'll be flying around, see a flock of pelicans and think, *Oh, they'd be good to eat*. Of course, when they try to take on a pelican, they don't stand a chance! All a pelican has to do is pull its beak open and go "Aarrrrrr!" for the pesky young sea eagle to quickly rethink its plan, turn around, and flee.

WHO'S DOING THE EATING?

Once you know that pelicans sometimes eat meals of the feathered variety, it can be concerning to see a pelican chick ducking its head inside an adult's enormous gaping bill. But don't worry! The chick isn't about to be eaten— it's clambering in to *get* a meal. Chicks can't hunt for themselves, so if they're hungry they snack on regurgitated fish paste from their parents' beaks. DELICIOUS!

GONE FISHIN'

Despite their bills being able to hold more than their stomachs, pelicans don't use them as lunchboxes to store snacks for later—they swallow their food as they catch it. Fresh is best!

▶ Most pelicans hunt by floating on top of the water and dipping their beaks in to find fish. Their bills have a lethal hook at the end that helps them to latch on to even the slipperiest of fish. Once they've caught something, pelicans squeeze the muscles in their bill to empty out all of the water they've scooped up with their prey before swallowing it whole.

▶ Many pelican species hunt and feed in large groups, working together to gang up on their prey. They get into formation, which is often a curved line, then beat their wings on the surface of the water and poke their bills around to herd fish into groups so they can pick them off. Sometimes they even direct the fish toward shallow water, where they're easier to catch.

▶ Pelicans are known for using their size to muscle in and snatch meals from other birds. But pelicans can get robbed, too! Gulls sometimes stand on a pelican's head, waiting until they catch a fish before ducking in to nab the pelican's meal for themselves.

SNEAKY!

WHO'S BiGGER—YOU OR A PELiCAN?

Pelicans are some of the heaviest flying birds in the world. **Dalmatian pelicans** are the largest, sometimes weighing in at nearly 33 pounds. That's over half the weight of a fully grown dalmatian—the dog kind, that is! They can also stand up to 6 feet tall, which is taller than some adult humans (including Beyoncé). Their wingspan is even more impressive, reaching over 10 feet!

SEE-FOOD DIET

Pelicans are carnivorous, and they're not particularly fussy eaters. They mostly eat fish but will also go after other water-dwelling animals such as yabbies, crayfish, frogs, and turtles. They've even been known to gobble down other birds, including seagulls, ducklings, and pigeons. Because they don't have any teeth, they swallow their prey whole— usually headfirst.

GRUESOME!

HUMMINGBIRDS

Most of the 338 hummingbird species don't sing or hum—they're named after the humming sound their wings make as they move at speeds too fast for your eyes to follow. Many hummingbirds have patches of iridescent feathers on their bodies, earning them the nickname "flying jewels." But they're not just beautiful! Relative to the size of their bodies, hummingbirds have the largest brains of any bird, and the second largest of any animal.

WHERE CAN I SEE A HUMMINGBIRD?

Hummingbirds live right across the Americas, from Alaska down to the very tip of South America. They're particularly common in South America. When people think of hummingbirds, they often imagine them in a rainforest, drinking nectar from an exotic tropical flower. Plenty of hummingbirds do thrive in tropical areas, but they're surprisingly versatile birds. Certain species can be found high up in cool mountainous regions where oxygen is scarce, and even in deserts!

A GROUP OF HUMMINGBIRDS IS CALLED A CHARM.

FLOWER EATERS

ALWAYS HUNGRY

HUMMINGBIRDS HAVE SPECIAL BODY PARTS THAT HELP THEM GATHER NECTAR.

Hummingbirds have a very high metabolism—higher than most other animals, including you. That means they burn through energy really quickly and need to eat regularly to keep their strength up. They can eat up to three times their body weight in food each day.

▶ Hummingbirds are omnivores, so even though nectar makes up most of their diet, they eat things like insects and spiders as well.

▶ Some hummingbirds can eat nectar from more than 1,000 flowers in a single day. They have excellent memories and are able to keep track of where the best nectar is, returning to those same flowers over and over again.

▶ Hummingbirds help to pollinate plants—they pick up pollen from flowers as they feed, carrying it to other flowers as they travel to eat. Some plants can only be pollinated by hummingbirds and couldn't survive without them.

▶ Each species of hummingbird has a slightly different beak that's perfectly suited to the specific types of flower they like to eat. Some hummingbirds have extra-long beaks so they can reach the nectar at the bottom of long, trumpet-shaped flowers. Beaks can either poke straight out or curve downward to fit the shape of certain flowers, too.

▶ Hummingbird tongues are often twice as long as their beaks! They're also almost completely clear, with a forked tip a bit like a snake's tongue, and they're hollow, too! Each one has two tubes, and when poked into flowers the tubes fill up with nectar. The tongues don't work like straws, though—hummingbirds can't suck nectar up through them. Instead, they have to pull their tongues inside their mouths to empty each load of nectar, so their tongues are constantly flicking in and out as they eat.

CLIMATE CHANGE

Climate change could have a huge impact on hummingbirds by destroying the forests they depend upon.

FANCY FEATHERS
AND DARING DIVES

MALE HUMMINGBIRDS OFTEN LOOK EXTRA SPECIAL, WITH BRIGHT PATCHES OF PLUMAGE OR ELABORATE TAIL FEATHERS. THEY USE THEIR FLASHY LOOKS, ALONG WITH IMPRESSIVE ATHLETIC DISPLAYS, TO ATTRACT A MATE.

▶ Many hummingbirds, like **ruby-throated** or **blue-throated hummingbirds**, have patches of vivid color on their throats that appear even brighter in certain lights, so the birds angle themselves to show their feathers off in the best possible way.

▶ Some males can fan out their throat feathers so that they're impossible to miss. The **calliope hummingbird** is one such bird, with beautiful pink neck feathers that can puff out into remarkable spikes.

▶ Some males, including the **marvelous spatuletail**, have very long, hair-like feathers on their tails, each one tipped with a brightly colored fan of feathers. They hover in front of females and wave their tails around to win over their mates.

▶ Both male and female **booted racket-tails** have the added feature of fluffy white feathers clumped around their legs—like teeny tiny boots.

▶ **Anna's** and **Costa's hummingbirds** make a series of outlandish dives to impress their mates, flying up into the air and hurtling down nearly 130 feet before heading back up to do it all over again. The wind moving through their feathers as they plummet downward makes a distinctive chirping sound!

HEADING ON VACATION

Although some hummingbirds stay put over winter, many species travel long distances to escape the cold—chasing after the sun and the flowering plants that supply them with nectar. **Rufous hummingbirds** have the longest journeys—they can travel close to 3,100 miles as they move from their summer home in Alaska to their winter home in Mexico.

STARTING A FAMILY

Hummingbirds build cozy nests out of various bits of plant matter. Depending on the type of hummingbird, the shape of the nest varies—some are rounded on the bottom, others are pointed. Sometimes the birds build their nests underneath overhanging leaves so that rain won't fall inside. Egg sizes vary between species, but they all have something in common— they're tiny!

A BIRD OR A BEE?

Hummingbirds are the smallest birds in the world. Their scientific name is Trochilidae—Greek for "small bird." The tiniest of them all is the **bee hummingbird**, which weighs a measly 0.06 ounces, about the same as a playing card. They can also be under 2 inches long—that's only a little longer than an Oreo! These bright green birds live in Cuba, where they're called "zunzuncito" because of the humming "zun zun" sound they make as they fly. Even the biggest hummingbirds are still quite small. The **giant hummingbird** might be giant compared with the bee hummingbird, but it's still only about 8 inches long, or the length of a large banana.

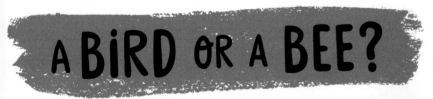

THE SMALLEST HUMMINGBIRD EGGS CAN BE AS SMALL AS TIC TACS.

SHAKE IT OFF

When hummingbirds get caught in the rain and need to dry off, they act a bit like a dog—shaking their head and body vigorously to send droplets of water flying. They twist their heads so violently during this process that their necks turn almost 90 degrees!

WING MASTERS

When it comes to flying, hummingbirds are unlike any other bird.

▶ Hummingbirds don't just flap their wings up and down; they make a complex rotating movement that gives them extra power. The chest muscles that make their wings move are so big they make up about 30 percent of their entire body mass.

▶ They can fly backward and even upside down!

▶ Hummingbirds are the only birds that can hover in the exact same place for more than 30 seconds—in fact, they can do this for minutes at a time!

▶ The fastest a hummingbird's wings can move is about 100 beats per second—so fast that their wings are just a blur.

OXPECKERS

You can get a lot of clues about what oxpeckers are like from their name—these birds are often found on large animals, including oxen, and they love to peck! Their scientific name, *Buphagus*, means "eater of cattle," which is slightly misleading—these tiny birds aren't exactly capable of devouring a cow! But the things they eat are still shocking in their own way . . .

WHERE CAN I SEE AN OXPECKER?

Oxpeckers are found only in Africa, where there are lots of large mammals to peck at and live on.

EXTREME NAPPING

Oxpeckers occasionally take naps on their hosts during daylight hours, holding tight as their hosts move around. Sometimes they even settle in and sleep, clinging to their hosts overnight.

A GROUP OF OXPECKERS IS CALLED A FLING.

STAY BACK!

Oxpeckers hiss when they're feeling threatened, which can be a helpful warning for their host animal that there might be danger nearby.

WHAT DOES AN OXPECKER LOOK LIKE?

There are two different species of oxpecker—**red-billed** and **yellow-billed**. Red-billed oxpeckers do indeed have red bills. Yellow-billed oxpeckers' bills are vivid yellow at the base, with bright red tips.

WHAT KIND OF FOOD CAN YOU FIND ON A GIRAFFE?

Oxpeckers cling on to their hosts and eat any insects they find. They eat a lot of different insects, including flies, maggots, and fleas, and they particularly love gobbling down ticks. The reason oxpeckers love ticks so much is that their real favorite food is blood. Ticks burrow into the host animal's skin so that they can drink its blood, and by the time the oxpeckers pluck them out they're like the bug version of a jam doughnut—crisp on the outside and full of oozy red blood in the center. Delicious! Blood isn't the only bodily fluid oxpeckers eat—they also happily suck down snot, spit, tears, and eye goo. Other less-than-appetizing snacks include dandruff and earwax. EWW!

AN UNCONVENTIONAL HOUSE

Oxpeckers spend most of their time hanging out with much larger animals. They like to perch on animals such as cattle, giraffes, rhinos, zebras, water buffalo, hippos, and antelope, and they particularly like hairy animals. Using their strong feet and sharp claws, these tenacious little birds can hold on just about anywhere, staying balanced at amazing angles.

Some animals, like elephants, don't particularly like oxpeckers buzzing around—just as you might wave away a fly that was trying to land on you, elephants will often shake off these birds.

CAN YOU LIVE YOUR WHOLE LIFE ON A WILDEBEEST?

Although oxpeckers can eat, sleep, play, and even mate on their hosts, there are times when they have no choice but to leave. For starters, there isn't any water on a host (none that is salt-free, anyway—tears don't count!), so thirsty oxpeckers have to leave. It's also really impractical to lay eggs on a moving animal. They'd just roll right off! Oxpeckers find holes in trees to nest in, lining them with grass and feathers, as well as hair that the birds have plucked right out of their host animal's skin.

WOODPECKERS

Woodpeckers are part of a family of birds called Picidae. They're famous for drilling holes into wood with fierce determination, but wood isn't the only surface at risk of being obliterated by their sharp beaks! It might seem, at first glance, that they're incredibly destructive birds, but woodpeckers can actually make trees healthier by drilling in and removing the pesky insects that are boring into the wood and hurting the tree. All of the birds in the Picidae family are called "woodpeckers," but some of them also have other names, such as **sapsuckers**, **piculets**, and **wrynecks**.

A GROUP OF WOODPECKERS IS CALLED A DESCENT, BUT A GROUP OF SAPSUCKERS IS SOMETIMES CALLED A SLURP.

WHERE CAN I SEE A WOODPECKER?

Woodpeckers don't live in Australia, New Zealand, New Guinea, Madagascar, or the polar regions, but they live just about everywhere else. They're particularly common in the Americas and Southeast Asia.

ALL KINDS OF SNACKS

Most woodpeckers eat lots of insects—they peck holes into trees with their sharp beaks so that they can gobble up the little critters living under the bark or inside the wood. But woodpeckers are a versatile bunch, and other types of food are often on the menu, too.

▶ Plenty of woodpeckers eat sap every now and then, but the woodpeckers known as **sapsuckers** are particularly mad about it. They drill lots of small holes into trees to get to the sap flowing below, which sometimes creates a spotty pattern on the tree's bark. They don't actually suck the sap through their beaks —they lick it up with their tongues.

▶ **Gila woodpeckers**, along with some of their close relatives, have been recorded using their sharp beaks to crack open the skulls of other birds' nestlings so they can eat the blood and brains inside.

▶ Some **golden-fronted woodpeckers** eat so much of the prickly pears growing on cacti that their little faces go purple from the juice.

▶ **Acorn woodpeckers** eat—you guessed it—acorns! They hide their food for later by pecking acorn-sized holes in trees and squeezing a single acorn into each one. Sometimes acorn woodpeckers can pack 50,000 nuts in a single tree, each one in its own little hole! Sometimes they find other places to drill into and hide acorns—like telephone poles, fence posts, or even wooden houses!

LIVING IN A TREE HOUSE

Woodpecker parents often drill holes into trees to nest in, but **bamboo woodpeckers** drill their nests into bamboo, and some desert-dwelling woodpeckers, like **gila woodpeckers** and **ladder-backed woodpeckers**, hollow out nesting holes in cactus plants! Some ground-dwelling woodpeckers, like the **Andean flicker**, dig hollows into the ground to nest in, and **campo flickers** will occasionally build their nests directly into termite mounds.

EXPERT TREE CLIMBERS

Most woodpeckers spend a lot of time in trees, hunting for food. Their sharp claws grip onto the bark, allowing them to walk up and down vertical surfaces such as tree trunks. Many species have particularly stiff tail feathers that help them balance against the tree, kind of like an extra leg. These feathers have sharp, spiky ends that can grip onto bark, too. **HANDY!**

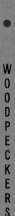

HOW BIG IS A WOODPECKER?

One of the largest woodpeckers is the **great slaty woodpecker**, which can grow to just over 20 inches tall. **Piculets** are the smallest of the woodpeckers, sometimes measuring less than 3 inches. They don't have the long, stiff tails that many other woodpecker species have—some barely have a tail at all!

CRITTER CATCHERS AND SAP SLURPERS

Woodpeckers have very long, agile tongues that can snake into freshly drilled crevices and holes to latch on to insects or sap. Woodpecker tongues aren't just attached inside their mouths like human tongues are—they wrap right around their skulls like an elastic band holding a lunchbox closed. Tongues can also be up to 4 inches long in some birds! Different woodpecker species have their own style of tongue, each one perfect for eating the particular kind of food they enjoy.

▶ **Sapsuckers** and other sap eaters have an oddly hairy tongue, a bit like a little brush, which helps mop up liquid foods.

▶ Woodpeckers that tunnel into wood for things like insect larvae often have a tongue with a barbed tip that helps catch onto their prey.

▶ Species of woodpeckers that forage on the ground for things like ants, like the **northern flicker**, have tongues with flat tips that help scoop up their food as it tries to scurry away.

DO WOODPECKERS EAT WOOD?

Woodpeckers don't eat the wood they excavate—in fact, they have some special features that stop woodchips or dust from getting inside their bodies.

▶ Woodpeckers have an extra eyelid on each eye that helps keep their eyeballs safe from flying debris, a bit like a carpenter wearing safety glasses while working. These eyelids have the added bonus of helping to keep the bird's eyeballs from bursting or popping out when they're drilling!

▶ Groups of bristly feathers near woodpeckers' nostrils keep wood shavings from getting caught inside the nostrils and blocking them up.

I'M WITH THE
BAND

Sometimes, woodpeckers peck at wood not because they're nesting or finding food—they just want to make a loud noise! Males are the most likely to drum, and each one has his own distinct style, just like human musicians do. This drumming behavior can help attract a mate, or warn off interlopers in their territory.

PROTECT YOUR HEAD

Woodpeckers can peck over 20 times in a single second, and sometimes over 10,000 times in the course of a day. Just thinking about that is enough to give humans a headache, so how do these birds do it day after day?

▶ Woodpecker skulls are very solid on the outside, but they have a thick, spongy layer of bone underneath the hard outer layer. This porous buffer helps absorb the impact of all that pecking before it makes it to the bird's brain.

▶ There is a lot of muscle built up around woodpeckers' necks, which helps stop their spines from getting hurt as they ricochet back and forth.

▶ Woodpecker brains are small, held snugly inside their skulls, and angled so that a flattened area faces the front. This flat area helps distribute the shocks across a wider surface.

▶ When they're drilling into a tree, woodpeckers move really quickly. Their beaks are actually only touching the tree for a millisecond or less with each hit, and this shorter period of contact helps keep their brains from being injured.

BIRD OR SNAKE?

When **Eurasian wrynecks** are feeling threatened they make a hissing noise, a bit like a snake, to scare away predators. That's not their only strange skill—they can also turn their remarkably flexible necks 180 degrees to look straight behind them, which is how they got their name.

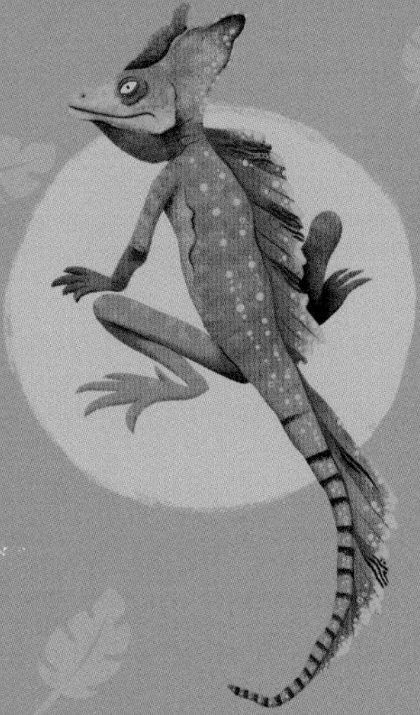

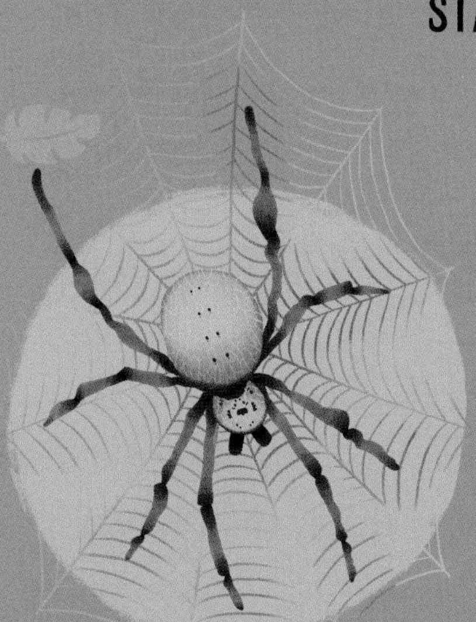

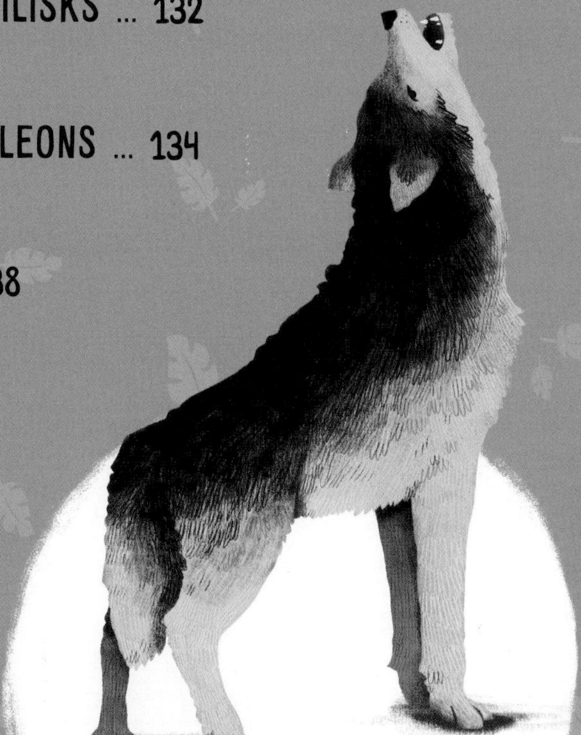

TREE KANGAROOS

You might think you know what kangaroos are. They're large, furry animals that bounce through the Australian outback, right? You might also think there's no way a kangaroo could ever climb a tree . . . but you'd be wrong! Most kangaroos *would* look incredibly awkward if they tried to clamber up a tree, but not tree kangaroos. As you can guess by the name, these fuzzy creatures are related to kangaroos—but they live in the treetops. And, despite their large, lumpy bodies, they're remarkably agile up there! So tree kangaroos can climb trees—but how else are they different from the land-dwelling kind? Read on and you'll know everything in no time (everything about tree kangaroos, anyway—not *everything* everything. That would be a much bigger book).

A GROUP OF TREE KANGAROOS IS CALLED A MOB.

WHERE CAN I SEE A TREE KANGAROO?

Tree kangaroos live in the rainforests of northeastern Australia and New Guinea, and in the alpine meadows of Papua in eastern Indonesia.

BUILT-IN RAINCOATS

Tree kangaroos have a special spiral-shaped patch of hair near their shoulders that helps rain flow off their furry coats instead of soaking through to their skin. This spiral of hair is in a slightly different place on each type of tree kangaroo, and the reason for that is pretty ingenious. Each type of tree kangaroo likes to snooze in a different position, and this built-in waterproofing system grows in the best possible place to keep rain off when they're sleeping in that pose.

NEW SKILLS

Tree kangaroos are descended from rock wallabies that learned how to climb trees. That's some pretty serious leveling-up!

FLANNERY FILE

I have been lucky enough to discover and name four species of tree kangaroos: **tenkile**, **dingiso**, **weimanke**, and **Seri's tree kangaroo**. The first three are native New Guinean names for tree kangaroos, but I named Seri's tree kangaroo after my best friend and companion in all my travels in New Guinea, Lester Seri. All of these tree kangaroos are found high in the mountains of New Guinea, in places so remote that other biologists hadn't found them. But the local people knew the animals well, and taught me a great deal about them.

Tree kangaroos are very hard to see in the forest. If they detect you, they will scramble around a tree trunk so that they are always on the opposite side of it from you, peeking around the trunk to make sure you aren't too close.

I have also cared for baby tree kangaroos whose mothers have been killed by dogs. They love to curl up with you at night, and to be carried around, making wonderful and affectionate companions.

CLIMATE CHANGE

Some tree kangaroos are found only in special rainforests or habitats growing near the summits of mountains where it's really cold. As the earth gets hotter, warmth-loving vegetation is growing ever higher on the mountains—so their habitat is shrinking. If we let climate change go on long enough, the habitats of these tree kangaroos will be pushed off the mountain summits and they will become extinct.

I'D RATHER BE **NAPPING**

Tree kangaroos can do death-defying leaps through the treetops, but they're actually pretty chill most of the time. They'd prefer to curl up on a branch, tuck their head into their folded arms, and do some heavy-duty snoozing.

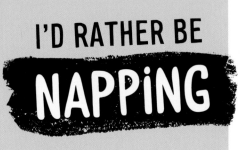

HOW DO THEY GET AROUND?

Just like other types of kangaroos, tree kangaroos hop when they're on the ground. But they can also hop along high up in the treetops! Some types of tree kangaroo also walk along branches, one foot in front of the other. That's very odd behavior for a kangaroo, and they're the only kind that does it. If you're a tree kangaroo, one wrong step could send you hurtling to the forest floor far below. The stakes are quite literally *high*. Tree kangaroos aren't too worried, though, because they can jump huge distances without hurting themselves. Really, REALLY huge distances, like 65 feet straight down to the ground from up in the treetops. That's the length of 2½ buses! If you had technology like Batman you could give that a go, but otherwise jumping that kind of distance would do some serious damage to a human.

ONE OF THESE THINGS iS NOT LiKE THE OTHER . . .

Tree kangaroos look pretty weird. They're a type of kangaroo, but they certainly don't look much like the standard, feet-firmly-on-the-ground kind. Tree kangaroos don't even look like other tree kangaroos. Each different species has its own distinct style. Take these two, for example—they barely look related!

▶ **Dingiso tree kangaroos** have fuzzy black-and-white fur that makes them look like small pandas.

▶ **Goodfellow's tree kangaroos** are chestnut-colored with a yellow underbelly and paws. They also have two parallel yellow racing stripes running down their backs and bright blue eyes!

YOU CAN TELL A FRIEND BY THEIR SPOTS

Each **Matschie's tree kangaroo** has a different pattern on its face, and each **Goodfellow's tree kangaroo** has a different pattern on its tail. Scientists think that these intelligent species are much more social than marsupials usually are, and that they use the different patterns and colored markings to recognize friends or family at a distance. So, just how smart are they? Relative to the size of its body, Goodfellow's tree kangaroo has the largest brain of any marsupial!

A BELLY FULL OF WORMS

Each type of tree kangaroo has its own favorite food. Most also have stomach worms that help them digest their food. After tree kangaroos have eaten, the worms wait for the partially digested food to hit the stomach, where they have their own feast. The **dingiso tree kangaroo** has far more worms than any other species—about 250,000 worms in a single stomach! These wiry worms are as thick as hairpins and twice as long. Imagine having a bellyful of those wriggling around inside you!

WHAT'S IN A NAME?

Tree kangaroos don't look anything like hares, and yet their scientific name is *Dendrolagus*, which means "tree-hare." That's a pretty puzzling name! Maybe the 19th-century Dutch biologists who came across them in New Guinea tried eating them and thought they tasted like hares.

BABY TREE KANGAROOS

Tree kangaroos are smaller than a baked bean when they're born, and the first thing they have to do is climb into their mother's pouch to do some extra growing. They make this precarious climb up in the treetops, using just their front arms to cling to their mother's fur, as their back legs haven't fully developed at this stage. They definitely deserve a long rest in a cozy pouch after such a stressful start to their lives!

STAR-NOSED MOLES

Moles are cool, but star-nosed moles are *extra cool*. Like other moles, they spend a fair bit of time digging tunnels under the ground and gobbling down bugs. Unlike other moles, they also like to swim in rivers and marshy areas! If these furry little creatures could only ride a bike they could complete a triathlon. Their swimming abilities aren't the first thing people notice about star-nosed moles, though—they're too busy staring at the mass of fleshy tentacles growing out of their noses.

WHERE CAN I SEE A STAR-NOSED MOLE?

Star-nosed moles only live in North America, so if you happen to live there you're in luck!

A GROUP OF STAR-NOSED MOLES IS CALLED A COMPANY (OR A FORTRESS, LABOR, OR MOVEMENT).

UNDERWATER ADVENTURES

Star-nosed moles use their giant paws as spades to excavate dirt, but they also use them as hairy, claw-tipped flippers to glide through the water. That means they can hunt both underground and in the water—they're a double threat! Like humans, star-nosed moles blow bubbles out of their noses underwater. Unlike humans, they breathe those same bubbles of air back in! The bubbles trap smells inside them, so when the mole sucks them back in they get to breathe in any nearby scents, which helps them track down prey. It's just like sniffing, but underwater!

CLING-WRAP BABIES

Baby star-nosed moles are completely blind when they're born, and their eyesight doesn't improve much as they grow up. Their ears and nose tentacles are also sealed with a clear film, kind of like cling wrap, which they can't hear or smell through. So, as babies, they have to get by without three major senses. The film isn't only there for the first few hours, either—it stays for a couple of weeks! Luckily, their parents stick around to look after them for about a month, and then they can fend for themselves.

ARE THEY REALLY A TYPE OF MOLE?

Star-nosed moles started evolving in a different way from other moles about 30 million years ago. This explains why they do strange, un-mole-like things, like swim! Their closest relative is the desman, which is a small, water-loving mammal from Europe. Aside from burrowing into riverbanks, desmans don't dig at all— they come onto land to sleep, but spend the rest of their time in the water.

FASTEST EATER

Star-nosed moles mostly eat insects and other creepy-crawlies, such as earthworms. They also gobble down the odd fish. They're extraordinarily fast when they hunt, locating and scoffing insects in less than two-tenths of a second. This record speed earns it the title of world's fastest eater—not bad for an animal that can't even see its food!

ALL TEETH

Star-nosed moles have an astounding 44 teeth crammed into their slim mouths. Thankfully, they never need braces!

IS THAT AN OCTOPUS ON YOUR NOSE?

Star-nosed moles get their name from their bizarre noses, which are star-shaped and look like the bottom end of a wriggly pink octopus. Their noses have 22 fleshy tentacles, and they're incredibly sensitive—kind of like a superhero version of a human hand. Your hand has 17,000 nerve fibers to help you feel the things you touch. That sounds like a lot, but each star-nosed mole has a whopping 100,000 nerve fibers in its nose! The entire nose is only as big as the tip of your thumb, so they're packing all of that power into a really tiny package, too.

Star-nosed moles are almost completely blind, so they rely on their nose tentacles to get around and find food. They nod their heads constantly underground, bumping their tentacles against the earth to get a sense of what their surroundings look like. They can also feel things moving nearby by sensing vibrations in the ground—even tiny bugs can't sneak past!

00:30

THE AMAZING EXPANDING TAIL

In winter the tail of a star-nosed mole can grow to four times its usual size! They need to build up body mass to be ready to breed when spring arrives, so they store a lot of extra fat in their tails.

A MOLE FOR ALL SEASONS

The cold doesn't bother star-nosed moles. They can tunnel in snow just as well as they can dig through earth, and they keep on swimming even when the water starts to freeze. Their thick fur repels water and acts like a cozy jacket in the chilly winter months.

SMALL BUT STOCKY

A fully grown star-nosed mole only weighs about 2 ounces, which is about the same as a tennis ball. They grow to about 6 to 8 inches long, or about the length of a chocolate bar.

WHAT'S IN A NAME?

Male star-nosed moles are called "boars" and females are called "sows," just like pigs! Their babies aren't called "piglets," though— they're "pups," just to keep you on your toes. Their scientific name is *Condylura cristata*, which means "crested knob-tail." Their tails aren't exactly their most eye-catching feature, so the common name—star-nosed mole—suits them better.

CUTE!

119

SPIDERS

Sure, some spiders are incredibly venomous, and they can move startlingly fast on their many legs but, believe it or not, most spiders are not out to get you. Most of the terrifying things spiders do—like liquefying their prey or eating their boyfriends—don't relate to humans at all. And we get to admire the amazingly detailed patterns in their webs, and watch them do surprising things, like shaking their butts as they dance.

ARE YOU SCARED OF SPIDERS?

WHY?

A GROUP OF SPIDERS IS CALLED A CLUTTER OR A CLUSTER.

HAPPY FAMILIES

Starting a family can be pretty brutal for a spider. Some spiders don't even survive the mating process! Many female spiders, including the **black widow spider**, eat their partners after mating. Male spiders are often much smaller than females, so they don't stand much of a chance if their partner decides to make a meal out of them.

Australian **crab spider** mothers feed their babies with insects they have caught, but when winter arrives it becomes much harder to find food. Then, unable to nurture them further, she offers them one last meal—herself.

THAT'S DEDICATION!

DO ALL SPIDERS EAT MEAT?

All but one species of spider are predators. Most of them eat insects or other spiders, but a few are big enough to hunt lizards, rodents, and small birds. Spiders can only eat liquids, so how do they manage to eat these creatures? There are a few different ways. Most spiders either inject venom into their prey or vomit digestive fluids over them. Both of these things help break down the body of their prey until it can be slurped up. Some spiders spin silk around their food before they inject it with venom. That way their food turns into liquid in a tidy little container that they can eat out of easily—kind of like how you eat out of a lunchbox. Although spiders don't have teeth, some do have serrated pincers near their mouths that can be used to help grind up solid foods into mush.

So what about the one spider that isn't a predator? The *Bagheera kiplingi* from Central America mostly eats the leaf tips of the acacia trees that it lives in, sometimes snacking on a small amount of pollen, nectar, or ant larvae.

LORD OF THE DANCE

WHERE CAN I SEE A SPIDER?

Spiders can be found just about everywhere in the world—the only continent they don't live on is Antarctica.

Some male spiders do elaborate dances to attract mates. One of the most incredible dancers is the **peacock spider**, a teeny-tiny spider with an amazingly colorful coat. These little guys scoot from side to side, stretching and shaking their legs. They often stick two legs straight up toward the sky, waving them up and down in a way that looks like they're clapping. The real showstoppers are their rear ends, though—these are the most colorful parts of the spider, kind of like the tail of a peacock, and they flip them up over their heads and wiggle them around as they dance.

CUTE!

ON THE HUNT

- The **ogre-faced spider**, also known as the **net-casting spider**, doesn't use its silk to spin a web—it creates a net instead, which it holds stretched out in its legs to wrap around unsuspecting prey that walks past.

- The *Arkys* **spider** appears to attract male moths by mimicking the pheromones of female moths, then grabbing the males when they get close enough.

- **Trap-jaw spiders**, not to be confused with trapdoor spiders, don't build tunnels or webs—they rely on their wildly fast jaws to catch their prey. These super hunters sneak up behind their prey and snap their mouths shut over them with the speed of a rubber band being released.

SOME SPIDERS DON'T BOTHER WITH BUILDING WEBS— THEY'VE COME UP WITH OTHER WAYS TO HUNT THEIR PREY.

- **Fen raft spiders** are relatively large spiders that live near bodies of water. They can walk across the water's surface by using the tiny hairs on their legs to spread their weight evenly. On top of their diet of insects and other spiders, these water-walkers also catch and eat tadpoles and fish!

- The **six-eyed sand spider** is a reclusive, crab-like spider that buries itself in the sand and ambushes prey that wanders too close. Sand grains adhere to it, providing a natural camouflage.

FLANNERY FILE

For more than 15 years I was the curator of mammals at the Australian Museum in Sydney. On one side of my office was the office of a snake expert and on the other side was the museum's spider expert. Accidents do happen in museums, and I've found myself, more than once, with a live snake lurking in my filing cabinet. Being surprised by a snake isn't exactly a pleasant experience, but the eccentric habits of the spider expert unnerved me even more. I'm not particularly afraid of spiders, but when I was dashing out of my office on an urgent errand and bumped into the spider expert, his hands full of deadly **funnel-web spiders**, I admit to feeling a little uncomfortable. He was a delightful fellow, but I dreaded visiting his office. Aquariums containing live spiders had been crammed into every corner, and the walkways between them were so narrow that the room was transformed into a den of oversized, hairy-legged creatures. Worst of all, he was so fond of his spiders that whenever I did come in he would reach into an aquarium and enthusiastically wave his latest spider in my face.

CLIMATE CHANGE

The impact of climate change on spiders is varied. Some will suffer population losses as their habitat shrinks, while other species' habitats will expand.

CAN SPIDERS FLY?

SPiDERS CAN'T FLY, BUT THEY CAN TRAVEL EXTRAORDINARILY LONG DiSTANCES THROUGH THE AiR USiNG A TECHNiQUE CALLED "BALLOONiNG."

Some spiders can even travel across oceans! So how does ballooning work? Spiders climb something tall, such as a tree or bush, and then spin a number of long strands of web. They use these web strands to form a kind of sail that catches the breeze, lifts them up, and carries them through the air. If the breeze is gentle they might not get far, but if they're caught up in a powerful wind they could land anywhere! Ballooning isn't just some kind of extreme sport for daredevil spiders, though—when spiders need to escape flooding or other threats, ballooning can literally save their lives. Sometimes huge numbers of spiders balloon at once, leaving their landing spot covered in wisps of spider web.

SPIDER EVOLUTION

Spiders have been around for at least 380 million years, and they're still going strong! There are 38,000 species of spiders living in the world today, and perhaps as many again are waiting to be discovered and named.

WONDROUS WEBS

Each type of web-spinning spider has its own special way of building a web, and each web is designed to make it very tricky for prey to avoid or escape them.

▶ The **giant trapdoor spiders** of Southeast Asia and Australia make webs that look like silken tunnels. The spider lives inside the tunnel, setting up a number of delicate threads at the doorway to detect passing insects. The web jerks as the insects touch the tripwires, and when the spider feels the disturbance, it stalks out to pounce on its prey.

▶ The webs of the **orb-weaver spider** can be decorated with special, highly visible silk structures. They reflect ultraviolet light, which may help the spiders attract insects to the web.

▶ Some spiders make ladder webs more than 3 feet tall. These are very effective for catching moths, because moths are covered in loose scales that prevent them from sticking to regular webs. It is only when they lose most of these protective scales through tumbling down a ladder web that they are finally caught.

▶ Some webs are made of extremely fine silk. They are not sticky but instead work by entangling the legs of insects.

▶ A spider web's tensile strength, or ability to not break under tension, is similar to that of steel!

THE NOTORIOUS FUNNEL-WEB IS ONE OF THE WORLD'S MOST DANGEROUS CREATURES. IT LIVES IN EASTERN AUSTRALIA, AND IT HANGS OUT IN THE BUSH AND THE CITY.

UP CLOSE AND PERSONAL WITH . . .
A FUNNEL-WEB SPIDER

During the breeding season, males leave their burrows to find mates. They sometimes even enter houses, where they love to lurk in slightly damp places, such as towels casually dropped on bathroom floors. They can be very aggressive, so you really don't want to surprise one—if frightened, it's likely to bite.

Their fangs are strong enough to penetrate human fingernails, or even pierce the skull of a small mammal, and they bite over and over again to soak wounds with their venom. If you're bitten by a funnel-web you'll suffer excruciating pain, as well as convulsions, foaming saliva, nausea, blindness, and paralysis. If the bite's not treated it can take an adult 30 hours to die an agonizing death, but babies will die after an hour.

Like all spiders, funnel-webs don't actually want to waste their venom on humans. Why? Because venom takes time to produce, so if they waste it on a human they might not have enough left for things they can actually eat.

EEEK!

125

BEARS

Are bears adorable fluffy friends? Or are they terrifying hunters with claws and teeth sharp enough to tear unsuspecting prey limb from limb? Well, they're both! And they're plenty of other things, too—like dedicated parents, wrestling-mad siblings, living vacuum cleaners, tree-climbing enthusiasts, and long-distance swimmers, just to name a few. There are eight different species of bear, living in places as diverse as sweltering tropical forests and icy tundra, mountainous regions and lowland forests.

READY TO RACE

Brown bears can move at nearly 30 miles per hour, which is easily as fast as a car—and much faster than you!

SOME SPECIES OF BEAR ARE SOLITARY, BUT GROUPS OF BEARS ARE OFTEN CALLED A SLOTH.

BIRD OR BEAR?

Sun bears and **spectacled bears** both spend a lot of time in trees, even sleeping up in the treetops. They're often too big to just sit on a branch, so they build the bear version of a nest—a platform made of sticks that they can curl up on.

CUTE!

HOW MUCH BIGGER THAN YOU ARE BEARS?

Polar bears are the biggest of all the bears. In fact, they're the biggest land-dwelling carnivores! Even though cubs start out weighing a measly pound, fully grown polar bears can eventually reach about 1,600 pounds. They can also grow to be nearly 8 feet tall, so they'd tower over adults—even the extra-tall ones, like basketball players!

COZY COATS

Polar bears have some of the thickest fur of all the bears. They even have fur on the soles of their extra-large feet, which makes padding around on the ice more comfortable. Their fur looks white, but it is actually clear. And each strand is hollow! These special features keep heat close to their bodies, and might even make it easier for sunlight to reach their skin so they can absorb vitamin D. Underneath all that fur their skin is black, and so are their tongues!

FRESH MOUNTAIN AIR

Pandas live in bamboo forests, usually quite high in the mountains. They can travel nearly 13,000 feet up into the mountains in search of food. **Spectacled bears** often live in particularly thick, lush jungles and are also great at living in high altitudes. They regularly climb over 13,000 feet into cloud forests.

STAY OFF MY LAWN!

- **Brown bears** often stand up on their hind legs and rub against trees to leave their scent on them. Leaving their scent can warn off other bears but can also help them to find a mate. They often rub so vigorously against the bark that it looks like they're dancing or scratching a particularly pesky itch.

- **Polar bears** also leave their scent for other bears to pick up on, and the way they do it is a bit gross. The sweat from their feet oozes onto the ice as they walk and leaves trails of smelly footprints wherever they go.

FLANNERY FILE

I once visited a bear reserve in Romania, where I hid in a very small camouflaged hut at dusk to watch a dozen bears feed on a dead sheep that had been left out for them. After night fell, I had to leave the hut and walk through the dark forest to get back to my car. My guide said that bears are more terrified of people than we are of them, but even though I knew we were safe it was still scary to walk through the bears' home at night!

RECORD-BREAKING NAPS

A lot of bears are up and about during the day, but others prefer to stay up all night.

- Despite their name, **sun bears** actually sleep during the day and are active by the light of the moon, not the sun!

- Bears often cozy up in some kind of den. Dens can be dug into the earth or made in caves and hollow trees. **Polar bears** dig theirs into the snow—it might still be chilly inside, but at least they're out of the bitingly cold wind.

- Not all bears hibernate, but plenty of them do—including **brown bears**. They settle into their dens and sleep through the winter, not even waking up to eat. All that time without a meal means they can lose half their body weight by the time spring arrives!

WHERE CAN I SEE A BEAR?

Bears are spread across the world—do any bears live near you?

- **Brown bears** are the most spread out, living in Asia, North America (where they're called "grizzlies"), and Europe.

- **Pandas** only live in China.

- **Sun bears** are found in Southeast Asia.

- **Sloth bears** live in South Asia.

- **Spectacled bears** are the only bears that live in South America.

- **American black bears** are only found in North America.

- **Asiatic black bears** live across Asia.

- **Polar bears** live only in the Arctic, in countries such as Canada, the United States, Greenland, Norway, and Russia.

CHAMPiON SWiMMERS

Bears can be great swimmers. Sometimes they get in the water to go after prey, but they often hang out in the water to cool themselves down, splashing and playing just for fun. **Polar bears** are particularly excellent at swimming. They have slightly webbed paws, which help them to paddle long distances, and the high percentage of fat on their bodies helps them stay afloat. Polar bears have been recorded swimming in the ocean hundreds of miles from land! They also hitch rides on floating ice to travel across bodies of water—some distances are too far for them to swim.

WHAT'S EVEN CUTER THAN A BEAR? A BABY BEAR! THEY'RE SMALL, THEY'RE FLUFFY, THEY'RE CUDDLY—WHAT'S NOT TO LOVE?

REAL LiVE TEDDY BEARS

- Bear cubs can weigh as little as a can of baked beans—sometimes even less!

- Cubs often play together, rolling around and tussling as they pretend to fight. These games aren't just for fun—they also help the cubs work out which of them are stronger and more dominant.

- **Panda** cubs are completely white when they're born.

- Sometimes **sun bears** stand up on their hind legs and cradle their cubs in their arms, just like a human mother.

- Baby bears are usually called "cubs," but can also be called "coy." Coy stands for "cub of the year," and cubs can be called that when they're in their first year of life. Once they're a year or two old they are called "yearlings" instead.

- **Sloth bear** cubs sometimes hitch a ride on their mother's back—not many other bear mothers put up with being used as a method of transport!

129

WHAT DOES A BEAR EAT?

People often think of bears as terrifying carnivores, but not all bears hunt for their food—some prefer plants, and plenty of the meat-eaters are also content to munch on berries or a bit of honey.

▶ **Pandas** mostly eat bamboo, only taking a break from it occasionally to eat a rodent or bird. As they've evolved, one of their wrist bones has become more like a thumb, which makes picking bamboo easier for them. Pandas spend more time eating than you do sleeping—12 hours out of every 24! They eat an impressive 22 to 44 pounds of food each day.

▶ **Brown bears** love to gobble down moths—they can sometimes eat 40,000 of these winged creatures in a single day. They also love eating fish, especially salmon—they can grab them right out of the water, and often dive under the water to catch them instead of waiting on the bank.

▶ **Spectacled bears** mostly eat plants, including cacti!

▶ **Sun bears** use their long tongues to scoop termites out of their nests and honey out of beehives. They love honey so much that they're sometimes called "honey bears"!

▶ **Sloth bears** eat ants and termites. Their claws are over 2½ inches long, and help them break open nests. They blow away the excess dirt (to avoid eating it), and then they suck the bugs right into their mouths! They have a huge gap between their front teeth for the bugs to pass through, and flaps to seal their nostrils to give their mouths extra sucking power. They're a bit like furry vacuum cleaners!

CLIMATE CHANGE

Six of the eight species of bear are vulnerable or endangered, especially **pandas** and **polar bears**. As sea ice melts and gets thinner in the Arctic, polar bears find it increasingly hard to move around their habitat and find food.

SCRATCHING AN ITCH

It seems to be quite rare, but some bears use tools to make their lives easier—including picking up rocks to scratch themselves, even going after barnacle-covered ones for an extra-rough surface to really get in there.

TRYING A NEW DIET

Studies of fossilized bones have shown that Europe's **brown bears** were all carnivores before the Ice Age, and only started eating plants later on. Back then, a type of bear called a **cave bear** lived in Europe, and it only ate plants. After they became extinct 28,000 years ago, brown bears didn't have to compete with them for plant foods, so they started eating a lot more of them. When farmers arrived in Europe 10,000 years ago, they began to kill any bears that ate farm animals, so lots of meat-eating brown bears died. The vegetarian ones survived and bred, so today most of Europe's brown bears are largely vegetarian.

BIG APPETITES

Bears that hibernate during cold months, like **brown bears**, eat a lot of extra food as winter approaches. They go into a special state called "hyperphagia" that makes them drastically change their eating habits so that they can keep on eating for up to 20 hours at a time. That leaves just 4 hours each day for them to sleep! They can eat over 90 pounds of food each day during this period, which is like eating 40 large pizzas.

   Polar bears don't hibernate, but they still eat astoundingly huge meals when they can. They gorge so they have enough fat to keep them going when food is scarce—sometimes they can go months without a meal, and by eating big when food is available, polar bears can last a whopping eight months without food!

DOG OR BEAR?

Dogs and bears are related, and 30 million years ago they looked a whole lot more similar than they do now. In fact, some bear ancestors looked more like dogs, and some dog ancestors looked more like bears! It took millions of years for bears to begin to resemble the bears of today, and for dogs to evolve into their wolf-like shape.

HOW BIG IS A BEAR'S YARD?

Male **polar bears** have the biggest territory of any bear. They roam around on something like 110,000 or 140,000 square miles! Female polar bears make do with quite a bit less—more like 50,000 square miles.

BASILISKS

WHERE CAN I SEE A BASILISK?

Basilisks live in Central America and northern South America.

When you hear the word "basilisk," you're likely to think of a giant serpent with magical powers. So what do those mythical beasts have in common with these cool forest-dwelling lizards? Well, they're both reptiles for a start.

The ancient Greeks believed a basilisk was a monster made with parts of a rooster, snake, and lion that could turn people into stone just by looking at them! The scaly crests on the bodies of basilisk lizards do give them a distinctly rooster-like air. And although these lizards can't turn you to stone, they can certainly make you freeze in shock and amazement when you see them literally walk on water!

A GROUP OF LIZARDS IS OFTEN CALLED A LOUNGE, BUT BASILISKS DON'T HAVE THEIR OWN SPECIAL GROUP NAME.

AS BIG AS A DOG

The average length of a basilisk is between 28 and 30 inches, which is longer than the average golden retriever! **Green basilisks** can grow even bigger, stretching to almost 3 feet. A whopping two-thirds of a basilisk's length is just their tail.

TREE CHANGE

Some basilisk species spend most of their time on the ground, whereas others prefer to lurk up in the treetops of their forest homes. They have sharp claws to help them grip onto bark, and they regularly climb more than 20 feet up into the trees.

One thing that all basilisks have in common is the desire to live near water, generally the banks of rivers. They rely on this watery back door as a method of escape if things get too dangerous on land!

TAKING A DIP

Although they can stay dry by running on the water's surface, basilisks are also great at swimming. They don't swim only for fun—they can hold their breath and hide under the surface for up to half an hour, which is a handy way of escaping land predators.

MIRACLE WORKERS

Basilisks can walk on water—which is how they earned the nickname "Jesus lizard." They usually walk on water to escape predators on land. It isn't a graceful walk—they stand upright and rotate their back legs rapidly, kind of like they're pedaling an invisible bike. Their arms stick out stiffly on either side and their whole body sways as they gallop along, head bobbing from right to left. Here are the mechanics:

▶ Their back feet are special—they're HUGE, which allows them to spread their weight over a wider surface (a bit like snowshoes). And their feet have extra flaps of skin on them; as they slam their feet down on the water, these flaps trap air bubbles that help keep them afloat.

▶ They need to move FAST to stop themselves from sinking—if they slow down, the air bubbles won't form and their feet will start to become submerged.

▶ Their tails play an important part, helping them to stay balanced and change direction.

▶ Basilisks usually start with a run-up on land, but they can also leap straight down from the trees onto the water below.

▶ They can run for a stretch of 30 to 70 feet across the water, and the youngest, lightest specimens are the fastest.

CHAMELEONS

If someone calls you a chameleon, they mean you're good at changing yourself in some way to suit a particular environment. But no matter how good humans are at switching things up to fit in, they can't truly compare to actual chameleons! These lizards are seriously incredible at blending in, but they're just as likely to be bright and flashy so they stand out. And if you think their skin is cool, wait until you hear about what's underneath it . . .

CAT OR LIZARD?

"Chameleon" is Greek for "on-the-ground lion"!

POINTLESS POISON

Some chameleons have venom glands, but they are atrophied and don't produce enough venom to do any damage to anything.

WHERE CAN I SEE A CHAMELEON?

About half of all chameleon species live in Madagascar, with the others sprinkled across small nearby islands and through Kenya, Tanzania, and other African countries. They also live in India, Sri Lanka, Spain, Portugal, and parts of the Middle East.

MOVING OVERSEAS

The oldest chameleon fossils are 60 million years old, and were discovered in China. However, there are no living chameleons left there today.

ARE THEY MAGIC?

Sometimes color changes are gradual, but they can also happen very rapidly—in minutes, or even seconds. Chameleons don't use magic to change color, but they do use crystals! They have different layers of skin, and each one does its own special thing.

- The top layer of skin is covered with cells that are filled with pigment. These cells expand and contract to make the chameleon darker or lighter—they only alter the shade, not the color.

- The lower layers of skin have cells called "iridophores," which are filled with small crystals. They change shape in reaction to the chameleon's mood. They reflect light differently, depending on how contracted or expanded they are, which is what changes the color of the skin. The shape of the cells affects the color of the skin, and so does the amount of space between each crystal-filled cell. The cells move further apart when the chameleon is excited and closer together when it's relaxed.

- There is a layer of skin even further down that only reflects a certain kind of light—infrared light. Scientists think this might help chameleons regulate their temperature.

- When it comes to starting families, males with the brightest colors are at an advantage—female chameleons are more likely to mate with them.

- For one particular chameleon, **Labord's chameleon**, there's no time to waste when it comes to having babies—this particular species only lives for a total of three months.

- Some chameleons, like **Jackson's chameleon**, have live babies, like humans do. Other species lay eggs. Imagine if some of your cousins hatched out of an egg!

- Chameleons can lay up to 100 eggs at a time. Up to 30 live babies can be born at a time, but it's often fewer.

- Chameleon eggs are usually buried in burrows that the mothers dig into dirt or rotting wood.

- Parents don't look after their babies—they don't even wait around to see them hatch! To be fair, eggs usually don't hatch for about a year, and the eggs of some species can take a whopping two years to incubate, so they'd be waiting a long time.

KEEPING AN EYE ON THINGS

Chameleon eyes are extraordinarily powerful. They have 360-degree vision, and each eye can point in completely different directions at the same time. They also work like camera lenses—they have a built-in function for zooming in to get a closer look at something in the distance.

HOW **BIG** IS A CHAMELEON?

The smallest chameleon is the **Brookesia micra**, which is often less than 1 inch long when fully grown—so they're small enough to sit on your little finger! The largest is the **Parson's chameleon**, which can grow to up to 27 inches. Even your entire arm isn't long enough for them to sit on!

LIZARD OR LEAF?

Some chameleons don't need to change color to blend in—their natural shape, size, and color already make them nearly invisible. **Decary's leaf chameleons** look just like brown leaves!

FLANNERY FILE

I love chameleons and have often seen them on my travels in Africa. Once I was riding a horse in Botswana and I saw a giant **ground chameleon**. It was gray and standing on a sand dune, pretending to be a dead stick. It was completely still, with its tail sticking straight up in the air, and I almost got off my horse to take a closer look, but was very glad I didn't when I saw the paw prints of a huge lion next to the chameleon! The prints were so fresh that sand was still dribbling into them, so I turned around and galloped off as fast as I could.

ALL THE COLORS OF THE RAINBOW?

Chameleons can't just pick any color to change into—each of the 200 species has a specific range of color options, so the idea that they can change color to blend into any background is a myth.

▶ When they're just chilling out, most chameleons are shades of brown and green—the colors that are more likely to blend in with their forest environments.

▶ It's not just their colors that can change—patterns, such as spots or stripes, can also appear on a chameleon's skin.

▶ Males are generally more likely to change color, and often have a wider range of colors than females. Sometimes males and females of the same species are very different colors.

FLASHY AND FIERCE

Changing color can help chameleons blend into their environment, but that isn't the main reason they do it. Color shifts also help chameleons communicate with each other. Their color shifts can say a lot about how they're feeling—if they're angry, or want to mate, or are trying to send a warning, for instance.

▸ Males are territorial and use their brightest displays to stand out and intimidate other males. Sometimes they turn bright red—a warning sign in most languages. In a standoff, one male will eventually concede defeat by returning to a duller color. Males can get physical if color-changing doesn't scare off another male. They will puff up, hiss, snap, headbutt, and charge each other, grappling until one backs down.

▸ Males get an extra-flashy set of colors, including various combinations of turquoise, blue, green, orange, yellow, and red, when they want to attract a mate. Females can communicate that they don't want to mate by changing color, often becoming darker with bright splashes of color. That can be particularly helpful when they're already pregnant.

▸ Sometimes male chameleons (especially smaller, younger ones) change color to look like females so other males won't become territorial and try to fight them.

UP IN THE TREES V. DOWN IN THE DIRT

▸ A lot of chameleon species spend the majority of their time in trees, using their prehensile tails to wrap around branches as they climb—a bit like a much longer, more flexible limb. When they're not using their tails they often curl them up into a tight spiral.

▸ A limited number of species spend more time on the ground, such as the **horned leaf chameleon** and **Gorongosa pygmy chameleon**. Some of these ground-dwellers climb up into trees for extra protection when sleeping, but otherwise they use camouflage to blend into leaf litter on the forest floor. Some of these species don't even have prehensile tails—in fact, theirs can be quite short and stumpy.

▸ Chameleons have very flexible ankles and wrists, plus specially shaped feet that help them grip onto branches and bark. They look like they only have two fat toes on each foot, but each toe is actually several smaller ones fused together into one mega toe. That's why what looks like one toe can have multiple claws on it!

SKUNKS

The smell skunks let off is called "musk"—but not the good kind. Their scientific name, Mephitidae, comes from the Latin name for an ancient goddess of noxious gases, like the stinky ones that waft out of swamps and volcanoes. So that gives you an idea of what they smell like! There's more to these animals than their smell, though. They can be strikingly beautiful and athletic.

WHAT IS A GROUP OF SKUNKS CALLED?

A group of skunks is called a "surfeit," which is a word that means an excessive amount of something. For some people, especially those with sensitive noses, even one skunk is too many, so a group of any size would certainly seem like a surfeit!

WHEN YOU THINK OF SKUNKS, YOU THINK **STINK.**

WHERE CAN I SEE A SKUNK?

Skunks live in South and North America. **Stink badgers**, despite their name, are a type of skunk. They live in the Philippines and Indonesia.

WHAT'S ON THE MENU?

Skunks use their claws to rifle and dig through leaf litter to uncover food, which often consists of insects. But they're not fussy. They also eat things like fruit, eggs, fish, reptiles, larvae, and small mammals such as mice or moles. Sometimes they even go after snakes!

Skunks are resistant to the venom of some kinds of snakes, so they have less reason to fear slithery predators than many other small, furry animals.

SUPER MOMS

Female skunks are very independent, preferring to raise their babies alone. They make this clear to their partners not long after mating—sometimes even chasing away the males! After mating, female skunks don't always become pregnant right away. The **western spotted skunk** often waits up to 150 days after mating to start growing babies inside her womb. The father is definitely long gone by then!

Skunk babies, also known as "kits," are completely blind when they're born. Their eyes are sealed shut for the first three weeks of their lives, so they count on their moms to feed and take care of them.

WHY THE STRIPES?

It is thought that the striped pattern on many skunks is connected to their defensive abilities. The white lines on their fur direct predators' eyes toward the source of their stink—their butts!

LOOK!

HOW BIG IS A SKUNK?

The **hog-nosed skunk** is one of the largest skunks, sometimes stretching over 2.5 feet—similar to the length of a labrador. A fair bit of their length comes from their tail, though, so even though they look big, they usually only weigh as much as 10 pounds.

That's barely half the weight of a wiener dog!

On the other end of the scale is the **pygmy spotted skunk**, which is often under 8 inches long. With its tail curled around it, you could hold one of these little critters in your hand!

FLANNERY FILE

A creature remarkably similar to skunks inhabits northern Australia and New Guinea. These **striped possums** (also sometimes known as skunk possums) are small, cat-sized marsupials strikingly striped in black and white. One type has a massively bushy tail like some skunks, and some New Guineans wear its black-and-silver tail as a false beard! The four known species of striped possum all live in the rainforest, and, as I discovered when studying them in New Guinea, they have a very strong smell that really is skunk-like, though not nearly as awful. You can locate where they have been feeding or denning in hollow logs or tree hollows by their smell. Luckily, they cannot spray their odor. But if you handle one, the stench can stick to your hands for days!

WHICH SKUNK IS WHICH?

Not all skunks have stripes! There are five main types of skunk, and the white on their fur can appear in all sorts of patterns, or not at all—some are black all over.

▶ The **striped skunk** has two long stripes down its back, while the **spotted skunk** is covered in swirls and splotches of white.

▶ **Hog-nosed skunks** can have stripes, but sometimes have one huge swath of white down their backs instead. They also have a particularly memorable nose—completely bare of fur and quite large, kind of like the snout on a pig or a hog.

▶ **Stink badgers** can have lots of different kinds of white marks, but often don't have any white markings at all. They also have much shorter tails than other skunk species.

▶ **Hooded skunks** have extra-long tails and super-soft fur, which is particularly long around the back of their head and neck. Sometimes they have small amounts of white on their black fur, other times they have a long patch of white from the top of their head to the tip of their tail.

HOW DO YOU GET RID OF SKUNK SMELLS?

Skunk musk can't be washed off easily—even taking a shower won't get rid of it. There are all sorts of strange things people use to try to get rid of the stink, including vanilla extract, tomato juice, and apple cider vinegar. None of those things are a match for skunk musk, though. One of the most popular remedies uses baking soda, dish soap, and hydrogen peroxide, but hopefully you never have to test it out!

A HOLE TO CALL HOME

Skunks spend most of their time on the ground, with the exception of **spotted skunks**—they can climb trees so well that they're sometimes called "tree skunks." Skunks often live in burrows underground or cozy up in hollow logs and crevices in rocks.

STINK

MOST PEOPLE KNOW THAT SKUNKS SMELL TERRIBLE. BUT WHY DO THEY HAVE SUCH A PECULIAR STENCH, AND WHERE DOES IT COME FROM?

- When skunks are feeling threatened by predators, they spray an oily substance out of two nipple-like areas just inside their butthole.

- Skunk stink takes days to wear off, but it isn't toxic. The point is to scare off predators, not kill them!

- If you get sprayed, you'll probably feel a burning sensation, plus you can temporarily lose your vision and have trouble breathing. It can also make you puke!

- Skunks can shoot their stink as far as 33 feet, but the closer the target, the more accurate their aim is.

- Skunks can spray out either a cloud or a concentrated jet of stink—a bit like adjusting the nozzle on a spray-bottle. The jet is usually used when they are close to an attacker and can aim right at their face. The cloud isn't quite as effective, but it's useful for covering a large area when the skunk can't aim as well, such as when it is running away!

- Skunk spray and onions contain some of the same type of chemicals, which helps explain why both can make your eyes water.

- Skunks often try to frighten off attackers using other means before resorting to using their smelly spray. They make hissing or snarling sounds, stamp their front feet, arch their backs, and raise their tails in the air. Some even charge their attackers. **Hog-nosed skunks** sometimes stand all the way up on their hind legs before crashing back down onto all fours.

- Some **spotted skunks**, like the **eastern spotted skunk**, do a handstand before they release their spray. They fan out their tails above them to look bigger, keeping an eye on their attacker to see if their intimidation tactic is working.

Sometimes they even charge at their attacker while upside down, moving quickly on their hands like some sort of stinky acrobat.

- Some people can't smell skunk musk—those people are rare, but lucky!

SLOTHS

There are two main kinds of sloth: the **two-toed** and the **three-toed**. It sounds like the difference between them is obvious—they have different numbers of toes, right? Correct! But that's not all. These sloths are actually very distant relatives, not two members of the same genus! That doesn't stop them from having heaps in common—they're slow, they like munching leaves, and they're prone to napping. Most people know those things about sloths already, but do you know what happens when you put one in water? Or what's special about the bones in their fingers, or their poo?

A GROUP OF SLOTHS IS SOMETIMES CALLED A BED.

WHERE CAN I SEE A SLOTH?

Sloths live in South and Central America.

SLOW MOVERS

Sloths are the slowest mammals in the world, without exception. Their climbing speed is usually only about 6 to 8 feet per minute at the most—sometimes even slower.

LIFE IN THE TREES

Sloths don't bother leaving their trees to mate—everything happens up in the treetops, from finding a suitable partner to giving birth. When they're ready to start a family, female sloths have a special way of announcing it. They yell! Their loud call can sometimes sound like a whistle or a scream. Sloths have one baby at a time and raise it high up in the trees. Since sloths don't have pouches, each tiny baby has to hold on tight to its mother's hairy tummy to avoid falling to the ground.

DEATH GRIPS

Sloths are famous for being lazy. They sleep for about nine hours a day, and they move very slowly (if at all) the rest of the time. But how can they possibly rest easy when they're way up high in the rainforest canopy? Sometimes they find a cozy fork to curl up in, but more often than not they fall asleep hanging upside down from a branch. They have to rely on their arms and claws to stop them from falling, and luckily for them both are incredibly strong. So strong, in fact, that even when sloths die, they rarely fall out of the trees. Their arms keep on clinging to the branch they were dangling from when they took their last breath.

HOW BIG IS A SLOTH?

Two-toed sloths are sometimes a little bigger than their **three-toed** counterparts, but both types usually weigh somewhere between 8 and 18 pounds—about the same as a small pug. They grow up to 27 inches tall, but their limbs are so long that they often look a lot larger! The **pygmy three-toed sloth** is the smallest sloth. It only lives on one island in Panama called Escudo de Veraguas, and can be as short as 19 inches. It weighs as little as 5.5 pounds, which is similar to a chihuahua.

CLAW OR SWORD?

Why are sloths so slow? It's to keep them safe from predators! They don't have many ways to protect themselves, so if they can avoid being noticed by a predator in the first place, they won't have to worry about outrunning them or fighting them off. Just about the only method of defense sloths do have is their claws, which can be a whopping 4 inches long. Sloth claws aren't anything like your fingernails—they're actually part of the sloth's finger bones covered in a fingernail-like sheath.

143

TEARS OF . . . BLOOD

Some **three-toed sloths** can occasionally be seen with red liquid leaking from their eyes. That sounds bad, right? But it's actually perfectly normal eye goop—a bit like the crusty gunk you get in the corners of your eyes in the morning. The reason it's red is that these sloths eat a particular kind of red-tinged leaf, and it dyes their eye goo.

DOWNSIZING

Ancient sloths were hugely different from the ones you can see today—emphasis on the HUGE. They weighed up to 7.7 tons, which is more than some species of elephant!

SWIMMING LAPS

You wouldn't expect sloths to be good at swimming, but they are! One extinct kind of **giant sloth** even swam in the Pacific Ocean off South America and ate seaweed.

Modern-day sloths often drop straight down from trees into water, paddling around and using their long front arms to cut through the water. They're actually three times faster in the water than they are on land! But in classic sloth fashion, they don't swim quickly all that often—they like to lie back and let the water hold them up. Being quite light makes floating easier for them, and the gas in their stomachs created by the digestion process also helps them stay afloat.

SUPER STOMACHS

Sloths are leaf connoisseurs—they eat HEAPS of them. **Two-toed sloths** eat quite a few different things aside from leaves, including insects, fruit, and even lizards. **Three-toed sloths** are much fussier by comparison—they eat leaves from just a few species of trees. Digesting all those leaves isn't easy, but luckily sloths have stomachs specially made to do just that. They are made up of four different parts and are packed full of powerful bacteria that help to break down the leaves and get the nutrients out. A sloth's stomach can weigh as much as one third of its entire body!

KEEPING COZY

Three-toed sloths often seek out the sun, climbing high up in the trees to sunbathe. It's important for them to stay warm, because sloths can't shiver to warm up—it uses too much energy!

THE ULTIMATE CAMOUFLAGE

As well as keeping still, sloths have another nifty trick that helps them blend into their leafy environment. Algae often grow on their fur, partly because they move so slowly, and the mottled green growth helps them look like just another plant.

COOL NAME,
WHERE'D YOU GET IT?

The scientific name for **three-toed sloths** is Bradypodidae, meaning "slow of foot" in Ancient Greek. The name for **two-toed sloths** is Megalonychidae, also from Ancient Greek, and translates to "great claw."

STRONG ARMS AND SMALL LEGS

Sloths spend most of their time in trees—there's plenty of food up there, and it helps them stay safe from the predators who can't climb! But there's another reason sloths don't really hang out on the ground—they're not built for it. Sloth bodies aren't all that strong, and they have a lot less muscle than other animals of a similar size. The muscles they do have are cleverly arranged to be in the most useful places for climbing trees—the front of their bodies, especially in their arms. Their back legs are really weak by comparison, so when they do make a rare trip onto the ground, they rely on their front legs to do most of the work in dragging their bodies forward. Their huge claws make gripping onto branches easier, but unfortunately they get in the way when they're trying to walk on the ground. It's a lot like someone with really long fingernails trying to use a touch screen. **AWKWARD!**

THE SLOTH VERSION OF HEAD LICE

You're not the only one who thinks sloths are pretty cool. A particular kind of moth might just be their biggest fan. These moths make their home in the sloths' fur, where they can eat the algae growing on them and drink their sweat. If you think that's gross, wait until you hear about where they lay their eggs. These weird moths can't think of a better place for their babies to hatch than in a pile of sloth poo. What a way to enter the world!

SOLENODONS

Solenodons are particularly odd-looking, with bare, scaly tails a bit like an oversized rat's tail and feet that are almost comically large. They also grunt like pigs! Solenodons are extremely ancient (as in, lived-at-the-same-time-as-dinosaurs ancient) and highly endangered. They're one of only two native land mammals left in the Dominican Republic, and they've survived this long partly because they spend a lot of their time hidden away, and partly because they have a clever and very surprising way of protecting themselves.

ARE YOU SURE THAT'S MILK?

Solenodon mothers feed their babies with milk, but it doesn't come out near their tummies or chests like many other milk-producing animals. Instead, solenodons have nipples near their butts, in the fold where their back legs meet their bodies.

SMELL YOU LATER

Solenodons have a strong, musty smell that oozes out of special glands in their skin. They have been described as smelling like goats or wet dogs!

WHERE CAN I SEE A SOLENODON?

One species of solenodon lives in Haiti and the Dominican Republic, the other lives in Cuba.

RUN OR HIDE?

Solenodons can climb trees but spend most of their time low to the ground—sometimes even underneath it! During the day they hunker down in dens dug into the earth, or occasionally inside a cave or hollow log. They're pretty awkward animals, with a slow, shambling gait, although they can work up a decent speed if they're under threat. Even at their fastest they still aren't graceful—they run on their toes, swerving from side to side instead of moving in a straight line. Sometimes when they're afraid, they stop moving altogether and tuck their heads in, possibly hoping that if they can't see the predator, the predator can't see them.

SUPER SCARY SPIT

Solenodon means "groove-tooth" or "pipe-tooth" in Ancient Greek, and they earned their name because they have an extra-special feature. They're one of the only venomous mammals in the world, and the only kind that inject venom using their teeth! They have two sharp fangs, a bit like a snake. The venom is actually a very toxic saliva, and it flows through special grooves in the solenodon's fangs to reach its target. For smaller animals, the side effects can be severe. They include paralysis, convulsions, and difficulty breathing. The venom isn't able to kill a human, but swelling and quite a lot of pain will bother you for up to a week if you get bitten. So if you ever find yourself near a solenodon, avoid its teeth!

FANG PASTE

A NOSE FOR FOOD

- Solenodons are called "insectivores," because they mostly stick to eating insects. Every now and then they'll branch out and eat a frog or lizard, or roots, fruits, and other plant matter.

- Solenodons hunt at night, using the claws on their oversized feet to dig through the dirt and find food. They also use their claws to tear into rotting wood, gobbling up the insects that live inside.

- The eyes of a solenodon are small and beady—just like a chicken's. Their eyesight is pretty terrible, so they can't easily spot potential snacks.

- Luckily, solenodons have great hearing. They hunt using echolocation, like bats do. They make clicking sounds that bounce off objects around them, from trees and rocks to other animals, echoing back so the solenodons can learn where nearby prey is located.

- Solenodons have an excellent sense of smell. They use their upturned noses to root around in the earth and their long, sensitive whiskers to help them sense their prey. Their noses have a special joint in them that makes them extra flexible, a bit like how you have joints in your knees and elbows, so they're perfect for poking into hard-to-reach nooks and crannies.

TIGERS

Not everyone has seen a tiger in person, but most people have seen plenty of pictures. They're big, they're stripy—what else is there to know? A lot! Including answers to pressing questions such as: What do tigers do with their leftovers? What does their pee smell like? And, most importantly, what does it mean when a tiger wags its tail?

WHERE CAN I SEE A TIGER?

Tigers live in China, India, Bangladesh, Cambodia, Thailand, Vietnam, Nepal, Malaysia, Bhutan, Myanmar, Laos, Indonesia, and Russia.

JUST LIKE THE MOVIES

Many people are convinced that tiger pee smells just like a big, buttery bucket of popcorn.

YUM!

A GROUP OF TIGERS CAN BE CALLED AN AMBUSH OR A STREAK.

CAN YOU OUTRUN A TIGER?

Tigers are a LOT faster than you. They can travel up to 40 miles per hour when they're in a serious hurry—easily as fast as a car.

HOW BIG IS A TIGER?

Tigers are the biggest felines in the entire world. **Siberian tigers** are the biggest of them all, weighing up to 800 pounds—about the same as five adult humans. They grow up to 11 feet long, and that's not even including their tail, which can sometimes extend nearly 3 feet on its own!

Sumatran tigers are the smallest, sometimes growing to less than half the length of their Siberian relatives. They are also considerably lighter, tipping the scale at a mere 300 pounds (mind you, that's still a lot more than you weigh!).

YOU CAN TELL A TIGER BY ITS STRIPES

Each individual tiger has a slightly different pattern of stripes—no two are the same, even if they're siblings. And they're not always orange with black stripes. They can be gold with pale orange stripes or white with pale tan stripes. And it's not just tigers' fur that's patterned—the skin below is just as stripy!

SHAVE CREAM

A YARD WITH A FENCE

Tigers mark their territory both with their scent and by scratching marks onto trees. They spread their scent by leaving puddles of pee and chunks of poo lying around—the stink of their urine can hang around for up to 40 days!

WHAT DOES A TIGER HAVE IN COMMON WITH A PET CAT?

When they're not using them, tigers can retract their claws back into their paws—a bit like a housecat. This helps keep their claws super sharp for when they need them—like when they're hooking into evasive prey.

FROM PRECIOUS BABY TO TERRIFYING BEAST

Tiger cubs can weigh less than 2 pounds at birth. At first, they're adorable little bundles of fluff that are completely reliant on their mothers for food and protection, but they mature quickly. By the time they're just one and a half years old, they're ready to start heading out to hunt.

WAGGING TAILS

A tiger's roar can travel an impressive distance—more than 1.9 miles! Tigers also use their long and expressive tails to communicate. But, unlike a pet dog, if a tiger is wagging its tail, it is NOT happy—it's often a sign of aggression. Even a twitching tail can be bad news—a relaxed tiger generally has an equally relaxed tail.

FAMILY TIES

Despite different appearances and habitats, the nearest living relatives to tigers are snow leopards. Tigers and lions are often lumped together, but they're actually not that closely related. It isn't just their stripes that set them apart—among other things, tiger brains are on average 16 percent bigger than lion brains! Tigers are extremely smart, learn quickly and have excellent memories.

ROOM TO SWING A CAT

Most tigers make their home in forested areas, where there is plenty of cover and lots of food to hunt. Tigers can climb trees but, despite often being surrounded by them, they generally prefer to keep their feet firmly on the ground.

Tigers usually like to live alone, and ideally their neighbors will live very far away—they're not the most sociable animals! **Siberian tigers** have huge territories—a single tiger can command more than 1,500 square miles. In places where real estate is more scarce, tigers are often forced to live much closer to each other—as many as 18 **Bengal tigers** can sometimes live in about 40 square miles.

ON THE HUNT

SPLISH SPLASH

Tigers often swim in rivers and lakes, and not just so they can hunt down animals in the water. They also like to splash around for fun, or to cool off when they get hot. They can swim up to 20 miles each day as they patrol their territory, and can easily swim across rivers that are 4 miles wide.

YOU CAN TELL JUST BY LOOKING AT A TIGER THAT THEY'RE PRETTY GOOD HUNTERS. THEIR HUGE TEETH AND SUPER-SHARP CLAWS KIND OF GIVE THEM AWAY . . .

- For animals of their size, tigers can be remarkably hard to spot. They're masters of stealth, relying on their striped coats to help them blend in with bars of shadow and light in their forest homes. They often slink low to the ground as they move, and their huge feet have plenty of padding to help them tread silently.

- Tigers usually hunt at night, and they're highly skilled at spotting even the tiniest movements of their prey. Their night vision is excellent—about six times better than yours.

- After stalking their target, they pounce and deliver a death blow, which for tigers is often a strong bite—usually around the neck area. Their teeth can be 3 inches long, and their jaws are powerful enough to snap the spines of their prey.

- Tigers usually hunt animals that are quite large, like deer, wild pigs, elk, antelope, and water buffalo. They also hunt animals that are pretty dangerous predators themselves, such as leopards, crocodiles, and pythons. They rarely eat humans, or even go near them.

- The average tiger meal weighs about 11 pounds, but tigers can eat up to 60 pounds of food in a single night. The animals they kill are often much larger than that, so what do they do with the leftovers? They don't have a fridge to pop them in, so they do the next best thing—cover the half-eaten corpse with leaves, so they can come back to it later.

- Sometimes tigers share their food. Once, an **Indian tiger** killed a large antelope and eight of her relatives came to visit over the next day or so to get involved in the feast.

151

WOLVES

The clichéd image of a lone wolf with its head thrown back, howling at the moon, is one that most people are familiar with. But wolves are far more fascinating than that—they are remarkably hardy creatures, and can have particularly odd habits, such as running marathons or taking long ocean swims.

SHADES OF GRAY

Gray wolves aren't always gray—they can be black, white, or any shade of gray between the two.

WHERE CAN I SEE A WOLF?

Wolves are one of the most widespread animals in the world. **Gray wolves** live all over the western hemisphere, from Arctic wolves in Greenland and parts of North America to sea wolves off the coast of Canada. **Red wolves** only live in one area of North Carolina, a refuge on the Albemarle Peninsula.

A GROUP OF WOLVES IS CALLED A PACK. EVEN A SINGLE PAIR OF WOLVES CAN BE CALLED A PACK AS LONG AS THEY HAVE THEIR OWN TERRITORY.

TOP DOG PARENTS

Wolves almost always live in groups, generally led by a dominant pair. These top dogs are called the "alpha male" and "alpha female." There are usually between six and ten wolves in a pack, and many of them are the grown-up pups of the alphas (that never left home!).

▶ The alpha pair are often the only wolves in the pack that have babies, but the other wolves are all involved in raising the pups. Pups can't see or hear for the first few weeks, so having a whole pack to look out for them helps keep them out of trouble!

▶ Milk is the first thing pups consume, then they move on to food that has been chewed up and spat back out by older wolves, until they're finally old enough to tackle solid food.

▶ Wolf pups are very playful and love to wrestle and leap around. Sometimes they even play tag or tug of war—games that help prepare them for hunting as an adult wolf.

▶ Baby wolves can't go to the toilet by themselves—their mother needs to lick them to help their bodily waste come out.

YUCK!

FLANNERY FILE

I've slept next to a wolf. I've fed a wolf. I've walked alongside a wolf. He was my best friend, and his name was Butch. It's not quite what you're thinking, though . . . Butch was my dog—a black labrador. Dogs are really just specialized wolf breeds. Wolves' scientific name, *Canis*, even means "dog" in Latin! I was 7 when I got Butch, and I had him for 15 years. He was a really big part of my life, and such a sweetheart— we shared every adventure together.

REAL OR MYTH?

Dire wolves were native North American wolves that preyed on the now extinct American megafauna. These wolves became extinct around 9,500 years ago, when their giant walking meals also died out—it's hard to thrive when there's nothing good to eat. They were really big, but the largest **gray wolves** living today are actually similar in size. After dire wolves disappeared, gray wolves came in from Asia and Alaska and filled the space their extinction had left.

OFF THE BEATEN TRACK

WOLVES LIVE IN A WHOLE LOT OF DIFFERENT HABITATS, BUT THEY USUALLY PREFER TO MAKE THEIR HOMES IN PLACES THAT ARE QUITE REMOTE.

- Wolves can live at temperatures as low as −40 degrees Fahrenheit and as high as 122 degrees Fahrenheit!

- Some types of **gray wolf** live near the beach and are surprisingly good swimmers! They are sometimes called "sea wolves," "rain wolves," or "beachcombing wolves." They live around the coast of British Columbia, often swimming over 7 miles through cold, choppy water to reach islands off the coast.

- Their diet reflects their closeness to the ocean and includes things like shellfish, crabs, clams, fish, barnacles, fish eggs, seals, and even dead whales that wash up onto the beach.

- Many wolves choose to live in wooded areas—trees make it easier to stay out of sight, and food is often more plentiful. Forests also have lots of good places to make dens for their pups, from hollow trees to dens dug into the dirt.

- Arctic wolves live in cold, unforgiving climates—places where ice and frozen ground mean they can't dig dens. They live in caves or rock crevices instead, relying on their extra layer of fur to stay warm in sub-zero temperatures. In some wolf habitats it can be dark for five months of the year! When spring finally arrives, bringing light and warmth, the wolves shed their underlayer of fur so they don't overheat, kind of like taking off your sweater so you're just wearing a coat.

CLIMATE CHANGE

The **Ethiopian wolf**'s habitat in the mountains of Ethiopia is shrinking due to climate change, and the Arctic wolf is also under threat—its icy habitat is becoming warmer and food is getting harder to find.

HAVING A **HOWL**

▶ Just as you talk to your family, wolves communicate with other wolves in the pack—by howling.

▶ Wolves often howl as a way of marking their territory— if a whole pack is howling in unison, it might be to let nearby wolves know they're on someone else's turf . . . so back off!

▶ Sometimes howls are a warning sign that a wolf is ready to attack, but not always—sometimes a wolf just howls because it hears another wolf howling, a bit like you might yawn if you see someone near you yawning.

▶ Howls can travel extraordinary distances—up to 6 miles—so just because you can hear a wolf doesn't mean it's particularly close by.

PAW PATROL

Wolves can have huge paws—the average wolf pawprint can be as big as a sandwich!

ON THE HUNT

▶ Wolves are carnivores and skilled hunters, often going after prey much larger than them such as elk, deer, moose, and caribou. The musk ox, which is eaten by Arctic wolves, can weigh ten times as much as the wolf hunting it!

▶ Wolves can eat up to 22 pounds of food in one go! Hunting large animals isn't easy, so when wolves make a kill, they don't let any of the meal go to waste—even if that means eating until they're ready to burst. Sometimes they don't eat for a week or more, so they really appreciate their meals when they can get them.

▶ Wolves won't turn their noses up at much—fish, birds, lizards, and snakes are all acceptable snacks. Meat is their main food source, but it's not unheard of for wolves to munch on fruit, such as berries, from time to time.

▶ Wolves often chase prey for a long time to tire it out so it's easier to kill. Sometimes they cover more than 12 miles in one go!

▶ Wolves often hunt as a group, using teamwork to bring down their prey. Hunting as a team means eating as a group, but not everyone gets an equal share—the dominant pair of wolves in the pack get to eat before everyone else, often snagging the best parts.

PRIMATES

Primates are a group of animals that includes monkeys, apes, lemurs, tarsiers, and . . . **YOU!** Yes, you're related to all of those animals—which explains why some of the things they do seem oddly human. Have you ever seen an ape holding hands with a friend, cuddling a baby, or flashing a big toothy smile? The resemblance can be uncanny. But despite the similarities, there are plenty of differences between you and your primate relatives. For example, would you eat a bug you'd just picked out of your friend's hair?

GOTTA FIND 'EM ALL

New species of primates are still being discovered around the world. Most of the new species are smaller primates, such as **lemurs** and **bushbabies**. But a new species of **orangutan** from Sumatra was named as recently as 2017!

WHERE CAN I SEE A PRIMATE?

Various types of monkeys live in Africa, Asia, and South America, and just one kind lives in Europe—the **Barbary macaque**, which lives in Gibraltar.

Great apes (aside from humans) live in countries across Asia and Africa, while lesser apes are only found in Asia.

Lemurs only live in Madagascar, plus on a few very small islands nearby.

WHO'S WHO?

Primates are a pretty big group, so it can be tricky to keep them straight. They're loosely divided into two groups—the **lemurs**, **lorises**, and **aye-ayes** sit in a group called the Strepsirrhini and the **monkeys**, **apes**, and **tarsiers** sit in a group called the Haplorhini. You fit into the second group, too.

▸ Although **gorillas**, **chimpanzees**, and **orangutans** are often called monkeys, they're actually all types of ape. So how do you tell the difference between apes and monkeys? Well, apes don't have tails, are able to walk on two legs, and are even smarter than monkeys (who are already pretty clever!). They're also usually bigger. There are two groups of apes— great apes and lesser apes. Great apes include **gorillas**, **orangutans**, **chimpanzees**, and **bonobos**. Lesser apes include **gibbons** and **siamangs**.

▸ There are heaps of kinds of monkeys, too! They're split into two broad groups: Old World and New World. Old World monkeys live in Asia and Africa, while New World monkeys live across South and North America. Old World monkeys can live on the ground or in trees, and they have special leathery patches of skin on their butts that make sitting on the ground more comfortable. New World monkeys always live in trees, and their flexible tails can be used to grasp tree branches—they're almost like an extra arm! Old World monkeys often have longer noses with small, close-together nostrils that usually face downward like yours, whereas New World monkeys have shorter noses with nostrils set further apart and facing more toward the sides.

▸ **Tarsiers** started to evolve in a separate direction from apes and monkeys way back when dinosaurs were becoming extinct, which is why they look quite different.

WHAT BIG TEETH YOU HAVE!

When a monkey smiles at you, it doesn't mean they want to be friends. It's actually a warning sign that means the monkey is feeling threatened.

KEEPING CLEAN

Primates often bond by grooming each other—brushing and stroking each other's fur and picking bugs out, too. Sometimes they even eat the bugs—and yet, they have quite strict hygiene standards. For example, **mandrills** avoid grooming monkeys that are infected with parasites. How do they recognize which monkeys are infected? By smelling their poop, of course! Because they stop grooming the infected monkeys until they're better, they stop the parasites from spreading.

CLEVER!

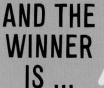

AND THE WINNER IS ...

The award for the weirdest-looking primate has to go to the **aye-ayes**! They have long, white hairs sprinkled over their darker fur that they can puff out to make themselves look bigger, plus outlandishly large ears. Their sharp incisor teeth keep on growing over time, kind of like fingernails do. And, speaking of fingers, aye-ayes have a totally bizarre middle finger that is longer than the others and looks like it is made purely of bone with just a thin coating of skin stretched over it. These weird digits are extra-sensitive, so they're what aye-ayes use to feel their way around.

WHAT DOES A MONKEY LOOK LIKE?

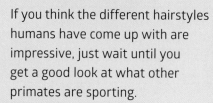

COOL!

If you think the different hairstyles humans have come up with are impressive, just wait until you get a good look at what other primates are sporting.

▶ **Golden lion tamarins** have small black faces surrounded by a thick, mane-like fringe of glossy orange fur.

▶ Mature male gorillas are sometimes called "silverbacks" because of the large patch of silvery fur on their backs.

▶ **Bonobo** hair is quite long, and it often parts naturally in the center of their heads and fluffs out around their ears in a style that looks oddly human.

▶ **Ring-tailed lemurs** are mostly gray or brown with cream underbellies, but their long, bushy tails are covered in black-and-white rings.

▶ **Golden snub-nosed monkeys** have thick orange fur and

BIGGEST AND SMALLEST

Great apes are the largest of all the primates, and **mountain gorillas** are the ultimate giants. They can be close to 6 feet tall and weigh about 485 pounds. **Orangutans** are smaller, under 5 feet and more like 440 pounds, but they deserve a special mention for being the biggest mammals to live in trees!

When it comes to monkeys, **mandrills** are the largest. They can grow up to 3 feet tall, which is the average height of a four-year-old child. Their weight is closer to a ten-year-old child, though—they can weigh more than 75 pounds.

The smallest monkey is the **pygmy marmoset**, which isn't quite 5 inches tall and only weighs about 3 ounces—about the same as a deck of cards.

If you think that's small, wait until you hear about **lemurs**. Although some of them can be quite large, **mouse lemurs** can be well under 2 inches tall and weigh less than 1 ounce.

bare blue faces. Their noses are so reduced that they look a bit like the nose cavities on human skulls.

▶ **Blue-eyed black lemurs** aren't all black—only the males are, with females having fur in shades of brown. Blue-eyed black lemurs are also the only primates other than humans that have blue eyes.

▶ **Emperor tamarins** have very long white mustaches that droop down on either side of their mouths. It's not just the male monkeys that sport these impressive 'staches—female monkeys grow them, too!

▶ **White-faced sakis** are very large, stocky monkeys. They grow black fur all over, except for a section of white fur

that puffs up all across their faces—only their eyes and noses poke through.

▶ **De Brazza's monkeys** have long white goatees and distinctive furry brown foreheads. The black fur on their heads is so neatly shaped that it looks like they've just been to the barber.

STRANGE EATING HABITS

PRIMATES HAVE SOME BIZARRE FOOD PREFERENCES—THERE'S NO ACCOUNTING FOR TASTE.

WHAT IS A GROUP OF PRIMATES CALLED?

A group of **monkeys** or **lemurs** is called a troop, and **gorillas** can be either a troop or a band (not the kind with instruments). A group of **chimpanzees** is sometimes called a community, and a group of **apes** is often referred to as a tribe, or sometimes a shrewdness.

▶ **Proboscis monkeys** only eat unripe fruit. Ripe fruit is packed with sugar, and as the sugar breaks down in the monkeys' stomachs it can make them swell up and even kill them.

▶ Male **gorillas** can eat 40 pounds of food each day. They mostly eat green, leafy plants.

▶ Many lemurs, including **red ruffed lemurs** and **mongoose lemurs**, love to eat nectar from flowers. They stick their noses deep inside to reach it, getting their snouts covered in pollen in the process. Mongoose lemurs also eat the flowers themselves!

▶ Some **red colobus monkeys** eat charcoal from burned trees, but not because they think it's delicious—it's thought that the charcoal helps get rid of the toxins that they eat when they munch on certain types of leaves.

▶ Up to 90 percent of a **bamboo lemur's** diet can consist of bamboo. Different species of bamboo lemur eat different parts of the bamboo, which means they don't have to fight over their food as much. Some prefer the young, tender shoots, others love the soft core of the bamboo stalk, which they have to shred their way through to.

▶ Some **macaque monkeys** living in Japan wash their food, such as potatoes, before eating it. Sometimes they use fresh water, but when they wash in salt water, they often dip their potatoes back in after each bite. Maybe they've realized salt and potato are the perfect flavor combination!

HUNTING AND FORAGING

▶ **Tarsiers** are excellent hunters. They can go after insects, birds, and even snakes! They are silent but deadly, leaping down onto their prey and using their sharp teeth to kill it.

▶ **Aye-ayes** tap on branches with their long middle finger to find the hollow insect tunnels under the bark. Once they find one, they use the same finger to tear into the wood and pull out the insects and larvae inside.

▶ "Don't poop where you eat" is a common saying, but **mouse lemurs** do exactly that! They poo near their homes and the seeds of the fruits they've gobbled down sprout into new plants, helped by the rich compost of the poo. The lemurs are eventually surrounded by the exact plants they like to eat, right outside their home. **CONVENIENT!**

ARE ALL TAILS EQUAL?

Lemurs have long, bendy tails that look like they would be perfect for clinging to branches or swinging through the trees. But they're not! Unlike those of New World monkeys, lemur tails can't grasp onto things—they're really only useful for balance.

PRIMATES OFTEN USE THEIR HANDS AND TEETH TO CRACK OPEN FRUITS, SEEDS, AND NUTS, BUT SOMETIMES THEY'RE JUST NOT STRONG ENOUGH TO DO IT ALONE—SO SOME OF THEM HAVE LEARNED TO USE TOOLS!

FLANNERY FILE

I had a terrifying interaction with a **gorilla** once. I was visiting a zoo in the United States and was taken behind the scenes to the area where the zookeepers fed the animals. I was walking along a corridor behind the gorilla enclosure when I suddenly felt an enormous rumbling. I thought there was an earthquake! Everything started shaking, and there was a deafening roaring noise. I turned around and came face to face with an adult male gorilla by the name of Caesar—he had thrown himself at the wire mesh fence and was staring straight at me. I felt my pulse speed up as my body went into fight or flight. This intimidating animal—who weighed over 400 pounds—was stomping, roaring, and baring his teeth at me, and there was just a wire mesh fence between us!

A TRUSTY TOOLBOX

▶ **Capuchins** smash open cashews by placing them on a rock and hitting them with another rock to reach the tasty nut inside. Stone tools can also be used to crack open fruit seed kernels and even different types of shellfish, like crabs. These monkeys use sticks to dig up things like roots and lizard eggs, or to fish hard-to-reach snacks out of narrow spaces, such as rock crevices.

▶ **Chimpanzees** mostly eat fruit, but will also eat insects, eggs, and even animals such as monkeys or wild pigs. They often use rocks to crack open the husks and shells of plants or animals, plus they poke sticks into ant and termite nests to scoop out the critters inside, spooning them straight into their mouths. They can also use leaves to scoop up water to drink!

161

CREATURE FEATURES

Not all primates have the same kinds of features—and some are a lot bigger than others.

- **Spider monkeys** have long, lanky arms and incredibly flexible tails. Their tails can grow to nearly 3 feet long, which far outstrips the length of their bodies.

- **Tarsiers** have HUGE eyes—each one is as big as their entire brain. For some species, such as the **Philippine tarsier**, each eye is bigger than their stomach.

- Male **proboscis monkeys** have simply enormous noses. The larger the nose, the more likely they are to attract mates. Their noses aren't just decorative—they can also be used to make loud honking sounds to assert dominance.

- **Orangutans** have ridiculously long arms that nearly reach the ground even when standing upright. Their arm span can be over 6 feet!

- Some **lemurs** store excess fat in their tails and back legs, so they can survive without food in times of rest. Sometimes, 40 percent of a **fat-tailed dwarf lemur's** body weight is packed into its tail.

FLANNERY FILE

I've had some really heartwarming experiences with primates. Once I went to the zoo with my wife and brand-new baby, and we were sitting outside the **chimpanzee** enclosure. Chimpanzees often interact with people quite a bit, but they also get bored and wander off if the people aren't doing anything interesting. This was a quiet morning at the zoo—no one was really around—so the chimpanzees were off doing their own thing. But when my wife started breastfeeding our little baby, every female chimpanzee in the enclosure stopped what they were doing and looked at her. They came over to the window and watched and watched. It was like they were thinking, *They do that as well?* It was incredible. They were completely mesmerized! Chimps are very chatty, but as soon as this happened, they started talking in a different tone—it seemed like they were saying, "Come over and look at this. It's amazing!"

MONKEY CHATS

Just like humans, groups of primates often like to chat. They communicate about all sorts of things, telling each other when they've found food, marking their territory, attracting mates or spreading the word that a predator is approaching. Not all of the ways they communicate are verbal—sometimes they use body language and gestures, but chattering is very common.

- **Bonobos** have one of the broadest ranges of sounds of all the apes, with about 40 different calls that include grunts, yells, squeals, growls, and screams, plus a particular squeaking sound that appears to mean different things depending on what the ape is doing when they make it.

- **Ring-tailed lemurs** use lots of vocal calls, but also use visual cues to stay in touch. They often hold their striking tails up in the air as they travel so it is easier for the group to see which way everyone is moving and stay together.

- **Chimpanzees** make a whole range of sounds, from hoots and yells to grunts. Sometimes they even laugh as they play together, including when they're being tickled! They also have very expressive faces, which they use to communicate, plus a whole lot of hand gestures.

- **Diana monkeys** have one of the most sophisticated monkey languages. They don't just have one alarm call, they have a different sound for each predator! They also combine different individual calls to say longer, more complex things—kind of like how you string words together to form sentences. Not only is their own language quite detailed, but they can actually understand the calls of other monkey species living nearby. They're fluent in multiple monkey languages!

- **Mountain gorillas** show their dominance using vocal calls such as hoots and roars, plus plenty of body language. They are often seen beating their chests or standing up on their back legs to appear tall and threatening.

- **Howler monkeys** have the loudest voices of any monkey. Groups of them often call all at once to mark their territory, and they're so loud that they can be heard nearly 3 miles away.

163

JUST ADD WATER

GIRLS RUN THE WORLD

Some primate species are dominated by males, but plenty of them go the other way. **Bonobos**, who are led by females, have some of the most peaceful communities of all the primates. They're good at sharing and usually coexist very happily. Most lemur species, including **ring-tailed lemurs** and **mouse lemurs**, also have dominant females. While males move from group to group, females will stay with the same group for their entire lives.

▶ **Japanese macaques** take outdoor baths in winter to stay warm. It gets very snowy where they live, so taking a nice long soak in a hot spring helps ward off the winter chill. Even though they like to stay warm, they still enjoy the snow—they actually like to play in it, sometimes even rolling up snowballs just like humans do.

▶ **Proboscis monkeys** are particularly good swimmers and can even leap down into the water from the trees. They have special webbing on their feet and hands to help them swim better, kind of like built-in flippers!

▶ Sometimes the last thing **chimpanzees** and **orangutans** want is to get wet, so they use large leaves as umbrellas, holding them over their heads to keep the rain off.

CLIMATE CHANGE

Deforestation is a big issue for primates, as they're losing many of the places they can live in. This is a particular issue for animals that have highly specific habitats, such as **lemurs** on the island of Madagascar. Some primates are found only in cool habitats on mountain summits. As the earth warms, they will be pushed ever higher, until there isn't anywhere else to go that will suit them.

Lots of primates help plants to grow and spread, because they eat their fruits and then poop them out in a handy pile of dung that helps the plants to sprout and grow. Unfortunately, even with all their eating and pooping they're no match for how fast humans are cutting trees down in some areas.

Bushbabies mark their territory using urine, but instead of peeing straight onto branches, they pee *into their hands* and then rub it on the trees.

BEGONE, PEST!

A range of monkeys, including **capuchins** and **spider monkeys**, have been known to rub crushed insects and the leaves of certain plants on their bodies. It seems they do this to deter insects from biting them—they do it more often when there are extra insects around.

Tamarin monkeys also use parts of plants to ward off pests—it is thought that they swallow large seeds to push out parasites that are living inside their bodies.

TAKING CARE OF A BABY

- Baby primates often just look like cuter, smaller versions of their parents, but not **François' langur monkeys**. As adults, they have silky black fur with two striking patches of white on their cheeks, but as babies they're bright orange all over! Their fur eventually changes to black as they mature.

- **Apes** often take care of their babies for much longer than many other animals—until they're at least seven years old, but sometimes into their teenage years.

- Lots of primates find new mates regularly, but not **gibbons**—they stick with their partner long-term, generally living together with their children.

- Baby **lemurs**, called "pups," are carried in their parents' mouths when they're really small. Once they get a little older they like to hitch rides by clinging to their mother's tummy or sitting up on her back—as if they're riding a motorcycle. Sometimes parents get grouchy, especially when the pups are old enough to walk, so they gently bite them until they get off!

- Some **lorises** and **lemurs** don't carry their babies around as they set off looking for food. Instead, they find a cozy place to leave them near where they're foraging, then come back to pick them up before heading home. It's a bit like dropping a kid at daycare before heading to work, only there are no adults in charge—the babies are usually left alone! This tactic works fine when the babies are too small to move by themselves, but once they get older they can sometimes wander off and need to be tracked down.

DESERT
& GRASSLANDS

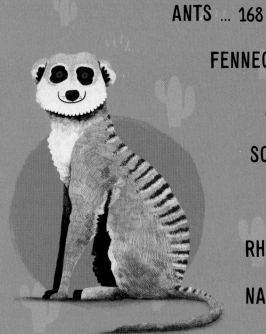

ANTS

A GROUP OF ANTS IS CALLED AN ARMY.

You've almost definitely seen an ant. In fact, you've almost definitely seen more than one because ants love to live and travel in groups. LARGE groups. The sight of ants pouring out of an anthill looks a bit like clowns getting out of a clown car—amazing and a little bit terrifying. How do they all fit inside their seemingly small anthill? We'll get to that.

Ants are great at teamwork, they're incredible builders, and they're really good at farming, too (just wait until you hear what kind of farming—it's gross). But farmer ants don't have anything on the ants that explode, or the ones that turn into zombies . . . or vampires . . .

WHERE CAN I SEE AN ANT?

Ants have colonized every habitable continent so if a human can live there, so can an ant! The only places that ants avoid are environments that even humans find tricky to live in, like Antarctica.

MUSHROOMS AND COWBOYS

Some ants take their chances on what they'll find to eat each day, but other ants like to know where their next meal is coming from. So they farm their food!

▶ **Leafcutter ants** create farms underground where they carefully tend to a certain type of nutritious fungi. They even make compost for the fungi by mashing up leaves! This type of fungus doesn't grow anywhere else in the world—in fact, it can't grow without the ants' constant care. The adult ants hardly ever eat the fungus, though. They grow it just to feed to their young, and they mostly eat plant sap instead. That's dedicated parenting.

▶ **Rancher ants** carefully tend herds of sap-sucking aphids—tiny pear-shaped insects. They move the aphids around so they get plenty of plant sap to eat, build shelters for them so they don't get wet when it rains, and fight off aphid predators, such as ladybugs. The ants sometimes even bite off the wings of the aphids so they can't escape. **RUDE!** So why do they do all this? The aphids produce a sugary substance called "honeydew," which ants love to eat. They milk the aphids by tickling them with their antennae until the honeydew comes out . . . of the aphids' butts! That's right, the ants are essentially drinking butt-milk. **GROSS!**

SMELLING THE WAY HOME

Ants lay down trails of chemicals called "pheromones" so other ants can follow them to find food or the way home. If you want to see how important these trails are, wait for a gap between ants marching in a line, then wipe your finger through the trail. As the incoming ants reach that spot, they will become confused and turn back, or wander around trying to sniff their way back to the path.

Even though we can't smell them, the chemicals used to mark these trails are extraordinarily strong to ants. Just 1 milligram of trail pheromone can be enough to create an ant superhighway so long it could wrap around the entire world 60 times.

ANT MANSIONS

Underground ant nests are enormous—there are some the size of whale skeletons! One species of **leafcutter ant** from South America has nests that can spread over thousands of feet. These nests can have nearly 2,000 rooms in them, some of which are so big that they could fit at least six basketballs inside. The ants have to dig out almost 4 tons of earth to make a home of this size—that much dirt weighs the same as 20 rhinos!

WORKING HARD

Ants live in large groups known as "colonies." You hardly ever see an entire colony at once, but it can be the size of a large octopus! Most ants in the colony are female workers. Each colony works kind of like a human town or city, with everyone doing different jobs to keep things running smoothly. Here are just a few jobs a worker ant might have:

BABYSITTER ANTS look after the ant eggs and baby ants, known as larvae.

EXPLORER ANTS go out looking for food.

ZOMBIES THAT DON'T EAT BRAINS

Zombie ants are carpenter ants that have been taken over by a deadly fungus. The aim of the fungus is to infect as many ants as possible. It starts by infecting an ant's body so it can control the ant's muscles—but it leaves the brain completely intact. This is where the fungus reaches incredible levels of evil masterminding—it accesses the knowledge inside the ant's brain about where other ants hang out, then it forces the zombie ant to walk there. Then the fungus makes the ant climb up high, where the fungus can bloom out of the ant's head and drift down to land on all of the other ants below, infecting them too.

DOCTOR ANTS

nurse sick or injured ants.

TRASH COLLECTOR ANTS

clear refuse out of the nest.

... OR HARDLY WORKING?

SO IF MOST OF THE ANTS IN THE NEST ARE FEMALE WORKERS, WHO ARE THE OTHERS?

▶ **Males:** These guys only have one job—to mate with the queen. After they've finished that task they die off pretty quickly.

▶ **The queen:** The queen's only job is to lay eggs. All her needs are taken care of by worker ants. Being pampered and fussed over by hordes of dedicated servants might sound kind of cool, but there are downsides to being the top ant. In some species, once the queen begins laying eggs she never moves again, laying 20 eggs every minute for all of her decade-long life. No fresh air, no stretching of her many legs—the worker ants might have the better deal after all.

THAT ANT IS GARBAGE

Trash collector worker ants smell of garbage, and the smell makes other ants really aggressive. If a trash ant sneakily tries to do a different job, its scent gives it away—and as soon as the other ants smell it, they shove the unlucky trash ant straight back to the dump.

FRIENDLY VAMPIRES

Dracula ants get their name because they suck the blood of their larvae! That sounds pretty brutal, but don't worry—they don't harm the larvae. In fact, dracula ants carefully tend to their young just like other ants—they just take a bit of blood in return.

UNDISCOVERED ANTS

There are currently 14,000 different species of ant in the world, but because they're small and really excellent at squeezing into hidden spaces, there could be another 14,000 types of ant still waiting to be discovered. Maybe even by you!

GUNSHOT WOUND OR ANT BITE?

The biggest ant is the **bullet ant**, which lives in the tropical rainforests of South and Central America. These ants can grow up to 1 inch long—that's more than 30 times bigger than their **leptanilline** relatives. Bullet ants get their name because being stung by one feels like being shot with a bullet. The pain of their sting makes you writhe and scream, throw up and even pass out. It's the most painful sting you can get from any kind of insect, and you won't feel better quickly, either— the pain lasts for a whole 24 hours.

OUCH!

SUPER STRENGTH

Despite their size, ants are wildly strong. They can lift 50 times their body weight and still clamber over difficult terrain. Imagine being able to lift 50 of your friends up over your head and then carry them all through an obstacle course!

BURIED ALIVE!

Undertaker ants recognize dead ants by their smell, not by the fact that they're not moving. When ants die, their rotting bodies produce something called oleic acid. When undertaker ants smell this acid, they carry the ant corpse to the cemetery. If a live ant gets any oleic acid on them they are promptly carried off by the undertaker ants too, despite the fact that they are still very much alive and kicking! If they try to leave the cemetery the undertakers will just keep on dragging them back until they have cleaned off the stinky acid.

STINKY ANTS

One ant species has been given the name **odorous house ant** because when they get squished, they release a disgusting scent that some people think smells like rotting coconut or blue cheese.

GROSS!

ANCIENT ANTS

Ants used to be wasps! They first evolved into ants around 140 million years ago.

SO FRESH AND SO CLEAN

Ants' antennae are coated in tiny hairs, and these hairs need to stay clean so that the ants can communicate and find their way around. It's not hard for ants to stay looking fresh, though—they have a built-in brush and comb set on their front legs! When they brush their legs over their antennae, the bristles clear out any dust or dirt.

CLEVER!

EXPLODING ANTS

Some ants can make themselves explode to scare predators away from the colony. They swarm around the invader and cling on to them, flexing their bodies until they literally burst open. One kind of exploding ant, the **_Colobopsis explodens_**, releases a lethal yellow goo when they explode, making them doubly as dangerous to predators. Strangely, this goo smells pretty delicious—like curry!

SMALL BUT DEADLY

The smallest ants are **leptanilline ants**. They're less than four hundredths of an inch long, which means one of these little guys could perch on the very tip of your pen and still have space to do an ant dance. But don't let their size fool you—these miniature ants are formidable hunters. Packs of these tiny creatures swarm together to take down and devour venomous centipedes much bigger than them!

STACKABLE

Just like acrobats, **fire ants** can stack themselves into towers and pyramids to get over obstacles. Sometimes more than 30 ants stack themselves on top of each other! Huge groups can also cling together to form ant rafts that can float across water. Their feet have special, extra-sticky pads on them that help them hold on to other ants.

FENNEC FOXES

These tiny, desert-dwelling foxes are smaller than a pet cat and their comically oversized ears would look more at home on a large dog. They're distractingly cute, but once the distraction wears off you'll probably have some questions. Such as, why would anything need ears that big? And how does a fur-covered fox survive in the baking hot desert?

A GROUP OF FOXES iS CALLED A SKULK OR A LEASH. (BUT FENNEC FOXES DON'T HAVE THEiR OWN SPECiAL GROUP NAME.)

Fennec foxes make purring sounds when they're happy.

CUTE!

WHERE CAN I SEE A FENNEC FOX?

Fennec foxes live in North Africa, including the swelteringly hot Sahara desert.

HIGH JUMP

Fennec foxes can jump up to 2 feet high, which is about three times their height!

CLIMATE CHANGE

Fennec foxes are perfectly adapted to live in a dry, hot environment, but as global warming makes the Sahara hotter it may be difficult for even this hardy fox to cope with the heat.

ANCIENT FOXES

The earliest fox fossils are seven million years old and come from Africa. The fennec fox is a very old species of fox—its relatives have probably been living in Africa's deserts for millions of years.

AREN'T YOU HOT?

For an animal that lives in the desert, fennec foxes have amazingly lush, furry coats. Even their feet are covered in thick hair! Although it seems wildly impractical, they actually rely on their fur to survive. The sun bakes down during the day, but the desert gets unbelievably cold overnight—so fennec foxes need all that fur to stay cozy after the sun goes down. Surprisingly, it comes in useful during the day, too—without a thick covering of fur their delicate skin would get burned to a crisp in no time! The fur on their feet is especially important for getting around in the desert. If you've ever tried walking barefoot on sand on a hot day you'd know why—sand gets UNBEARABLY HOT in the sun!

NIGHT FOX

Even though they're great at keeping themselves cool, fennec foxes get uncomfortably warm if they hang out in the desert in the middle of the day. So they don't! They use their furry feet to dig underground dens where they can curl up and snooze through most of the day, heading out to prowl at night once it's cooler.

GRANDMA, WHY ARE YOUR EARS SO BIG?

The only part of a fennec fox that isn't tiny is its ears. Each ear can grow to an astounding 6 inches long, which isn't that far off the height of the entire animal. So, why ARE their ears so big? All the better to hear their prey with! Their hearing abilities are so powerful that they can pick up the sound of tiny insects moving deep underneath the sand. Once they've found the precise location by listening carefully, they can dig at exactly the right place to uncover a delicious snack. Their bat-like ears also help fennec foxes to survive in their sandy, super-hot desert homes by radiating heat away from their bodies to control their internal temperature.

ARMADILLOS

A GROUP OF
ARMADILLOS
iS CALLED
A ROLL.

Armadillos are strange-looking creatures, with a mix of hair and armoured plates covering their stocky bodies. The Spanish name for them means "little armored one" and the Aztec name translates to "turtle-rabbit."

They come in a whole range of colors, including black, red, brown, gray, yellow, and pink (read on to find out why pink armadillos are pink—it's surprisingly icky). Some armadillos can roll up into a ball, which makes them look a bit like rocks. And their vocal abilities are incredible!

WHERE CAN I SEE AN ARMADILLO?

Nearly all armadillos live in South America. Only one type, the **nine-banded armadillo**, lives in North America.

PLATING UP

Most armadillos are covered in a protective armored shell that's built out of a number of overlapping plates—a bit like old-fashioned knight's armor.

▶ Each type of armadillo has a different type of shell—some only have a few plates, others have more. They usually have two main plates—one over their butts and one over their shoulders, and then a number of more flexible bands in between. Some armadillos are named after how many "bands" of armor they have, like the **nine-banded** and **three-banded armadillos**.

▶ Most armadillos have armored sections over their tails, heads and feet, but their bellies are just soft skin. The **three-banded armadillo** is the only kind that can roll into a ball so that its entire body is protected. Armadillos that can't roll into a ball have to find other ways to protect their delicate stomachs from predators. They run and hide in their burrows when they're in danger, or dig holes to hunker down in so that only their shells are exposed.

▶ **Pink fairy armadillo** shells are different—they're the only armadillo whose shell is mostly separate from their bodies. It is only connected along the spine by a little bit of skin! Their shells aren't solid, so they're not very useful as armor. But they are useful for regulating body heat. There are blood vessels just underneath the shell's surface, which can take in warmth or chilliness from the air or soil. By pumping blood into their shells or draining it back into their bodies, these armadillos can control their temperature. And their shell's shade of pink can actually change depending on how much blood is oozing around near the surface!

SCREAMING
IN THE FACE OF DANGER

One type of armadillo has earned the name **screaming hairy armadillo**. You can probably guess how—it has a particularly hairy tummy and is known for the piercing shriek it lets off when it's threatened. But even if these armadillos are screaming in terror, they won't necessarily run from danger. They're actually pretty brave! Like other armadillos, these noisy creatures have been known to throw themselves on top of snakes, cutting them with the sharp edges of their armor.

FUZZY
TUMMIES

Armadillo bellies are covered with hair, and each different species has its own hairstyle. On the **pink fairy armadillo** the hair is plentiful and fluffy, while on the **screaming hairy armadillo** the hair is long and wiry. Armadillo hair is very sensitive and helps them to feel things as they move around, kind of like how a cat uses its whiskers.

GIANTS
AND FAIRIES

The largest armadillos are called, appropriately enough, **giant armadillos**. They can grow to 5 feet long, which is the length of four bowling pins laid out in a row, and weigh a hefty 120 pounds. That's the same weight as eight bowling balls! The smallest armadillos are teeny tiny, and have an adorable name, too—the **pink fairy armadillos**. They can be just 3 ½ inches long, which is little enough to hold in your hand. They only weigh 3 ounces, which is a little less than two golf balls.

HIGH
JUMPERS

Armadillos are known for jumping when they're startled, and it's not a small jump—they can shoot over 3 feet into the air! Seeing an armadillo jump that high would stop most predators in their tracks for a moment at least, giving the armadillo a chance to bolt away and find somewhere to hide.

BABY ARMADILLOS

Nine-banded armadillos hardly ever have just one baby at a time. In fact, they're the only mammal that regularly gives birth to identical quadruplets! Baby armadillos, called "pups," are born without the armor that their parents have. Over time, their leathery skin hardens to form the protective shell they're famous for.

KEEPING COZY

Armadillos have barely any fat on their bodies, so they can get cold really easily. They also have a low metabolic rate, which means they don't produce much of their own body heat. If it gets too cold they can die, so armadillos prefer to live in warm places. Plus, it's easier to find food in warm places, and armadillos need to eat pretty regularly when they're awake. Insects don't keep you full for long!

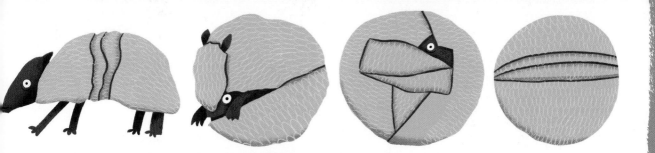

SWIMMING CHAMPS

Armadillos don't look like they could power through laps in the local pool, but they're surprisingly good swimmers! They can hold their breath for up to six minutes, which helps them walk along the bottom of rivers and streams to reach the other side. They can also swim along the surface of the water instead—if they gulp in enough air, they become buoyant enough to float near the surface as they paddle across.

I'D RATHER BE SNOOZING

Most armadillos regularly sleep for 16 hours each day, only rousing themselves in the morning, evening or at night to rustle up something to eat. The **giant armadillo** is even sleepier than the rest—it can sleep for 18 hours at a time!

SNIFFING AND SCARFING

Armadillos have an excellent sense of smell, which is very lucky because their eyesight is terrible. They rely on their noses to track down food—usually some kind of insect. They have a particular passion for ants and termites, which they latch on to with their long, flexible tongues. Their spit is extra sticky, making it tricky for insects to escape. They keep their noses buried in the soil a lot of the time, sniffing out things to eat. It's hard to breathe when your nose is full of loose soil, so sometimes they hold their breath as they dig.

TOOTHY WONDERS

Giant armadillos have up to 100 teeth crammed into their jaws.

A BUTT BUILT FOR DIGGING

Armadillos have strong paws and sharp claws that help them tunnel for their prey or build burrows to sleep in. **Pink fairy armadillos** live underground, like moles do. In fact, it's very rare to see one aboveground, as they're up and about when you're asleep. These particular armadillos have a special body part that helps them with all that digging—a butt plate! This plate is a solid patch at their rear end that they use to pat down all of the loose earth they dislodge as they dig with their paws. The butt plate pushes the loose soil to the back and compacts it, keeping a clear path ahead of them.

SCORPiONS

Scorpions have a reputation for living in exceptionally hot places and stinging anything that comes near them. That's not entirely correct, though. Scorpions do thrive in the desert, but did you know they can also handle freezing temperatures? And they are packed with venom, but they're more likely to go after their prey using their pincers (although that fact might not be much of a comfort!). Scorpions have a lot of other qualities that might surprise you—they love smoothies, like to take a spin on the dance floor, and do something really weird with their vomit.

HOW BIG ARE THEY?

The smallest scorpion is the **Microtityus minimus**. It can be tricky to spot because it's less than half an inch long. The biggest scorpion in the world is the **Heterometrus swammerdami**. It's a massive 9 inches long, which is the width of a full-sized soccer ball (but a lot less fun to play with).

A GROUP OF SCORPIONS IS CALLED A BED.

HUNTING AND EATING

- Scorpions can't swallow solid food. Instead, they tear hunks of flesh off their prey, then vomit their stomach fluids over them. This turns the solid food into a meat smoothie.

- Scorpions can slow down their metabolism so that they can stay alive when there isn't much food around. If they have to, scorpions can survive by eating just one insect for an entire year!

- Scorpions usually try to catch their prey with their pincers instead of using the powerful stinger on the end of their tails. It might seem strange for a hunter to avoid using their strongest weapon, but scorpions don't actually have a constant supply of venom. Once the venom has been used up it can take a whole week for their bodies to make more, so it needs to be saved for special occasions. **DELICIOUS!**

GIANT SEA SCORPIONS

About 400 million years ago the ocean was home to an ancient relative of scorpions. These salty creatures were called "Eurypterids" and grew to an enormous 8 feet long—that's as long as a surfboard! Luckily for us, modern scorpions are much smaller.

CAN A SCORPION KILL YOU?

There are about 2,000 different species of scorpion and fewer than 40 of them have venom strong enough to kill a human. That doesn't mean you should go and cuddle the other 1,960 types, though! Even a non-lethal scorpion sting packs a powerful punch.

WHERE CAN I SEE A SCORPION?

Scorpions live on every continent except Antarctica.

CAN I HAVE THIS DANCE?

The average pair of scorpions waltz around together for about half an hour before they mate. If a scorpion couple REALLY love dancing they might keep tearing up the dance floor for two hours!

FLANNERY FILE

Once I was riding my motorcycle around Australia, and we stopped to camp in the outback overnight. I was sleeping on the ground because it was really hot, and a scorpion stung me. It paralyzed my arm, so I couldn't grip onto anything—which meant I couldn't ride my motorcycle! I had to get a lift to the nearest doctor, who was half a day's ride away, on the back of someone else's bike. I couldn't feel my arm for about a day, but I wasn't seriously harmed—eventually the feeling came back and I could go and pick up my abandoned bike.

POO FREE

Scorpions produce almost no poo—just a teeny-tiny bit of nitrogen-rich waste.

SNEAKING UP ON A SCORPION

Scorpions are almost impossible to sneak up on because their senses are ridiculously sharp.

▶ Scorpions have six pairs of eyes, so they don't have a single blind spot. Their eyes can pick up on even the tiniest movements around them by tracking changes in the light.

▶ Scorpion claws are covered in tiny hairs that can sense things moving nearby. They also have a slit-shaped organ on the upper part of each leg that is so sensitive to vibration it can pinpoint the footfall of a beetle nearly 3 feet away.

▶ Scorpions have highly sensitive comb-shaped organs called "pectines" under their bodies. These organs are packed with nerve endings and are capable of smelling and tasting things from the ground as the scorpion walks.

THIS SKIN IS SO LAST SEASON

Baby scorpions start out with soft skin that hardens over time. Even after they've grown up scorpions can't rely on their tough skin to protect them, because they shed the outer layer up to seven times each year. When they shuck off their old skin the skin underneath is silky-soft, so they have to lay low until it has a chance to harden into the usual armor-like coating.

HITCHING A RIDE

A baby scorpion is called a "scorpling"—which is super cute for something that can grow up to be so dangerous! Scorpion mothers carry their hordes of scorplings around on their backs like the insect versions of school buses.

CLIMATE CHANGE

Scorpions will probably survive climate change better than most living things, including us. They're very hardy and have already survived for 430 million years, making them among the most ancient of land creatures.

FLANNERY FILE

I once camped near Lake Eyre in the Australian desert. It hadn't rained for a long time, but that night we had a brief shower. When I got out of my tent and turned on my flashlight I saw that there were hundreds of transparent scorpions, about the length of my thumb, walking over the sand. There were so many it was hard to step between them. When I looked closely, I could see some of their internal organs through their skin!

PACKED WITH VENOM

The **yellow Israeli scorpion**, also known as the deathstalker, has about 100 different types of venom! Even so, its venom is rarely powerful enough to kill a healthy adult human.

ELEPHANTS

Elephants hang out in deserts, grasslands, and forests, squirting water out of their trunks, stamping around and snacking on various plants. But those aren't the only things worth knowing about them! For example, did you know that there used to be elephants the size of ponies? Or that they like playing catch? If they're feeling extra rebellious, elephants might even gang up to cause trouble for nearby hunters.

PRETTY COOL!

WHERE CAN I SEE AN ELEPHANT?

Asian elephants live in Southeast Asia, **African elephants** live across sub-Saharan Africa and **African forest elephants** live in the central and West African rainforest.

ANCIENT ELEPHANTS

Elephants once lived on every continent except Australia and Antarctica, and there used to be dozens of different species, from the pony-sized **dwarf elephants** of Crete to the huge **woolly mammoths** and **mastodons** of North and South America.

SUPER NOSES

Elephant trunks are actually noses, but they're much more versatile than a human nose. Their noses have an astounding 100,000 muscles and can do a whole lot of useful things:

▶ Elephants can drink through their trunks, but it's not like drinking through a straw. They use their trunks to pick up water, which they then squirt into their mouths.

▶ Elephants use their trunks to communicate with each other, like how humans use sign language or baseball players use hand signals to call a play.

▶ Trunks can be used like a hose and sprinkler, with elephants sucking up water and then spraying it over themselves to cool down or wash off.

▶ Elephants tear branches off trees with their trunks. Why? To use as flyswatters!

▶ Elephants' trunks are strong enough to uproot entire trees to throw at predators! But they don't just throw things to protect themselves. They often use their trunks to throw objects around for fun, like how we play catch with a ball or frisbee.

ELEPHANTS ARE HUGE

Elephants are the largest land animals in the world. **African elephants** can grow nearly 13 feet tall and weigh up to 24,000 pounds, and babies can weigh 220 pounds when they're born. To put that in perspective, you probably weighed about 8 pounds as a newborn!

A GROUP OF ELEPHANTS IS CALLED A HERD.

WHAT'S IN A NAME?

There are three types of elephant: **African elephant**, **African forest elephant**, and **Asian elephant**. The Asian elephant's scientific name is *Elephas maximus*, which means "largest elephant" in Latin. That's pretty funny, because Asian elephants are actually smaller than African ones!

WHAT ARE TUSKS FOR?

Tusks are kind of like the elephant version of a pocketknife—they're strong, pointy and can do a whole lot of nifty things. **African elephants** have the biggest tusks.

- ▶ Tusks are perfect for digging up roots to eat or drilling down to reach underground water.

- ▶ Elephants can use their tusks to strip the bark off trees so that they can munch on it.

- ▶ If an elephant needs to intimidate or fight predators, or even other elephants, tusks are perfect for the job. As you can imagine, being on the other end of a pair of long tusks would be pretty terrifying!

CONSERVATION STATUS

ENDANGERED

Asian elephants are endangered and African elephants are threatened.

MOVE OVER, MICHAEL PHELPS!

Elephants are excellent swimmers. In fact, they're the best swimmer of any land mammal—except for professional human swimmers! They are able to float quite well in the water, and can also use their trunk like a snorkel and swim with their body completely submerged underwater.

CLIMATE CHANGE

Different elephant species used to breed with each other, and sharing their genes in that way helped them become stronger and more able to adapt to living in different places. Scientists worry that because the last three living elephant species no longer breed outside of their own species, they may be less adaptable and more vulnerable to climate change.

MUD BATH

Elephants love to swim in water, but they'll also wallow around very happily in a pool of mud. A mud bath helps elephants to keep cool and rid themselves of bugs. The mud has another special benefit, too—it coats their skin and helps protect them from the hot sun. Yes, even elephants can get sunburned!

FLANNERY FILE

Once I was in a bush camp in Botswana, and there was a little swimming pool there. A young elephant came right into the camp and started playing with a hose that was being used to refill the pool. The people running the camp were a bit nervous—they said an elephant had never come into their camp before. But it turned out to be harmless—and hilarious. The elephant was having so much fun! He grabbed the end of the hose out of the pool and squirted himself all over, and then started waving it around wildly and squirting everything else! I was standing a few yards away from him, so I got completely drenched.

FULL OF FEELINGS

Elephants are incredibly clever, sensitive creatures. They have excellent memories and can recognize up to 1,000 other elephants! They have been known to remove spears from wounded friends and cry when a loved one dies, just like humans do. They often bury their dead; in one case, a group of elephants broke in and raided a shed filled with the body parts of illegally slaughtered elephants, removing the ears and feet (which were destined to be turned into umbrella stands) and burying them.

GOT MILK?

Baby elephants survive on their mother's milk for two years. When they're being weaned they throw tantrums that rival those of the wildest two-year-old humans, screaming, trumpeting, and poking their mothers with their tiny tusks.

WAAAH!

RHINOCEROSES

Rhinos are big and tough, but they also have plenty of habits that are more likely to make you laugh than run away in terror—including prancing around in poo slippers and having tongues that lick like an overexcited labrador.

MONSTER RHINO

The world's biggest ever land mammal was closely related to today's rhinos. The *Indricotherium*, now extinct, is thought to have been up to 25 feet tall. It probably weighed more than 30 tons, which is the weight of eight particularly large **white rhinos** put together!

ODD RELATIVES

They don't look alike, but rhinos' nearest relatives are actually tapirs and horses!

COMM-POO-NICATION

Rhinos make all sorts of sounds when they're talking to each other, including roars, honks, bleats, grunts, and snorts. They also use their poo to communicate and mark their territory. They build huge piles of poop called "dung middens," coming back time after time to go to the toilet in the same place. **Greater one-horned rhinos** are particularly likely to do this, and their middens can be up to 3 feet high and 16 feet wide. That's longer than some small cars! After doing their business, they stomp their feet in their poo and walk their scent all through their territory, warning other rhinos to keep away. Definitely do *not* try this at home.

HOW BIG IS A RHINO?

Greater one-horned rhinos are the tallest of all the rhinos, measuring up to 6 feet from toe to shoulder—that means they'd tower over plenty of basketballers. When it comes to weight, first place goes to **white rhinos**—they can weigh up to 9,000 pounds, which is more than twice the weight of some cars. They could crush you like a bug!

EW!

A GROUP OF RHINOS IS CALLED A CRASH, OR SOMETIMES A HERD.

WHERE CAN I SEE A RHINO?

Rhinos once roamed in many parts of the world, but they now only live in a handful of places. All rhino species are under threat of extinction due to deforestation and poaching.

▶ The **Sumatran rhino** lives in Indonesia and Malaysia.

▶ The **Javan rhino** lives in Indonesia.

▶ The **white rhino** lives in South Africa, Botswana, Kenya, Namibia, Swaziland, Zambia, Zimbabwe, and Uganda.

▶ The **black rhino** lives in Kenya, Namibia, South Africa, Swaziland, Tanzania, Zimbabwe, Zambia, Botswana, and Malawi.

▶ The **greater one-horned rhino** lives in India and Nepal.

NO BABYSITTER REQUIRED

Female rhinos are called "cows," males are called "bulls," and babies are called "calves"—just like cows! Rhinos are pregnant for 15 to 16 months. Rhino moms are extremely caring and very protective of their babies, but mothering duties usually only last for two to five years. At that point the cow is ready to have another calf, so her current baby has to start taking care of itself.

FLANNERY FILE

I have touched the rarest rhino on Earth: the **Sumatran rhino**. There are only a couple left in captivity, and this one was in a zoo in Cincinnati, Ohio. It was a really big rhino, and the particularly amazing thing about it was that it was covered all over in thick, black hairs. It was very striking. The rhino seemed to appreciate being touched—it leaned into my hand a little as I stroked its flank. Meanwhile, I had this lump in my throat because it was so beautiful, and so endangered. The Sumatran rhino is the nearest relative to the **woolly rhinoceros**. I couldn't stop thinking about the woolly rhinoceros and how we've already lost it to extinction, and about how the Sumatran rhino might become extinct soon too, and then we wouldn't have any hairy rhinos anymore.

PASS THE SALT

Rhinos are big, tough vegetarians. They love to munch on soft new leaves and juicy shoots, plus stems, twigs, grasses and fruit. Rhinos consume about 110 pounds of food each day, which is like eating 110 bunches of kale (rhinos really love their greens). They don't only love plants, though—they're also mad about salt! Every few months they travel to "salt licks," which are places where salt naturally builds up. The rhinos lick at the salt with the same enthusiasm that you would eat a bag of salty potato chips.

SALT

FRIEND OR FOE?

Rhinos are known for being tough, but most species only fight to protect their young or defend themselves. If there is plenty of food, water, and salt to go around, rhinos can be quite social with each other. It's usually only if resources are scarce that they start to defend their territory more aggressively (except for **black rhinos**—they have bad tempers!). African rhinos don't have incisor teeth, so they use their horns for defense, while Asian rhinos regularly use their sharp lower teeth when they feel threatened. When two animals fight, injuries can occur. Sometimes even deaths. When it comes to black rhinos, the chance of one of them dying in a fight is particularly high— about half of all males die in combat, and around a third of females. No other mammal is as likely to die in a fight with a member of its own species.

WHO'S WHO—AND HOW LONG WILL THEY BE HERE?

The name "rhinoceros" comes from the Greek words for "nose" and "horn." All species have at least one nose-horn, and some have two—those ones look particularly impressive! Tragically, their horns are prized by poachers, who often kill rhinos to take their horns. Many species of rhino are in danger of becoming extinct as a result.

▶ **Black rhinos** and **white rhinos** aren't actually black or white—they both have gray skin! So, how can you tell the two species apart? The most obvious difference is that black rhinos have a pointy lip that helps them pluck fruit and leaves straight from the trees. White rhino lips are much squarer in shape, which is perfect for grazing on the ground.

▶ **Sumatran rhinos** are one of the oldest living mammal species on Earth (which explains why they look so prehistoric). They're also critically endangered.

▶ **Greater one-horned rhinos** have super-long lower teeth. They can grow up to 3 inches long! They love swimming, and will often duck underneath the water to find food. They can even eat underwater!

▶ The **Javan rhino** has a known population of just 67, so they really need our protection.

▶ There are two species of white rhino: **northern** and **southern**. The **northern white rhino** is the rarest mammal on Earth. They have been killed in huge numbers for their super-long horns, which reach up to 6 feet in length. There are now only two in existence. Both are female—and neither one is fully fertile. The only hope for the survival of the species lies in new technologies that might be able to produce sperm cells from skin cells that have been taken, frozen, and kept in laboratories. The **southern white rhino** hasn't been so badly targeted by poachers, but it is still endangered.

NAKED MOLE RATS

Naked mole rats are one of those animals that people can't agree on. Some people think they're horrifically ugly, others find these rodents fascinating. Although they do look pretty odd—a bit like a pale, wrinkly sausage with teeth and the odd hair—their appearance isn't even the weirdest thing about them. They're one of the few cold-blooded mammals in the world, they live in colonies that are eerily similar to ants' colonies and they have some surprising uses for poo.

WHERE CAN I SEE A NAKED MOLE RAT?

Naked mole rats live in the east African desert—Somalia, Ethiopia, and East Kenya.

HOW BIG IS A NAKED MOLE RAT?

Naked mole rats are usually a little under 4 inches long and weigh 1 to 1.2 ounces, about half the weight of a tennis ball. The queen is significantly longer and heavier, generally weighing at least double any other naked mole rat in her colony and sometimes reaching nearly 3 pounds—the weight of a particularly small chihuahua.

THE SUPREME RULER

Naked mole rats live in large groups—there are usually around 75 in each colony, but there can be up to 300! Each naked mole rat has its own job within the colony, and the rules of who does what are strictly enforced. One of the riskiest things a naked mole rat can do is challenge the hierarchy of its colony. Breaking the rules is inexcusable behavior, and the punishment is often death (or exile, which for naked mole rats pretty much means death—they're not built to live alone). So, who's who in the colony?

▶ **The queen:** Naked mole rats are led by an all-powerful leader, and it's always a female. The queen is a fair bit larger than the rest of her colony, but she's not born that way; she starts out life just like all the others and has to fight her way to the top. It's her job to eat all the best food and have lots of babies.

▶ **The dads:** Not every male gets to be a father—a small handful of males in the colony are in charge of mating with the queen.

▶ **The security guards:** These naked mole rats are tasked with keeping the entire colony safe from outside threats.

▶ **The workers:** This group of naked mole rats do most of the work to keep the colony going. They dig tunnels for everyone to live in, gather food, and look after the queen's babies.

HOME SWEET HOME

Naked mole rats don't really know the meaning of the phrase "personal space"—they live packed tightly together in huge underground burrows. The burrows are a mass of winding tunnels, with separate rooms for eating, sleeping, and going to the toilet. Naked mole rats can dig closer up near the surface where the earth is heated by the sun to warm up, or deeper down if they need to cool off. Their legs are quite small and not all that strong, so they mostly use their powerful teeth for digging away at the soil, only using their feet to clear away the loose dirt. There often isn't much room to turn around in the narrow tunnels, but, luckily, naked mole rats are great at running backward!

PRECIOUS POO

Poo isn't just a waste product for naked mole rats—it is a treasured resource that they *eat*. The roots they eat are hard to digest, so by eating their poo they have a chance to get extra nutrients from their food that weren't digested the first time around.

Poo is more than a food source, too—naked mole rats roll around in the colony's communal toilet so that they all smell the same, which helps them tell outsiders apart.

BRAINWASHING THE BABYSITTER...
WiTH POO

Although naked mole rat colonies can have hundreds of members, only the queen has babies. All of the other females produce a special hormone that stops them from getting pregnant. The hormone only works when they're living under the rule of a queen—if any of the females leave the colony, their bodies go back to being ready to have babies very quickly. The queen has to keep on having babies each year in order to stay in power, but she doesn't take care of them all by herself—after about a month, the workers step in. They're really good at babysitting, and there's a bizarre reason for that—they eat the queen's poo, which is full of special hormones that make the workers act like mothers and take extra good care of the babies.

FOREVER YOUNG

Many small rodents don't have particularly long lifespans—take mice, which usually only live for a year or two. Naked mole rats are different, though. They can live for over 30 years, which is an incredibly long time for a rodent of their size. They usually stay fit and healthy right into old age, and they're also naturally resistant to certain diseases, such as cancer.

POOP

BREATHING IS OVERRATED

Oxygen is very scarce in naked mole rat burrows, partly because they're underground, but also because the oxygen has to be shared by everyone living there—and there are a lot of them. If you tried to move in with a colony of naked mole rats, you'd die—there simply isn't enough oxygen for humans to survive in that kind of environment. Naked mole rats are able to thrive, though, and that's due to a special skill they have— when oxygen is running low, they can stop breathing for up to 18 minutes! When they stop breathing, they keep producing energy to survive by using a substance in their bodies called fructose, which is a type of plant sugar that makes energy without using up oxygen. No other mammal has this ability. Your body uses a different kind of sugar, called glucose, which creates a lot more energy, but also uses up lots of oxygen.

TENDER OR TOUGH?

Naked mole rats live in hot, dry deserts, but they aren't bothered by their harsh climate. Despite looking delicate, naked mole rats are actually super tough. They don't feel pain the same way as other animals do— in fact, they barely notice it. When they touch hot, acidic or spicy things they don't feel the same discomfort that you would, which lets them focus on important things like finding food.

FUSSY FEEDERS

Because naked mole rats rarely leave their burrows to venture out into the dangerous world, their diet is quite limited. They eat the tubers, roots, and bulbs of certain plants that poke down into the soil, and it can take a lot of digging to find a suitable one. Naked mole rats are well suited to underground foraging. Their lips can seal behind their teeth to keep dirt out of their mouths when they're using their mouths to dig! Workers often band together to find food, lining up to dig tunnels in unison. Once they find a suitable tuber, the naked mole rats can be set for food for months, or even a year in some cases. The tubers can be very large, so even though they're being eaten by the naked mole rats, the plants often don't die. Instead, the tubers keep regrowing the parts that are being gnawed on.

HIPPOPOTAMUSES

The name "hippopotamus" comes from Ancient Greek and means "the horse of the river." Hippos certainly do love rivers—they spend about 16 hours in the water every day! However, they're not related to horses—not even a little bit. They're related to the group of aquatic animals known as cetaceans, which includes whales, porpoises, and dolphins.

A HIPPO IN THE CITY?

Prehistoric hippo bones have been found in many parts of the world, including Asia, Africa, Europe, and the Mediterranean. The bones of prehistoric hippos have even been found buried underneath Trafalgar Square in London!

WHERE CAN I SEE A HIPPO?

There are two hippo species left in the world: the **common hippo** and the **pygmy hippo**. The common hippo can be found in East Africa, south of the Sahara. The pygmy hippo lives in very restricted forested parts of West Africa.

A GROUP OF HIPPOS IS CALLED A BLOAT.

CAR CRUSHERS

Hippos are the second largest land animals in the world (elephants sneak ahead to take first place). At their largest, hippos can be over 5 feet tall from toe to shoulder and measure easily over 13 feet from snout to rump—the length of a small car. Hippos can weigh well over 9,000 pounds at their biggest—the same as more than *two* cars!

TERRITORIAL TERRORS

Hippos live in herds that are led by one dominant male. There are usually about 20 hippos in a herd, with females and babies making up most of the numbers and a couple of less dominant males rounding it out. If another alpha male invades the herd's territory, the herd leader and his sidekicks will bare their huge teeth, grunting, snorting, and splashing the water in a display of terrifying ferocity. They don't just fly off the handle at other hippos, though—any intruders, including humans, will be warned off in this way, or even attacked. So, take care to avoid hippos in the wild!

SLINGING SCAT

Hippos use their poo, also called "scat," to mark their territory. They swat their poo with their tails as it comes out, splattering it far and wide. The sound of scats being slapped echoes down the river, warning other hippos of their presence.

WHAT DOES A HIPPO EAT?

Hippos can be pretty aggressive when they're defending their territory, but their eating habits are far from brutal. Hippos like to eat grass, young plant shoots, tender leaves, and the occasional piece of fruit. Although they spend most of their daylight hours in the water, they tend not to eat water plants. When the sun sets, they take a long walk inland, munching on all the food they find along the way. Once they're full, they return as a group to their water hole. They often have to travel up to 6 miles inland to find a full meal, because their appetites are very healthy—they can eat 75 pounds of grass in just one night. In times when food is hard to find, hippos can store food in their stomachs and live off those supplies for three weeks if they have to.

EMUS

A GROUP OF EMUS iS CALLED A MOB.

Emus aren't your average birds. Their bodies are so huge and oddly shaped that their puny wings can't possibly lift them off the ground. Their stomachs are full of more than just food, the sounds they make are as far from a "tweet" as you can get, and they take the idea of dedicated parenting to a whole new level.

I AM YOUR FATHER

Mother emus leave soon after laying eggs—the fathers sit on the nest for eight weeks, keeping constant guard. They don't leave to eat, drink, or even poo, so by the time the eggs hatch the fathers are weak and very skinny. When they crack out of their shells, the chicks have downy feathers with brown and cream stripes and are small enough to cup in your hands.

CUTE!

WHERE CAN I SEE AN EMU?

Emus only live in Australia.

WHAT IS THAT SOUND?

Emus often make grunting sounds, and they're known for hissing when they feel threatened. But the most astounding noise they make is a deep, booming call that sounds like drums being played. Emus have an inflatable pouch in their throat that they expand or deflate to make these distinctive calls. They're so loud that you can hear them more than a mile away! Females are more likely to make these thunderous sounds, especially around mating season when they're defending their territory or competing for a mate.

FLANNERY FILE

If you see an emu in the distance, lie down on your back and pretend you're riding a bicycle upside down. Emus will be so curious about the strange movements you're making that they'll come straight over to investigate. I do it whenever I'm out in the bush and see emus. It works fantastically! If you're in the opposite situation and you want an emu to *go away* instead of coming closer, there's a trick for that too. Just stand up and raise your hand above your head, with your hand curled and pointing forward in the shape of an emu's head. They'll get intimidated and go away, because you look like a taller emu!

NO TIME TO CHEW

Emu stomach acid is strong enough to dissolve just about anything they gobble down. They're mostly herbivorous, and prefer seeds and the young, tender parts of plants. Aside from super-strength stomach acid, emus have another trick to help them digest their meals. They swallow a whole heap of stones, which end up in a part of their stomach called the gizzard. These stones grind up their food, meaning emus can gulp down big mouthfuls and let the stones do the "chewing" later on.

NiFTY!

ON THE RUN

Emus don't usually stick around to tangle with predators. They can't fly away, so it's lucky they're pretty fast on the ground—they can keep pace with a car, hitting speeds of up to 30 miles per hour! Instead of running in straight, predictable lines, they zigzag wildly.

GIRAFFES

Giraffes are very relaxed animals. They like hanging out in groups, munching on leaves and taking the occasional nap. But every now and then, you'll see giraffes doing something very odd—like picking their noses or tasting pee. And things that are easy for you, like having a drink or blowing your nose, are a whole lot more awkward for giraffes!

A GROUP OF GIRAFFES IS CALLED A TOWER.

BIG-HEARTED

A giraffe's heart weighs over 24 pounds. It takes a massive heart to pump blood through their long limbs and all the way up their necks!

WHERE CAN I SEE A GIRAFFE?

Giraffes live across Africa.

STARTING A FAMILY

▶ How does a male giraffe find out if a female is ready to start a family? He drinks some of her urine! By sniffing and tasting a potential mate's pee, males can work out if she's ready to have a baby, or even if she's already pregnant.

▶ When a baby giraffe (also known as a "calf") is born, it is much more developed than a human baby. It plops out and falls a good 5 feet down to the ground, but it doesn't get hurt—in fact, it's walking around within half an hour! Within 10 hours, it's running and keeping pace with its mom, and it's not long before it can gallop at up to 35 miles per hour.

▶ Mothers band together to take care of their young, forming giraffe kindergartens so that most of the parents can go out foraging while a small number stay back to keep an eye on the calves.

WHAT'S THAT SMELL?

Giraffes are particularly stinky creatures, but not because they're unclean—it's thought that the smell is a tool for keeping insects and parasites away.

TIP-TOP TONGUES

The first thing you notice about a giraffe is probably its long neck, then possibly its lanky legs. But those aren't their only oddly elongated body parts—a giraffe's tongue (which is a dark, purply black) can be over 20 inches long! That's at least five times longer than your tongue—probably even more. They need extra-long tongues so they can reach leaves from high-up branches, but they also use that extra length to reach up and lick the snot out of their own noses.

YUCK!

The closest living relative of the giraffe is the okapi. An inhabitant of dense African jungles, the okapi was not discovered by scientists until 1901. I once touched an okapi when I was at a zoo in America. They have much shorter necks than giraffes, but they're still big animals, and very striking. They're purple and white, and their coat is very short and unbelievably soft, like velvet. It was such a lovely feeling to be able to pat one of them!

WHAT'S THAT SONG?

When you ask someone what sound a giraffe makes, chances are they have to stop and think about it—giraffes aren't known for being particularly noisy. But that doesn't mean they're silent! They moo when they're in distress and grunt or snort if startled, plus they spend a solid chunk of their evenings humming. It's thought that the humming is a way of communicating with each other, but its purpose is still a bit of a mystery to scientists.

CLIMATE CHANGE

Climate change is causing habitat loss for giraffes—flash floods and droughts kill off their food sources, forcing them to move on in search of leaves to eat. This sometimes causes fragmentation: a group breaks up, losing their safety in numbers and making it harder to reproduce. They are also affected by the drying of waterholes.

WHAT DOES A GIRAFFE EAT?

WHAT TIME DOES A GIRAFFE GO TO BED?

Getting a solid night's sleep isn't high on the to-do list for giraffes. They generally only lie down to sleep deeply for about ten minutes per night, with a few five-minute naps sprinkled throughout the day. They don't even bother to lie down for those naps—it takes a lot of effort for such a gangly animal to lie down and then get back up. Instead, they nod off standing up—and they do it with their eyes open, too!

multivitamin—they get a big dose of calcium, phosphorus, and other minerals from gently gnawing on and licking bones.

▶ While they may be perfectly built for reaching leafy snacks from the treetops, their body shape isn't nearly so helpful when it comes to drinking. When they arrive at a water hole, giraffes need to be fairly sure there are no predators nearby, because the stance they use to drink is hard to get out of in a hurry! They splay their long legs as wide as possible, then bend their necks right down to the water so they can lap it up. Luckily, they only need to drink once every week or so—they get most of their hydration from juicy leaves.

▶ Giraffes spend most of their time eating leaves—they can eat up to 130 pounds of food per day. They don't just chew and swallow like you though—they chew, swallow, then spit their food back up before chewing it again, repeating until the leaves are a dense, gloopy lump called a "cud."

▶ Giraffes are sometimes seen licking animal carcasses. This is their equivalent to taking a

LOOONG LEGS

A giraffe's super-long legs measure up to 6 feet—so if one of your parents stood next to a giraffe, they may not even reach its belly! Males can be up to 20 feet tall, with females generally standing a little under 16 feet. Giraffes weigh up to 5,000 pounds—that's more than a car!

203

LIONS

In some ways, it isn't hard to see why lions are called "kings of the jungle" (although they're actually far more likely to live in grasslands than in jungles!). The impressive mane that most males sport looks a bit like a crown—but don't underestimate lionesses just because they don't have manes! They might not be kings of the jungle, but they're certainly queens of the hunt. Despite the geographic distance, **Asiatic lions** and **African lions** aren't completely different species—these two groups are related.

BIG . . . BUT FAST

Lions are super speedy—they can race along at over 50 miles per hour, which is easily as fast as a car. They're also incredibly agile— they can launch their hefty, muscular bodies an impressive 36 feet into the air.

A GROUP OF LIONS iS CALLED A PRiDE.

WHO HUNTS?

- Male lions are protectors of the pride, while female lions are in charge of hunting.

- Lionesses love a challenge. They tend to hunt animals that are bigger than them, and sometimes faster too. In Africa, that includes zebras, antelopes, and wildebeest. In Asia, sambar deer and buffalo are some of the larger animals on the menu.

- If lionesses want the best chance of snagging a meal, they need to team up. That's why they usually hunt in packs. Sometimes they hunt alone, but usually only if something tasty wanders right past their nose—then they can't help the impulse to attack!

- Lionesses rely on their endurance to chase down their speedy prey.

Once their prey is completely exhausted, the lionesses will corner it and take it down.

- **African lionesses** prefer to hunt in the evening, when the moon isn't fully out yet. They use the low visibility to their advantage, sneaking up on their prey and pouncing before it has a chance to escape.

- Lionesses are usually only about a year old when they join in on their first hunts. They tail their older relatives to learn the tips and tricks of a successful hunter.

- Not every lion in the pride gets to eat at the same time—the most powerful ones eat first and get all the best bits, with cubs being left to eat last and comb over the pickings.

THE GANG'S ALL HERE

Cats are usually quite solitary creatures, but lions are different—they live and work in tight-knit groups.

- In **African lion** prides, there are often about four times more females than males in a group—about 12 females to 3 males. Girl cubs usually stay with the same pride for their whole lives, but it isn't safe for boy cubs to stick around— the adult males in the group often see them as a threat and attack them. Once they're old enough, they usually leave and try to take over a different pride.

- Male and female **Asiatic lions** spend most of their lives in two separate prides, generally only coming together to mate.

FLANNERY FILE

I once had a student who was researching the first documented case of black rats in Botswana. He wanted to find out why these rats had started living in Botswana, so he went to a garbage dump to try to catch some of them for his studies. It was night-time, and all he had with him was a little flashlight and a pocket knife. He had his head down, searching, and when he finally looked up, a lioness was staring straight at him. She was only 30 feet away, so he knew that if he ran, it would be the end of him. Luckily, he remembered there was a little outhouse about 150 feet away. He figured if he could make it there, he would be safe. He backed away slowly, with the flashlight and the knife pointed at the lioness. When he got close enough to the outhouse, he turned and ran. But when he reached it, he realized it had no door—it was completely open on one side! He began screaming and shouting, but nobody could hear him. He was working with some friends, but they were back at the camp, which was about 300 feet away, and they couldn't hear him over the sound of the generator running. Finally, after a couple of hours, his friends started asking each other, "Where's Chris? He hasn't come back yet!" They went out to look for him, and eventually found him huddled up in the outhouse, looking terrified. All around the outside were the paw prints of the lioness. She'd been circling him, and had only left when his friends' car approached!

FAMILY SIZED

African lions can reach nearly 6 feet in length, plus nearly another 3 feet on top of that if you include their tails. That means that all up, they can be one and a half times as long as your bed. They can weigh up to 420 pounds, which is probably more than you and two adults combined. **Asiatic lions** are even bigger! They can weigh over 485 pounds and be as long as 9 feet from head to rump.

KEEPING CLEAN

Lions enjoy preening each other: licking each other's heads and rubbing their necks together. It's partly practical—it's impossible to lick your own head (go ahead, try it!)—but it also seems to be an affectionate gesture that helps them bond.

LIONS THROUGH HISTORY

Lions evolved from jaguar-like ancestors between two and three million years ago.

- Some of the world's oldest art shows pictures of lions—32,000-year-old paintings in a cave in France show lions living alongside now-extinct animals, such as mammoths and woolly rhinos.

- Lions used to live on every continent except for Australia, South America, and Antarctica. They lorded it up in England, France, and even Los Angeles, but now their territory is much more limited.

- **European cave lions** survived until 14,000 years ago. They were bigger than modern lions and lacked a mane, and some of them may have had faint stripes.

- **American lions** became extinct 11,000 years ago. They were the largest lions ever, with males sometimes weighing more than 1,000 pounds.

WHOSE CUB IS WHOSE?

- Lions can reproduce at any time of year, but females living together in the same pride regularly have babies at the same time and share the work of raising the cubs. Lionesses often babysit big groups of cubs, a bit like a cub kindergarten, and cubs will drink the milk of any mother lion in the pride—not only their mother.

- Baby lions are usually called "cubs," but can also be called "lionets." **CUTE!**

- If a male lion appears on the scene and tries to take over a pride, he usually kills all the cubs. Brutal! The mothers don't let that happen without a fight, though—they often band together in groups and fight back heroically to protect their cubs.

- Cubs are super playful. Mothers will sometimes join in with the games, but dads are more likely to get annoyed and swipe them away.

WHERE CAN I SEE A LiON?

African lions live in Botswana, South Africa, Kenya, and Tanzania, with the majority grouped in a park called the Serengeti National Park in Tanzania, where they are protected from hunters.

There is just one area left in the world where **Asiatic lions** live: the Gir Forest in India, which is a wildlife sanctuary where the lions are protected and able to live in peace.

ROADRUNNERS

Roadrunners are members of the cuckoo family that have become terrestrial, meaning they spend pretty much all of their time on land. Their scientific name, *Geococcyx*, means "cuckoo of the earth" in ancient Latin. Despite being earth-bound, they can still get around! You might have seen a cartoon version stirring up a cloud of dust as it shoots across the desert, and the animated version does share some similarities with the real deal. For example, they do live in the desert, and they are incredibly fast! There are two types of roadrunner, the **greater** and the **lesser**. The greater is bigger, and has a longer bill, but otherwise they're quite similar.

ROADRUNNERS GENERALLY TRAVEL IN PAIRS RATHER THAN BIG GANGS, BUT WHEN A GROUP OF THEM GET TOGETHER THEY'RE CALLED A MARATHON OR A RACE.

WHERE CAN I SEE A ROADRUNNER?

Greater roadrunners live in Mexico and the southwestern US. **Lesser roadrunners** live in Mexico and Central America.

WELCOME HOME!

TRUE ♥ LOVE

Roadrunners mate for life. Some couples stick together year-round, but others go off and do their own thing for most of the year, only meeting up when it is time to mate and raise a new set of babies. When these pairs reunite there is much excitement, with special calls and dances. The male performs a mating show, parading before his mate with his head held high, then bowing right down and fanning his wings and tail out. When it's time to mate, the male will often present a dead mouse or some other gruesome offering to the female. She doesn't think it's gross, though—she's delighted!

BUILT FOR SPEED

Roadrunners have to be lightweight to move as fast as they do—the heavier ones still often only weigh about the same as a soccer ball. **Lesser roadrunners** are usually about 18 inches long and **greater roadrunners** are a little larger—more like 22 inches on average.

SOAKING UP THE SUN

Because they don't migrate for the winter, roadrunners have had to develop some clever tricks to live through the colder months. During winter nights, they lower their body temperature and become very still to preserve energy. As soon as the sun comes up, they splay out their feathers, exposing a little patch of bare skin on their back to absorb as much of the sun's heat as possible.

RAISING BABIES IS A
TEAM SPORT

ROADRUNNER PARENTS WORK TOGETHER TO RAISE THEIR YOUNG, WHICH IS RARE FOR CUCKOO SPECIES.

▶ The natural habitat of roadrunners includes dry, scrubby deserts with cactuses or shrubs for nesting in. The father goes out to hunt for building materials for the nest, and then the mother is in charge of putting it together. She cleverly weaves items such as sticks, leaves, snakeskin, and dung into a large, fairly flat nest that can reach over 16 inches wide and about 8 inches thick.

▶ Sometimes roadrunners abandon their nest after one use and build an entirely new one the next year, but sometimes they renovate instead! They mend parts that are worn and add new flourishes, so it's as good as new for the next set of eggs.

▶ It only takes about 20 days after mating for mothers to lay 2–6 smooth, white eggs. Mothers keep the eggs warm during the day, then the fathers take the night shift so their partner can stretch their legs. Parents keep this routine up until their eggs hatch, and then they keep working in shifts for another three weeks or so to take care of the newly hatched chicks.

▶ Roadrunner hatchlings aren't anything like you were as a baby—after just three weeks, they're ready to learn how to run, hunt, and fly—although they never get very good at that!

AN UNLIKELY NEIGHBOR

Roadrunners generally live in secluded desert habitats. But these plucky birds have also become increasingly used to living in suburban areas filled with humans. If you live in the same area as roadrunners, one could quite possibly pop up in your backyard!

ON THE RUN

Roadrunners can reach speeds of up to 25 miles per hour, which isn't that far off the record for human footspeed—27.8 miles per hour, set in 2009 by Usain Bolt. They have long tails that they use for braking and balancing, and they steer by tilting their tail or small wings to quickly switch direction. This is a useful tactic when running away from predators, such as coyotes.

ON THE HUNT

You don't come across picky roadrunners; basically, if they can catch it, they'll eat it. Their diet includes frogs, snakes, lizards, centipedes, scorpions, caterpillars, beetles, crickets, and even other birds' eggs and chicks. They're one of the only predators fast enough to take on rattlesnakes.

Roadrunners tenderize larger animals by picking them up in their beaks and thumping them against rocks or other hard surfaces. This breaks down the prey's bones and makes them a manageable meal for these fearsome birds!

Roadrunners also nibble on seeds and such fruits as sumac and prickly pear, particularly in the winter when their preferred prey is a little harder to find.

X MARKS THE SPOT

Roadrunners have zygodactyl feet, which means two of their toes point forward and the other two point backward, creating a super cool, X-shaped footprint.

WHAT DOES A THIRSTY ROADRUNNER DRINK?

Roadrunners don't drink much water—they get most of the hydration they need from guzzling the blood of their prey. Blood is wet like water, but not nearly as refreshing—it's too salty! Luckily roadrunners have special glands in their eye sockets to ooze out the excess salt.

FLANNERY FILE

Once I was in Arizona, visiting a research institute, and I was really curious about the roadrunners that lived in the area. I was out walking when I saw one with a snake in its mouth, and I was so excited that I jogged toward it. The roadrunner got nervous—it dropped the snake and ran off. I was disappointed, but I went over to at least have a look at the roadrunner's abandoned meal. It turned out that the snake was actually an incredibly rare species that no one at the research institute had ever seen before! They were delighted that I had accidentally found such a rare specimen.

CAMELS

Whether they have one hump or two, camels are awesome-looking creatures. Their humps make a beautiful silhouette against a desert horizon, rising and falling with their strangely graceful, bobbing walk. But not everything about camels is elegant—in fact, some of the things that come out of their mouths are far from it!

WHERE CAN I SEE A CAMEL?

Dromedaries live in North Africa and the Middle East and **Bactrians** can be found in the rocky central deserts of East Asia. **Wild Bactrians** live in Northern China and Southern Mongolia. There are also lots of feral camels in the Australian desert.

ALL-WEATHER CREATURES

Camels can survive all sorts of harsh conditions that would be wildly unpleasant for you. They can deal with temperatures as low as -22 degrees Fahrenheit and as high as 122 degrees Fahrenheit.

A GROUP OF CAMELS iS SOMETiMES CALLED A CARAVAN.

THAT'S WILD!

The most common camels—**dromedaries** (with one hump) and **Bactrians** (with two humps)—aren't actually wild animals. Both species were domesticated thousands of years ago. Although plenty of these two species do live in the wild, they're descendants of domesticated animals. The only truly wild camels left on Earth are a third species: the **wild Bactrians** of Northern China and Southern Mongolia. These camels are critically endangered; there are only about a thousand remaining.

BACK OFF!

When a camel feels threatened, it spits at the source of threat—which can sometimes be a human! Their spit is combined with the contents of their stomach to make something a bit like a spit and vomit soup, and it is a very stinky concoction indeed.

THE ULTIMATE PACKED LUNCH

Camels travel around with something a lot like a lunchbox attached to their backs. Or in the case of **Bactrians**, two lunchboxes!

▶ The humps that stick up on camel backs aren't just decorative—they're packed full of fat. When camels eat, any extra fat gets stored away for later. The camel can metabolize the fat in its hump, deriving more than 1 gram of water for every gram of fat metabolized.

▶ When food is scarce, camels can live off the fat they saved in their humps for up to seven months!

▶ Camels hardly sweat at all, even when they're tramping around the desert in up to 122°F heat. That means they can go a lot longer without water than other big animals that sweat heavily—like horses, for example.

▶ **Dromedaries** have specially shaped red blood cells. Unlike your red blood cells, which are round, dromedaries' oval-shaped red blood cells keep their blood flowing even when they're super dehydrated.

▶ As long as there's plenty of succulent herbage around, camels don't actually need to drink—they can get enough hydration to survive just from the water in plants.

▶ When camels do find a water source, they become an incredible rehydration station, and can drink up to 30 gallons of water in 13 minutes. They can rehydrate faster than any other mammal!

▶ Once camels get to the seven-month mark without a meal, their humps start to look pretty saggy. When they get really empty, they actually flop over to the side! Once their stores of fat build up again, their humps go back to standing tall.

213

MEERKATS

A GROUP OF MEERKATS IS CALLED A MOB OR A GANG.

Meerkats are really cute—they're small and fluffy, with big eyes and adorable little paws that they hold in front of their tummies when they stand up. But for something small and seemingly sweet, they can also be terrifyingly tough. You don't have anything to worry about when it comes to meerkats, but plenty of other animals do—even dangerous predators, such as snakes and scorpions, can be destroyed by a fearsome meerkat.

WHERE CAN I SEE A MEERKAT?

Meerkats live in deserts and grasslands across Africa.

HOW BIG IS A MEERKAT?

Meerkats weigh 2 pounds at most, so even the heaviest ones are lighter than a chihuahua! The biggest meerkats are about 1 foot long, and they can stretch a little taller when they pop up onto their back legs to survey their territory, or to let the exposed skin on their bellies soak up some sun.

ON THE ALERT

Meerkats hunt in gangs, with a small number put in charge of keeping a lookout for danger. Sentries take it in turns to keep watch for about an hour at a time. They make peeping sounds when the coast is clear; if they whistle or bark, the hunting group know they're in trouble and need to make a break for the nearest underground tunnel or find some other way to evade a predator's notice. The warning noises differ depending on whether the predator is creeping up on the ground or swooping through the sky, and there's also a whole range of sounds that let the rest of the hunting team know if the threat is minor, major or somewhere in the middle. That way, the mob can decide whether to run and hide, duck down and remain still, or form a dense group and try to look collectively intimidating.

BUILT-IN SUNGLASSES

Meerkats have big, adorable eyes with black markings around them. This marking isn't just decorative; it reduces the sun's glare so that they can keep an eye on their surroundings. They have such good eyesight that they can see things moving almost 1,000 feet away!

CLIMATE CHANGE

Climate change is making the Kalahari Desert, where many meerkats live, warmer and drier. A drier habitat makes it more difficult for meerkats to feed, grow, and reproduce.

SAFETY IN NUMBERS

One meerkat by itself can't do all that much damage, but a whole hissing mob of them is much more dangerous. If they gang up on something like a snake, they can frighten it away or even kill it!

SUPREME RULERS

MEERKATS ARE SOCIAL ANIMALS, WITH UP TO 50 INDIVIDUALS LIVING TOGETHER IN ONE BIG GROUP.

▶ Not all meerkat mobs are the same—just as your family is probably a bit different from the one living next door to you. Some mobs are more helpful toward each other and fight less, whereas other mobs will be more competitive and aggressive.

▶ One thing all meerkat mobs have in common is their strict hierarchical structure—a lucky few get all the perks, while the rest are forced to be hard-working (and often undernourished) underlings. It's not worth challenging the rules, though—meerkats that try to change the system can end up in a deadly fight with their rulers.

▶ Meerkat rulers often kill the babies of lowlier meerkats in the group. If that isn't brutal enough, they then either banish the parents or force them to babysit and feed the rulers' babies now that their own babies are gone.

▶ Meerkat groups might be tough, but they're not all bad. The strong cooperative group dynamic helps them to survive in a world where plenty of predators think a small, fluffy meerkat is a perfect snack.

ROOM FOR ONE MORE

Meerkats live in burrows made up of lots of little underground rooms that are connected by a network of tunnels. When they go to sleep, they stack themselves up in cozy piles. It can get chilly in the desert overnight! Meerkats don't just share their homes with each other—their burrows are also used by animals such as Cape ground squirrels and the meerkats' close relative, the yellow mongoose.

SCARY SNACKS

Meerkats eat insects, lizards, eggs, and sometimes even small birds, plus more dangerous critters such as spiders, snakes, and scorpions. They have a very clever system for eating scorpions without getting poisoned.

▶ First, they bite off the tail and spit it out. That gets rid of the venomous stinger. Then they rub the scorpion in the sand, cleaning the venom off its hard outer shell, which is called an exoskeleton. And just like that, they've transformed a deadly critter into a nutritious snack!

▶ Meerkats train their pups to eat scorpions by using a four-step process. First, they offer them dead scorpions and show them how to get rid of the poison. Second, they give them live scorpions, but make sure they've already removed the dangerous stinger. Third, they put them to the test by giving them injured scorpions to kill and clean. The fourth and final step is letting them loose on completely healthy scorpions, so they can try out their new skills.

STARTING A FAMILY

▶ In some meerkat groups, the rulers are the only ones that get to have babies.

▶ The whole gang is usually involved with rearing babies, including the mother, the father, and any siblings.

▶ Mothers don't always feed milk to their babies. This job is usually given to a babysitter—someone lower in the group's hierarchy.

▶ Meerkat pups are born with curled-up ears and closed eyes, which don't open until about two weeks after they're born. A few days later, they're allowed to leave their burrow to see the world for the first time.

▶ Sometimes meerkats that are low in the pecking order will kill the babies of the rulers (or other high-ranking meerkats) in an attempt to climb the social ladder.

DUNG BEETLES

There are thousands of dung beetle species, and they come in many different shapes and sizes. But there's one thing they all have in common—poop. They love the stuff! They're born into it, roll on it, sleep in it, dance on it, dig in it, and even eat it. It might sound gross at first, but it's actually pretty cool what a dung beetle can do with poo!

WHERE CAN I SEE A DUNG BEETLE?

Dung beetles live on every continent of the world, except Antarctica.

CLIMATE CHANGE

These incredible insects can help reduce greenhouse gas emissions by digging carbon-rich poo into the soil.

HOW BIG ARE DUNG BEETLES?

The largest dung beetle in the world feeds on elephant dung and would probably take up most of your hand, while the smallest is just a fraction of an inch long.

WHICH POO?

- Dung beetles usually prefer to eat the dung of herbivores, but certain species prefer carnivore poo. In fact, 11 different species of American dung beetle like human poo best of all!

- One type of Australian dung beetle (**Onthophagus parvus**) loves eating wombat poo. It clings to the fur near a wombat's butthole until poo comes out, then drops down to the ground to pounce on the fresh cubes of excrement. Delicious! Other dung beetles do the same thing, but they hang out near sloth or monkey butts instead.

ARE DUNG BEETLES USEFUL?

Dung beetles do a vital job when they move poo around. As they dig into the ground to bury the poo they've collected, they're doing two things: helping air get into the soil, which makes it healthier, and spreading the nutrient-rich poo through the soil instead of leaving it to harden above ground. Poo mixed through the soil is great—it helps plants to grow, which is why gardeners often use manure on their plants. Poo left on the surface of the ground isn't nearly as good—it attracts flies and other parasites, plus when it lands on plants, sunshine and fresh air can't get to them anymore.

WHO'S WHO?

There are four main types of dung beetle, and you can tell them apart by looking at what they do when they come across poo.

1 **Tunnellers**, also called "Paracoprids," dig their way through piles of dung and into the soil beneath it to make a burrow. They pick up bits of dung as they go, then hang out underground and snack on their poo collection (plus lay their eggs in it).

2 **Dwellers**, also called "Endocoprids," hang out on piles of dung, eating and laying eggs.

3 **Rollers**, also called "Telecoprids," don't hang out at a dung-pile for long. They take a chunk of the poo and roll it into a big ball, then roll it away to a quiet, safe place. They usually face backward as they roll, using their back legs to push the dung.

4 **Dung thieves**, also called "Kleptocoprids," are tiny dung beetles that sneak around stealing dung balls that rollers have already made. **RUDE!**

STUBBORN STARGAZERS

Dung beetles like to move in straight lines when they're racing away with a ball of dung. Instead of detouring if they come across an obstacle, they climb up and over the object in their path. Some dung beetles use the light from the sun, moon, or Milky Way to steer straight. Every now and then they climb on top of their dung balls and do what looks like a little dance, but they're actually taking a good look at the sky so they know which way to go.

WHO ATE DINO POO?

Pieces of fossilized dinosaur poo from 70 to 80 million years ago have evidence of dung beetle tunnels inside them.

WHY POO?

Of all the favorite foods to have, poo seems like an odd choice. It's basically what's left after someone's body has digested all the good bits of their meal—so how can it be of any use to a beetle? Well, lots of animals don't actually get all of the nutrients out of their food as they digest it, especially if they eat things that are hard to break down. So there's still plenty of goodness left in their poop.

FLANNERY FILE

A number of years ago, a tiny type of dung beetle that was really good at cleaning up carnivore poo was introduced to Australia. They introduced it to the city of Sydney to clean dog poo off the streets. Once the beetles got to work, it was quite amazing. You'd be walking along, and suddenly you'd see a piece of dog poo moving on the street. The first time it happened, I thought, *What's wrong with my eyes? Surely that poo can't be moving?* But it was! There was a little dung beetle behind it, working hard to roll the poo to a bit of dirt where it could be buried. The project didn't work out in the end—I think the climate wasn't quite right for the dung beetles—but, for a while, we had moving poo on the streets of Sydney.

BORN INTO A LIFE OF POO

POO IS INVOLVED IN JUST ABOUT EVERY ASPECT OF A DUNG BEETLE'S LIFE—INCLUDING FINDING A MATE AND RAISING A FAMILY.

▶ A **roller dung beetle** male shows a female he likes her by offering her a big ball of poo. If she's interested, she often clambers on top of the ball. The male then pushes the ball, with the female riding on top, to a pleasant patch where the new couple can start their family.

▶ **Tunneler dung beetles** build their burrow before mating. The female usually does the excavating, with her future mate standing guard and fighting off any other males that try to enter the tunnel.

▶ Some species lay their eggs inside balls of poo called "brood balls" and then seal them up with their own spit and poo. The babies hatch into little grubs and eat their way out of their poo ball—it's like being born right in the middle of a big bowl of your favorite food!

ON THE HUNT

Some dung beetles, such as **Deltochilum valgum**, hunt live prey. They go after millipedes—grabbing them and biting off their heads before digging in to their feast.

HOW MUCH POO CAN YOU PUSH?

Dung beetles are stronger than any other beetle in the world. In fact, relative to their body weight, they're stronger than any other animal on the planet—including you. It might seem outrageous that a beetle is stronger than an elephant, or a rhino, or a horse, but it's true. **Onthophagus taurus**, a type of horned dung beetle, can roll more than 1,100 times its own weight in poo. No other creature on Earth can push something that weighs that much more than them!

RATTLESNAKES

Fear of snakes is pretty common, but when it comes to rattlesnakes, there's so much more to be amazed by than there is to be scared of. Sure, they make intimidating rattling noises, have incredibly fast reflexes, sharp fangs, and oodles of venom—but they don't want to hurt you! They can't eat you, so they really have no interest in biting you unless they feel threatened. Rattlesnakes are a specialized kind of viper, and they're beautiful to look at, with their colorful ridged scales and striking geometric patterns.

A GROUP OF RATTLESNAKES IS REFERRED TO AS A BED OR A KNOT.

WHERE CAN I SEE A RATTLESNAKE?

Rattlesnakes live in North and South America. The state of Arizona has the greatest number of different species.

SNAKE SCARF

The biggest rattlesnake is the **eastern diamondback**, which can weigh over 10 pounds and stretch to nearly 8 feet long. If you draped one of them across your shoulders, both ends of its body would probably reach the ground!

WARNING SIGNS

DO SNAKES LAY EGGS?

Rattlesnake babies grow inside eggs, but these eggs never get laid or hatch like chickens' eggs do. Instead, they sit inside the mother's body until the babies have hatched and are ready to come into the world. Baby rattlesnakes are born with a thin membrane around them that they have to pierce before they can feel the fresh air.

Rattlesnakes have strong venom, but they need to make sure they save plenty of it for killing their meals. If they're feeling threatened, rattlesnakes will try to warn the intruder off before resorting to biting them.

▶ Hissing is a snake's go-to tactic for telling other animals to back off. But don't bother hissing back! Snakes can't hear sounds in the air; they can only "hear" things by sensing vibrations in the ground. If you want to alert snakes to your presence as you walk through their territory, stamp your feet. It warns them that you're nearby and gives them a chance to slither off before you get close enough to frighten them.

▶ Rattlesnake tails have a number of loose pieces at the end that clatter against each other when they move. They're made of keratin—the same thing as your hair and fingernails—but they look more like bones from a human spine stacked on top of each other. They can make a clear, harsh rattling sound, or a noise like a bunch of bees buzzing furiously. Some rattlesnake species can rattle their tails more than 50 times in a single second!

SUPERSIZED MEALS

Rattlesnakes munch on things like mice, birds, squirrels, lizards, and even other snakes. They have a range of clever hunting techniques to capture their prey:

▶ Rattlesnakes use their sensitive tongues to taste the air around them and pick up traces of nearby food.

▶ Hunting in the dark is easy for rattlesnakes, because they have special pits underneath their eyes that are extra-sensitive to heat. These pits help them track down the warm bodies of their prey.

▶ Rattlesnakes often chase their food, but they also hunt using ambush techniques: lying in wait and striking when an unsuspecting creature wanders too close. Sometimes they keep their bodies still and gently wiggle the tips of their tails like bait to lure in prey.

▶ Many species of rattlesnake eat their food alive. They'll often paralyze it with their venom first, so it doesn't wriggle around as it goes down!

▶ Swallowing an animal whole is tiring work. Rattlesnakes generally take a few days to break down a meal inside their body, and they can go a couple of weeks between meals once they're fully grown.

▶ Rattlesnakes have sharp, hollow fangs that they use to inject venom into their prey. Their fangs are on hinges, so they can fold in and out of their mouths in the same way that a door can swing open and closed.

▶ When they're getting ready to strike, rattlesnakes harness all their power (plus look taller and more terrifying!) by raising their heads into the air and coiling their bodies like a spring.

▶ Even when they're dead, rattlesnakes can still be dangerous, because their instinct to bite doesn't stop working right away. Even hours after death, a rattlesnake can still inject venom into anything that gets too close—and its head doesn't even need to be attached to its body!

▶ Rattlesnake venom causes certain parts of the body, such as muscle and skin, to rot. It also causes internal bleeding and makes it harder for blood to clot. Bites can be very painful and need to be treated by a doctor, but are rarely fatal to humans.

DEATH BITES

FLANNERY FILE

I once had a close encounter with a particularly large snake on a research trip in Papua New Guinea. I was about to board a tiny plane to travel to a different part of the island, when some locals arrived with an enormous chest. I peered through the wire lid and saw the biggest snake I had ever laid my eyes on! It was a **Boelen's python**, which is a very rare mountain-dwelling snake. It was incredibly riled up—at one point it even struck the top of the chest, sticking its fangs right through the wire. I wanted to take the snake with me so I could study it properly, but the chest was too big to fit on the small plane. If I wanted this fierce, 10-foot-long snake, I was going to have to wrangle it into a sack instead. And it wasn't easy! The snake writhed around violently as I lifted it, wrapping its thick coils around me until my arms and legs were bound together. I thought I was done for, but luckily my friend Ken helped me bundle the snake into the sack. The pilot of the plane was *very* unimpressed when he found out what was inside the wriggling sack, but he eventually allowed us to bring it along for the ride—as long as Ken held it on his knee for the whole trip!

QUIET BABIES, NOISY ADULTS

As rattlesnakes grow, their skin gets too tight—so, just like you have to get new clothes after a growth spurt, rattlesnakes have to shuck off their old skin and grow a new one. Each time they shed a layer of skin, rattlesnakes develop a new rattling piece at the end of their tail! That's why very young rattlesnakes don't make the same sounds as their older relatives—they haven't shed any layers of skin yet, so they don't have a proper rattle. Instead, they have a little nub on the end of their tail called a "button."

WRESTLEMANIA

Male rattlesnakes go to extreme lengths to find the right mate. As well as traveling long distances, they compete with each other—often by wrestling. You might wonder how a creature without arms or legs can possibly wrestle, but rattlesnakes are masters at it! They wrap their flexible bodies around each other, squeezing and writhing around until the weaker snake is defeated and slithers off in disgrace.

MONITOR LIZARDS

You might think you haven't heard of monitors, but chances are, you're familiar with a few of them. There are heaps of different species, and they're often called by other names—like **goannas** or **komodo dragons**. These super-smart, cold-blooded lizards are remarkable in many ways! They can run, dig, swim, and climb trees —and they do all of these things exceptionally well. Add in a huge appetite and a healthy dose of venomous spit, and you've got an animal worth monitoring!

WHERE CAN I SEE A MONITOR?

Monitors are native to parts of Africa, Asia, and Australia, and some have been introduced into parts of the Americas.

A GROUP OF MONITORS iS CALLED A BANK.

ARE YOU ON THE MENU?

THERE ARE MANY TYPES OF MONITOR LIZARD, AND THEY ALL HAVE THEIR OWN OPINIONS ABOUT WHICH FOOD TASTES BEST.

▶ Monitor meals include anything from small spiders and insects to huge prey, such as water buffalo.

▶ Some monitors mix plants into their diets, but it is much more common for meat to be the focus. The **Northern Sierra Madre forest monitor** is a special exception—aside from the odd insect, it survives almost entirely on fruit!

▶ Monitors think snails and eggs are tasty snacks, and their strong teeth can crush the shells without any trouble. They don't bother to spit the shells out after breaking them—they swallow the whole slimy mess!

▶ Many monitors eat their prey whole—they have a hinge in their jaw that helps them fit even quite large animals into their mouths. When eating ridiculously big prey, monitors tear it apart and eat it in chunks.

▶ Cannibalism isn't unheard of for monitors. They often target monitors smaller than them, but some will even go after lizards that are bigger.

▶ **Komodo dragons** have enormous stomachs, and appetites to match—they can eat 80 percent of their body weight in one meal. That's why they go after oversized prey like pigs, water buffalo, goats, and deer. They can even eat humans that happen to be in the wrong place at the wrong time!

CAN I BORROW YOUR NEST?

Many monitors, like **savannah monitors**, **perenties**, and **Nile monitors**, lay their eggs right in the middle of termite mounds! The mothers dig into the mounds to lay their eggs, but they don't bother covering them back up—the termites do that part of the job. The eggs are in no danger from the termites—they're actually kept warm by all of the activity around them!

If there are no male **komodo dragons** around, females can fertilize their own eggs and they will eventually hatch into perfectly healthy baby lizards. Oddly enough, when there is no father involved, all of the babies will be born male.

TAKING A DIP

All monitors are good swimmers, even the ones that live on land. Many of them can seal their nostrils so they don't inhale water while swimming, and they can even walk along riverbeds.

I'M GOOD HERE

Ridge-tailed monitors sometimes wedge their tails into rocks when a predator is bothering them—that way they can't be moved!

HOW BIG IS A MONITOR?

The size difference between the smallest and largest monitors is more extreme than with any other group of land animals. Some of the biggest monitors are **komodo dragons**, which can stretch over 10 feet—that's nearly one and a half times the height of LeBron James! They're heavier than any other lizard on the planet, weighing up to 330 pounds. **Crocodile monitors** can actually be longer than komodo dragons—they can stretch up to 16 feet—but they're much lighter. **Pygmy monitors** are the smallest, with some species only growing to 8 inches—that's just half the height of a bowling pin. They often weigh under an ounce—not even as much as a house mouse!

FLANNERY FILE

My friend John went to a Catholic boys' school when he was little. All of the teachers, who were called "brothers," wore black robes. One of John's teachers loved to take his students on bushwalks, but he would often get lost. One day, John and his classmates were lost in the bush with this old teacher. He was standing there muttering to himself, trying to work out the way home, when a huge goanna rushed up to him, climbed up his black robes and sat on his head! The goanna must have mistaken him for a burnt tree stump. The boys weren't sure whether they should be afraid or laugh— the teacher wasn't hurt, but he must have looked completely hilarious!

READY TO RUMBLE

Monitors often stand up on their back legs to get a better look at their surroundings—but they also adopt this human-like pose to look intimidating, or to fight. When two monitors tussle, they pop up on their back legs and wrap their arms around each other in what looks like a hug. But don't be fooled! They're squeezing each other HARD. They can also wrestle and snap their jaws while wrapped in an embrace, inflicting serious injuries on each other.

SECOND-HAND SKIN

Even though they're heaps bigger than the average reptile, monitors still shed their skin. A new layer of skin forms, and they shuck off the old one. Imagine coming across an enormous, empty sheath of monitor skin—it might be big enough for you to fit inside!

VIOLENCE, *SPEED*, MOMENTUM

Monitors are excellent hunters—their strength, speed, and tracking ability all work in their favor. Oh, and they have venomous spit.

▶ Even the smaller monitor species have remarkably powerful limbs, and the bigger species—such as the **komodo dragon**—are heavily muscled and have tails big enough to knock your feet right out from under you.

▶ Monitor tongues are forked like a snake's, and they flick them in and out of their mouths to pick up traces of their prey from the air, ground, or water.

▶ Unlike fang-sporting snakes, monitors have rows of sharp, serrated teeth that can tear through flesh and create huge wounds.

▶ All monitors have venom in their spit, but for most species it wouldn't be enough to kill a human outright—it would just cause infection and pain. Their venom works by lowering their prey's blood pressure and preventing the blood from clotting, so it streams out extra fast. The gaping wounds that monitors inflict also help the blood to spurt out more rapidly. So, when it comes to "death by monitor," although venom helps with the kill, blood loss is the ultimate cause of death.

▶ Some monitors, like **Nile monitors** and **goannas**, will occasionally work together to steal eggs from other animals' nests—including crocodiles. One monitor acts as the decoy, leading the mother away from her nest. Meanwhile, the other monitor tears into the nest. The decoy then sneaks back to join its partner-in-crime for an eggy feast.

▶ Some monitor species actively hunt their prey over long distances, but many larger species prefer to ambush their meals. The colors and patterns on their scaly skin help to camouflage them as they wait to spring out and attack.

GLOSSARY

ALGAE

Algae are a large and wide-ranging group of organisms, most of which are aquatic. Some are microscopic, while others (like many types of seaweed) can grow to be very large. They can be found in both salt water and fresh water.

ALPHA MALE/FEMALE

The alpha is the most powerful individual in a group of animals—the leader. There can be alpha males or alpha females, and some groups of animals are led by a pair of alphas—both male and female. Alphas usually gain leadership by fighting and defeating the former alpha.

AMPHIBIAN

Amphibians are small vertebrates that live in a wet environment. Amphibians include frogs, salamanders, and newts.

APEX PREDATOR

Apex predators are also called alpha predators or top predators. They are on the top of the food chain, which means that they have no natural predators to fear. They play an important role in maintaining a balanced and healthy ecosystem.

AQUATIC

Aquatic animals are those that spend all or most of their time in the water.

ARBOREAL

Arboreal animals are those that spend all or most of their time in trees.

ATMOSPHERE

Atmosphere is the gases surrounding a planet, held there by the planet's gravity. Earth's atmosphere is a very thin layer of air between the earth's surface and the edge of space.

ATROPHY

Atrophy is the wasting away or degeneration of a part of the body. It can happen for many reasons, including the body part no longer being used or a lack of nutrition.

BACTERIA

Bacteria are microscopic single-celled organisms. They can be found in many different places: in the soil, air, and water, as well as on and inside plants and animals—including humans. Some bacteria are beneficial to us, whereas others are destructive.

BIOLUMINESCENCE

Bioluminescence is the production of light by a living organism. This glowing light is created by chemical reactions inside animals' bodies, and can be helpful in many different ways, from scaring off predators to finding food or a mate.

BLOOD CELLS

Blood is made up of blood cells, plus a liquid element called plasma. There are three kinds of blood cells: 1. red blood cells absorb oxygen from the lungs and transport it around the body, 2. white blood cells fight against disease and infection, 3. platelets help to clot the blood and heal wounds.

CANINE

A canine is an animal belonging to the Canidae family, or dog family. This includes wolves, jackals, hyenas, coyotes, foxes, dingoes, and domestic dogs.

CANNIBALISM

Cannibalism is the act of eating a member of the same species. More than 1,500 species are known to do this. Some species will only turn to cannibalism when other foods are scarce, but for others, scarcity has little or nothing to do with the practice of eating each other.

CARBON

Carbon is a chemical element. It is one of the building blocks that plants and animals are made from, making it essential to all life on Earth. All organic compounds are considered "carbon-based." Carbon can combine with other elements to make new compounds.

CARBON DIOXIDE

Carbon dioxide is a compound made up of one carbon atom (C) and two oxygen atoms (O_2). It is a greenhouse gas, which means it traps the sun's heat close to the earth instead of allowing it to move out into space. Too much carbon dioxide causes the earth to overheat and, as the weather changes, many plants and animals are negatively affected. This is called global warming, or climate change.

CARBON EMISSIONS

When we burn carbon-rich fossil fuels, we release a huge amount of carbon into the air. The carbon then bonds with oxygen to produce carbon dioxide. Over time, the amount of carbon in the atmosphere has risen drastically due to the increased use of fossil fuels.

CARNIVORE/ CARNIVOROUS

Carnivores are animals that exclusively or primarily eat meat—either by killing their meal or by scavenging carcasses.

CETACEANS

Cetaceans are a group of aquatic mammals that includes whales, porpoises, and dolphins. Many of them live in salt water.

COLD-BLOODED AND WARM-BLOODED ANIMALS

Warm-blooded animals, or endotherms, use their metabolism to generate the right amount of heat to keep their bodies at the right temperature. Cold-blooded animals, or ectotherms, aren't able to control their body temperature using their metabolism. On cold days, their metabolism drops along with their body temperature, which slows down their physical movement. Endotherms generally need a steady food supply to keep their metabolism generating heat, while ectotherms can often survive long periods without food, thanks to their ability to slow their bodies down and wait out the colder months.

COLONIZATION

In zoology, colonization is when animals or plants move into a new habitat and make it their home.

COLONY

In zoology, a colony is a group of animals or plants of the same kind that live together, and often rely on each other to survive.

CONTINENTS

A continent is a large landmass, and one continent often includes multiple countries. The continents of the world are Europe, Asia, Africa, North and South America, Australia, and Antarctica.

CRUSTACEANS

Crustaceans are a diverse group of invertebrate animals. All crustaceans originally came from the sea, but some (such as slaters) have adapted to terrestrial life. All crustaceans have antennae and a tough exoskeleton. Crustaceans include such animals as shrimp, crabs, lobsters, crayfish, and krill.

CURRENTS

Ocean currents are sections of water that constantly flow in a particular direction. Some currents run along the surface of the water, while others run through the ocean's depths. Currents are affected by the wind, the earth's rotation, the temperature, differences in salinity (salt content of the water) and the gravitational pull of the moon.

DEFORESTATION

Deforestation is the permanent destruction of forests. People clear the land to graze farmed animals such as cattle, as well as to build or to harvest wood any other tree products (such as palm oil). Deforestation causes habitat loss for many animals and can lead to the extinction of species that need the forest to survive. It also reduces the number of trees taking CO_2 out of the atmosphere, which means that our atmosphere fills up with more greenhouse gas emissions.

DOMESTICATED SPECIES

Domesticated species are animals that have been bred to benefit humans, often over many generations. Animals are often domesticated so that humans can use parts of their bodies (such as flesh, skin, fur, or bone), or things that they produce (such as milk or eggs), for food, clothing, and decoration. Animals are also often domesticated to use as labor or to keep as pets.

DROUGHT

Drought is a prolonged period with much less rainfall than usual, or no rainfall at all. Drought causes rivers and lakes to dry up, which leaves many animals without water to drink. It causes plants to die, which can result in habitat loss and less food for animals to eat. Many animal populations are threatened by drought, and climate change is increasing the instances of drought around the world.

ECHOLOCATION

Echolocation is the use of echoes and soundwaves to find out where an object is in space. Many animals use echolocation to hunt and navigate, like dolphins, whales, bats, and some bird species.

ECOSYSTEM

An ecosystem is a finely balanced environment, in which all the living things (plants, animals and other organisms) and nonliving things (like rocks and the weather) work together to maintain the system's health.

EXOSKELETON

An exoskeleton is the hard, shell-like covering around some animals that functions to support and protect their body. All insects and crustaceans have exoskeletons; their skeleton is on the outside of their body. Some animals, such as turtles and tortoises, have both an exoskeleton (their shell) and an endoskeleton (the bones inside their bodies).

FELINE

Felines are members of the Felidae (or cat) family. They are all carnivorous mammals. Felines include lions, tigers, and domestic cats.

FERAL ANIMALS

Feral animals are domesticated animals that have been released into the wild and continued to reproduce there—for example, feral cats, goats, camels, and dogs. Feral animals can often endanger the lives of wild animals by preying on them.

FORAGING

When an animal searches for food in the wild, this is called foraging.

FOSSIL FUELS

Fossil fuels are made from fossilized plants and animals that have been buried under the soil for millions of years. Fossil fuels include things like oil, coal, and natural gas.

FUNGI

Fungi are a large group of of organisms that include mushrooms, molds, and mildews. They are more closely related to animals than they are to plants. Fungi consume organic matter to survive, breaking down dead or living organic matter into molecules that they use for energy and reproduction.

GENES

Genes are made up of DNA, and they're the things that make each animal in the world unique. They exist inside the cells of living things, like plants and animals, and are passed on from parents to their offspring. In humans, the combination of genes passed on by both parents can determine the appearance of their child, through things such as eye or hair color.

GREENHOUSE GAS EMISSIONS

Greenhouse gases absorb the heat that radiates off the earth's surface and bounce it back, trapping heat in the atmosphere rather than releasing it into space. The main greenhouse gases are water vapor, carbon dioxide, methane, and nitrous oxide. Fossil fuels are the biggest human cause of greenhouse gas emissions.

HERBIVORE/ HERBIVOROUS

Herbivores are animals that have an exclusively or primarily plant-based diet.

HIBERNATION

Hibernation is a type of deep rest that some endotherms, or warm-blooded animals, go into. Hibernation often occurs when animals don't have access to enough food or when it's too cold—certain species of animal hibernate over winter every year. During hibernation, body temperatures drop and metabolisms slow down as animals become inactive.

HIERARCHY

Hierarchy refers to a power structure within a group of animals. An alpha or an alpha pair is generally at the top of the hierarchy, with other members of the group having varying degrees of power below them. Omegas are the least powerful members of the hierarchy.

HORMONES

Hormones are chemicals inside plants and animals that help all of these living things to function. In plants, hormones help to control growth, as well as the production of flowers or fruit. In animals, hormones are used to send messages to different parts of the body to help it operate. Hormones affect all sorts of things, like growth, sleep, temperature, hunger, and much more.

HUNTING

For animals, hunting is the activity of killing and eating other animals. For humans, hunting also includes killing animals, but not always for food.

HYPERPHAGIA

Hyperphagia is a hugely increased appetite, and usually prompts eating a lot more than usual. Many animals go into hyperphagia to prepare themselves for hibernation (a period in which they don't eat at all).

INCUBATION

Incubation is the process of keeping eggs at the right temperature while embryos grow inside them. Different animals incubate their eggs in different ways, such as sitting on them or burying them in sand, dirt, or plant matter.

INVERTEBRATE

Invertebrates lack a backbone; they either have a gooey, spongy body (like jellyfish and worms) or they have an exoskeleton (like insects and crabs).

KERATIN

Keratin is a strong, fibrous protein. It is the main substance that forms body parts like hair, nails, hoofs, horns, feathers, and the outermost layers of skin and scales.

KRILL

Krill are tiny swimming crustaceans. They eat phytoplankton, a microscopic type of plankton that generally grows near the ocean's surface. Krill are the main food source for hundreds of different animals, including fish, whales, and birds.

LARVAE

Many animals begin their life as larvae before eventually growing into their adult form. Larvae generally look completely different from their parents, and often need very different conditions to survive. For example, tadpoles are the larvae of frogs, and caterpillars are the larvae of butterflies.

MAMMALS

Mammals are a very broad class of animals. Some walk,

some swim, and some fly, and their diets can vary from carnivorous to herbivorous, but they all have a number of traits in common, including that they have hair or fur, feed their young with milk, and are warm-blooded.

MARSUPIALS

Marsupials are a group of mammals. Most female marsupials have a pouch where they keep their babies when they're very young, so that they can continue to grow and develop in a safe, warm place. Some marsupial species are herbivores, others are carnivores, and there are also some omnivorous species. Most of the world's marsupials live in Australia and South America.

MEGAFAUNA

The word "megafauna" means "giant animal." It is most commonly used to refer to animals from the Pleistocene epoch (the end of the last ice age), which are the larger ancestors of animals alive today. However, species that are alive today can also be referred to as megafauna —common examples include elephants, rhinos, hippos, giraffes, lions, bears, and whales.

MEMBRANES

A membrane is a thin layer of tissue. Membranes can be found inside all living things—each cell inside a plant or animal is surrounded by a membrane—but membranes can also be found in many other places. Some animals are born completely surrounded by a membrane, which they then break out of, and other animals have protective membranes underneath their eyelids that help keep their eyes safe.

METABOLISM

Metabolism refers to the chemical reactions that happen inside an organism to keep it alive. There are many different metabolic reactions, but the main ones involve releasing energy or using energy. For example, an animal's metabolism digests the food it eats and converts that food into a form that can be released as energy. Animals also use their energy to grow and repair their bodies.

MIGRATION

Migration is a movement from one place to another. Animals often migrate each year at about the same time, and different species migrate for different reasons. Migrations commonly occur as animals travel to places where food is more plentiful, or the weather is better, or to places where they can find a mate or breed.

NOCTURNAL

Nocturnal animals are active during the night and rest during the day.

OMNIVORE/ OMNIVOROUS

Omnivores are animals that eat a variety of meat and plant matter.

ORGANISM

An organism is an animal, a plant or a single-celled life form.

OXYGEN

Oxygen is a gas that makes up part of the air we breathe. It's highly reactive, which means it bonds easily with other elements (for example, carbon). Animals rely on oxygen to survive—they breathe it in and use it to convert nutrients into energy, releasing carbon dioxide as a waste product of this process. Plants exist in perfect symbiosis with animals, as they absorb carbon dioxide and release oxygen.

PARASITE

A parasite is an organism that makes its home in or on an organism of another species, relying on it for food, shelter, and everything else it needs to live. The organism that a parasite makes its home on is called its "host."

PECTINES

Pectines are comb-like structures found on many animals. They can be used for many different things, including grooming, filtering food, and as a sense organ to help the animals feel their surroundings.

PHEROMONES

Pheromones are a type of hormone—a chemical that some animals release to communicate with other members of their species. Pheromones can be released for many reasons, including to attract a mate, to mark pathways leading to home or food, and even as a warning sign.

PIGMENT

Pigments are colored chemicals in the tissues of animals. Some animals produce their own pigments, whereas others get them from their food.

PLANKTON

Plankton are small living things—comprising both plants and animals—that drift along in the ocean and other bodies of water. Plankton is an essential food source for many animals, and certain types of plankton are also vital for releasing oxygen into the atmosphere.

POACHING

Animal poaching is the illegal capturing or killing of animals.

POLLINATION

Pollination is the way that plants reproduce to create seeds and fruits. Pollination involves the movement of pollen from the male part of a flower (the anther) to the female part (the stigma). Some plants self-pollinate, meaning that the transfer of pollen happens within a single flower, or between different flowers on the same plant. The other form of pollination is cross-pollination, where pollen travels between different plants. Things like wind and water can help pollen to travel between plants, but many plants rely on "pollinators"—animals such as birds and insects—to transfer their pollen.

POLLUTION

Pollution is the introduction of harmful materials or substances into our environment. The three main types of pollution are water, air, and land pollution. Some examples of pollutants are microplastics in the ocean, greenhouse gas emissions in the atmosphere, and pesticides used in agriculture.

PREDATOR

In zoology, "predator" usually refers to an animal that hunts other animals for food. Parasites are also a kind of predator. Predators are essential to a balanced ecosystem.

PREHENSILE

A prehensile body part is one that can grab on to things. Many different body parts can be prehensile, including tails, noses, hands, and feet.

PROBOSCIS

A proboscis is a long, flexible snout or feeding organ. Many insects use a proboscis to eat, like some moths and butterflies, but larger animal species can also have a proboscis—like elephants and solenodons.

SANCTUARY

A wildlife sanctuary is a carefully designed environment where endangered wild species are brought to live and be protected from human threats, such as poaching. Proper sanctuaries are as much like the animals' natural habitats as possible: they have the right climate, and contain the right variety of plant and animal species.

TERRESTRIAL

Terrestrial animals are those that spend all or most of their time on land.

TERRITORY

An animal's territory is the area of land or water that it lives in, claims as its own and defends against trespassers.

TIDE

The tide is the periodic rise and fall of the ocean. Changes in the tide are caused by the earth spinning around, and by the gravitational pull of the sun and the moon.

VERTEBRATE

Vertebrates are animals that have a spine and a well-developed skeleton inside their bodies.

WILD SPECIES

Wild species are animals that have evolved without human interference and live and reproduce independently from humans.

INDEX

ACKNOWLEDGMENTS

I'd like to thank Jane Novak for suggesting this project
to me, and the fantastic team at Hardie Grant Egmont,
especially Ella Meave. Without their dedication, this book
would never have seen the light of day. I'd also like to thank
Sam Caldwell for his brilliant illustrations, and Pooja Desai
and Kristy Lund-White for their magnificent design work.
I owe much gratitude to my wife Kate Holden and our son
Coleby. They put up with long absences as I wrote this book.
Many colleagues helped me with information, among whom
Kris Helgen and Luigi Boitani
deserve special mention.

ARE ZOMBIE JELLYFISH REAL?
CAN TURTLES LIVE IN TREES?
WHAT'S IT LIKE TO WRESTLE A PYTHON?

Tim Flannery has the answers. Introducing some of the most spectacular and unusual creatures on Earth, from water to sky and the forests and deserts in between, he offers in-depth and often bizarre facts about extraordinary animals that live in each habitat. Flannery ties concepts of climate change, evolution, conservation, and taxonomy to each animal's profile, firmly connecting the animal and its environment while sparking wonder at its role in the natural world.

Did you know that lions once roamed North America, or that albatrosses sleep-fly? Have you ever heard a piranha bark, or wondered how the sloth got its name? Packed with vibrant illustrations and guided by real-life anecdotes from one of our greatest science communicators, *Weird, Wild, Amazing!* teaches readers to cherish and delight in our planet's ecosystems with Tim Flannery's signature mix of humor and wisdom.

WILD!

© Al Bloom

Tim Flannery, FAA, is an internationally acclaimed scientist, explorer, and conservationist, and one of the world's leading writers on climate change. He has published more than thirty books, including the international bestsellers *The Weather Makers* (2005) and *Here on Earth* (2010). His research has led to a dinosaur, an extinct kangaroo, and a parasitic worm being named after him. He lives in Melbourne, Australia.

© Emily Fenna

Sam Caldwell is an illustrator based in London. His art has appeared in the *Guardian*, the *Independent*, and *Granta*.

Jacket design by Yang Kim
Jacket art © Sam Caldwell
Printed in Canada

Norton Young Readers
An Imprint of W. W. Norton & Company
WWW.NORTONYOUNGREADERS.COM